MARIUS: ON THE ELEMENTS

Published under the auspices of the

CENTER FOR MEDIEVAL AND RENAISSANCE STUDIES

University of California, Los Angeles

Publications of the
CENTER FOR MEDIEVAL AND RENAISSANCE STUDIES, UCLA
1. Jeffrey Burton Russell: Dissent and Reform in the Early Middle Ages
2. C. D. O'Malley: Leonardo's Legacy
3. Richard H. Rouse: Serial Bibliographies for Medieval Studies
4. Speros Vryonis, Jr.: The Decline of Medieval Hellenism in Asia Minor and the Process of Islamization from the Eleventh through the Fifteenth Century
5. Stanley Chodorow: Christian Political Theory and Church Politics in the Mid-Twelfth Century
6. Joseph J. Duggan: The Song of Roland
7. Ernest A. Moody: Studies in Medieval Philosophy, Science, and Logic
8. Marc Bloch: Slavery and Serfdom in the Middle Ages
9. Michael J. B. Allen: Marsilio Ficino: The *Philebus* Commentary
10. Richard C. Dales: Marius: On the Elements

A Critical Edition and Translation
By RICHARD C. DALES

MARIUS:
On The Elements

UNIVERSITY OF CALIFORNIA PRESS
Berkeley, Los Angeles, and London
1976

The emblem of the Center for Medieval and Renaissance Studies reproduces the imperial eagle of the gold *augustalis* struck after 1231 by Emperor Frederick II; Elvira and Vladimir Clain-Stefanelli, *The Beauty and Lore of Coins: Currency and Medals* (Croton-on-Hudson, 1974), fig. 130 and p. 106.

University of California Press
Berkeley and Los Angeles, California

University of California Press, Ltd.
London, England

ISBN: 0-520-02856-2
Library of Congress Catalog Card Number: 74-16707
Copyright © 1976 by The Regents of the University of California

Contents

Preface	vii
Introduction	1
Some Observations on the Milieu of Marius' *De Elementis* by Brian Lawn	41
Marius On the Elements: Book One	46
Marius On the Elements: Book Two	106
Bibliography	185
Index	191

Preface

I first came across Marius' *De elementis* by accident in 1960. I was editing Robert Grosseteste's *Commentary on the Physics* and checking British Museum MS Cotton Galba E. IV to see if Grosseteste might have known any of the treatises on the elements described by Haskins in *Studies in the History of Mediaeval Science*, pp. 92-94. He had not, but my attention was caught by the tables of the elements in round arches, in the manner of Canon tables, and as soon as I had the time, I returned to the Cotton manuscript. It has been a rich mine. I transcribed and translated Marius as a diversion while I was editing Grosseteste's *Hexaëmeron* and became so intrigued by it that I interrupted work on the *Hexaëmeron* in order to study it thoroughly.

I have received much assistance from colleagues, friends and generous scholars whom I had not previously known. The debt I owe to Dr. Brian Lawn of London is much greater than can be discharged by a few words in a Preface. He supplied me with extensive help on Marius' sources, convinced me that Marius was not a Salernitan, and wrote a most persuasive argument that Marius was working in Montpellier when he wrote *De elementis*. I am including his remarks on this point as an appendix to the Introduction. C. H. Talbot has checked the Latin text, caught some errors, and corrected the translation in several places. Mlle. Marie-Thérèse d'Alverny has also checked the text, made some valuable suggestions concerning the sources, and made several corrections in the translation. I am especially grateful to Rodney Thomson of the University of Melbourne, Australia, who abandoned his own edition of *De elementis* when he learned that I was farther along and made his work accessible to me. Other scholars have provided me with copies of their unpublished works. Dr. Wolfgang Stürner, of the

University of Stuttgart, furnished me a copy of the draft of his edition of Urso of Calabria's *De commixtionibus elementorum*, and Dr. Joan Cadden, now of Harvard University, sent me a Xerox of her Columbia University Master's thesis, a partial edition of the anonymous *Compendiosus tractatus de philosophia et eius secretis*, which, it turned out, made extensive use of Marius *On the Elements*. I have also benefitted from the criticism of John F. Benton, Marshall Clagett, Lynn T. White, Jr., and Kevin Robb, and from the editorial expertise of Richard Rouse. I am most grateful to the University of Southern California for giving me financial assistance in the form of a Research and Publication grant and a sabbatical leave during the Spring of 1972. And finally I must express my heartfelt thanks to The Graduate School of the University of Southern California and to the Center for Medieval and Renaissance Studies of UCLA for subsidizing the publication of this text. I owe a special debt of gratitude to Dr. Carol D. Lanham of the Center for the meticulous care with which she checked my typescript and proofs. She has saved me from several egregious errors of transcription and translation and has made many helpful suggestions.

Introduction

The twelfth century remains a rich field for historians of science. In spite of the considerable amount of work which has been done in the past century, it is still not possible to make many reliable generalizations. There are too many sources unidentified, too many translations unascribed, too many channels of influence uncharted, and too many twelfth-century writers still unstudied for us to have a full picture of what actually occurred, much less explain why it occurred. But at least one thing is clear: During the twelfth century there was an intense interest in the world of nature, a great amount of energy and intelligence expended on its study, and a spectacular increase in knowledge of it. Whether this was due primarily to the translations of Greek and Arabic works or to forces operating within European society; whether the twelfth century was credulous, naive, non-rigorous and dominated by magic and astrology, or the reverse; whether its science was independent of technology or closely tied to it; all are questions which cannot yet be given definite answers. But each closely studied text provides us with more reliable data on which to construct our answers.

Some time during the third quarter of the twelfth century, a scholar and investigator of nature named Marius composed a treatise on the elements. It is the only one of his writings which survives, and in a unique copy at that. It is a most remarkable work, employing experiments in a sophisticated if not quite rigorous way, marking a significant advance in the theory of matter, studying with great subtlety the nature of a compound, utilizing a quantitative table to explain how the great variety of the world could arise from just four elements, eschewing magic, and exhibiting a thoroughgoing naturalism in its attitude toward the physical world. This treatise throws much new light on the nature and quality of twelfth-century science and forces a rethinking of the standard accounts of the history of chemistry in the Middle Ages.

The Author

There is no incontrovertible evidence concerning Marius' life, where he taught and wrote, or his dates. Rodney Thomson has presented a case for his having been a teacher at Salerno,[1] arguing from an entry in "Boston of Bury's" *Catalogus,* a death notice in a Salernitan Necrology, the contents of the manuscript in which *De elementis* is contained, and the general character of *De elementis* itself. A work entitled *De humano proficuo*, which Marius tells us in *De elementis* (below, p. 179) that he had written, is listed in "Boston of Bury's" *Catalogus scriptorum ecclesiae* and ascribed to Marius Salernitanus.[2] "Boston of Bury" was undoubtedly Henry of Kirkestede,[3] *armarius* of Bury St. Edmunds from about 1360 to 1380, at which time our manuscript was housed there. It was Kirkestede who inscribed it with the library's press mark, *ex libris* and table of contents. The first folio of *De elementis* is now missing but may well still have existed when Kirkestede knew the book. If so, the name Marius Salernitanus would likely have been contained in the running title across the top margin of the page. It has been shortened simply to Marius in the succeeding folios. One wonders where Kirkestede learned of "Marii Salernitani *De humano proficuo,*" since aside from the reference in *De elementis* there is no trace of it and no evidence that such a book ever existed in England. Thomson suggests that Kirkestede's source was *De elementis* itself—a plausible suggestion; but one may then ask why *De elementis* is not listed in his catalogue. If

---

[1] Rodney Thomson, "*Liber Marii De Elementis*: The Work of a Hitherto Unknown Salernitan Master?" *Viator*, III (1972), 179-189. Mrs. Jacqueline Reuter is currently writing a thesis under the direction of R.W. Hunt at Oxford, in which she attempts to prove that the author of "Marii *De elementis*" is Petrus Alphonsi; she dates it *ca.* 1120.

[2] Cambridge University Library Add. MS 3470, p. 107. The *Catalogus* is reprinted in somewhat condensed form in the Preface to Thomas Tanner, *Bibliotheca Britannico-Hibernica*, ed. D. Wilkins (London, 1748), pp. xvii-xliii. Marius Salernitanus is listed, but without the title of any work, in Tanner, p. xxxv.

[3] Richard H. Rouse, "Bostonus Buriensis and the Author of the *Catalogus Scriptorum Ecclesiae*," *Speculum*, XLI (1966), 471-499.

it was the source of his knowledge of *De humano proficuo* and of its author Marius Salernitanus, it seems that he would have listed it too. It is also possible that the codex contained *De humano proficuo* at the time Kirkestede made his catalogue and was subsequently lost. In any case, Kirkestede got the name Marius Salernitanus from some place, and this Marius is also the author of our *De elementis*. This evidence carries considerable weight.

A second bit of Thomson's evidence is the Necrology of the church of San Matteo of Salerno, in which many Salernitan masters held prebends, which lists a "Marius medicus" as having died in the year 1206 or 1217 (the list is fragmentary and one cannot be sure of the exact year).[4] However, there is nothing in *De elementis* to indicate with certainty that Marius was a *medicus*. Dr. Talbot, in his comments to me on the text, expresses the opinion that Marius was probably a monk; he points particularly to the phrase "in cordis armario" (below, p. 85), the general tenor of the conversation on page 177 below, and the closing words of the treatise: "Qui ipsum super huius seculi universa composita sullimavit, sit benedictus in secula seculorum. Amen."

In the third place, Thomson argues that the contents of the manuscript in which *De elementis* is contained suggest that Marius was a Salernitan. Of the twenty-six works it once contained, about twelve have a clear connection with Salerno, including Constantine the African's *Liber graduum* and two translations of Nemesius of Emesa's *De natura hominis*, one by Alfanus of Salerno and the other anonymous. The works of Salernitan masters had quite a wide currency, however, and their inclusion in the Cotton manuscript cannot be considered as proof that Marius was also a Salernitan. The works of two Englishmen, Wiscard and Picot, are also included in the collection. It was clearly put together in England from various

---

[4]C.A. Garufi, *Necrologio del Liber Confratrum di S. Matteo di Salerno* (Rome, 1922), p. 211.

sources and not transmitted *in toto* from Salerno or anywhere else.

Finally, Thomson argues that the character of the work itself suggests Salerno. It contains several of the physical questions which also appear in the collections of Salernitan questions, and the answers are sometimes similar to those in the prose questions or are obviously based on sources which the authors of those collections used. It makes extensive use of Constantine the African's *Pantegni* and displays the naturalistic outlook so characteristic of Salerno, as well as a strongly experimental bent.

There is therefore quite a strong circumstantial case for Marius' being a Salernitan. However, there are several major difficulties with this identification. First, there is the matter of sources not used by Marius which he would certainly have known if he had been working at Salerno. Of these, the most difficult to explain away is Nemesius of Emesa's *De natura hominis,* which was known to almost all the Salernitan writers and which contains material directly applicable to Marius' topic. Nor is there any trace in *De elementis* of the "elementatum" theory.[5] This doctrine, apparently originated by William of Conches, quickly found its way to Salerno, where it was incorporated into the teaching of Urso and Maurus, the two leading Salernitan masters of the late twelfth century, and generally considered to be a Salernitan doctrine. As such it was attacked as an absurdity of the "Salernitani pueri" by the anonymous author of a *Compendiosus tractatus de philosophia*

---

[5]The word *elementatum* seems to have appeared at about the same time in John of Seville's Latin translation of Abu Ma'shar's *Introductorium in astronomiam* (1133) and William of Conches' *De philosophia mundi* (before 1129). Richard J. Lemay, *Abu Ma'shar and Latin Aristotelianism in the Twelfth Century* (Beirut, 1962), pp. 179-184, argues that John was William's source, but Peter Dronke, "New Approaches to the School of Chartres," *Anuario de estudios medievales*, VI (1969), pp. 128-129, shows that the dates make this highly unlikely. John used the word to mean "something composed of the elements," and with this meaning it occurs frequently in the Middle Ages. Theodore Silverstein, "Elementatum: Its Appearance among the Twelfth-Century Cosmogonists," *Mediaeval Studies*, XVI (1954), 156-162, has pointed out that William of Conches, in his *De philosophia mundi*, used the word in a restricted sense to refer to the first four material bodies made from pairs of the first four true elements, the immaterial qualities hot, cold, moist and dry, which, being simple, cannot be apprehended by sense but only by reason, and that William's theory was taken over from this work by other twelfth-century writers, including the Salernitans.

*et eius secretis*⁶ (written in northern France in the late twelfth or early thirteenth century). This author also used much material from Marius' *De elementis,* including his table of the proportions of the elements in mixed bodies, so apparently he did not consider Marius to be a Salernitan. Then there is the form which Marius' treatise took, that of a dialogue between student and teacher. This form of presentation was not used at Salerno, and one should look for models of this type to John Scotus Eriugena, Adelard of Bath and William of Conches. Third and most important, there is the matter of the sources Marius did use which a Salernitan writer would not have. He had read several Arabic authors and had a very high regard for them. Several of these I have not been able to identify. But he did use Algazel's *Metaphysics* extensively; and Isaac Israeli's "Chapter on the Elements" (or the ps.-Aristotelian *De Elementis* on which it is a commentary) is the source of much of his Aristotelian knowledge (see especially below p. 83). Marius also used Eriugena's *De divisione naturae*, from which he derives his knowledge of St. Gregory of Nyssa's doctrine of form (below, p. 89), and Gundissalinus' *De anima* (below, p. 181). These sources indicate that Marius was working not in Salerno, which was proud of its Greek tradition and hostile toward Arabic works, but rather in a French center which had close contacts with the translators of Spain and a strong interest in Latin Neoplatonism, probably Chartres, Montpellier, or some other town with similar intellectual interests. The French hypothesis is strengthened by the fact that the only two works we know to have used *De elementis* directly were written in northern France.

But there are also difficulties with this identification. There are references in *De elementis* to coral growing under the sea and to palms, carobs and orange trees. These would not have been seen in northern France, although there were coral beds

---

⁶Vatican MS Barb. lat. 283, fol. 61v. See Theodore Silverstein, *Medieval Latin Scientific Writings in the Barbarini Collection* (Chicago, 1957), p. 79. A portion of this work (fols. 61v-74r) has been edited by Joan Cadden, *De Elementis: Earth, Water, Air and Fire in the Twelfth and Thirteenth Centuries*, unpublished M.A. thesis, Columbia University 1968. I am indebted to Dr. Cadden for furnishing me a copy of her thesis.

near both Salerno and Montpellier, and although these references may have come from literary sources rather than personal observation, (coral, in fact, is mentioned in the *Liber Apollonii*) they are presented as data of personal experience. A clue to the solution of this problem is Marius' statement to his student that he had travelled widely (below, p. 165). It is not necessary to restrict Marius' entire life and work to one locality. We may account for the pro-Salernitan evidence by assuming that Marius had been born there and very likely ended his life there, and that he was known as Marius Salernitanus among the northern Europeans. His literary activity, however, must have taken place somewhere else, and although Spain is possible, France is much more likely.

There remains the problem of his dates. In an earlier study,[7] I attempted to date Marius by placing his work in the course of development of the schools of Salerno and concluded that 1150-1170 was the most likely time for him to have been writing. However, since it now seems that Marius was not working at Salerno, my previous arguments are irrelevant. Still, the dating is not much affected. Of the Arabic works Marius knew, Isaac Israeli's "Chapter on the Elements" (or ps.-Aristotle *On the Elements*, the work on which this was a commentary) is not known to have existed in Latin, aside from Marius' use of it, so it provides us with no guide to his dates. Al-Kindi's *De quinque essentiis* is usually said to have been translated by Gerard of Cremona between 1167 and 1175.[8] But we do not know when Gerard began his translating activity; none of the MSS attributes this translation to Gerard; and in any case, as we show below (p. 25) Marius probably received his knowledge of Al-Kindi at second hand. The only two works he definitely used which are later than 1150 are Gundissalinus' *De anima* and translation of Algazel's *Metaphysics*. It is still not necessary,

---

[7] Richard C. Dales, "Marius 'On the Elements' and the Twelfth-Century Science of Matter," *Viator*, III (1972), 191-218, especially p. 210.

[8] A. Nagy, ed., *Die philosophischen Abhandlungen des Jacqūb ben Ishāq Al-Kindi* (Münster i. W., 1897). *Beiträge zur Geschichte der Philosophie des Mittelalters*, II. 5, p. XIV.

Introduction

therefore, to place Marius later than 1170. He did not know Gerard's translations of the works of Avicenna or Alfred Sareshel's translation of Avicenna's *De mineralibus*. He knows none of Aristotle's natural philosophy at first hand. And the dialogue between student and teacher was a form rapidly going out of fashion after the middle of the twelfth century. All the evidence points to Marius' having written during the third quarter of the twelfth century, probably the decade of the 1160s.

The Manuscript

Marius' *De elementis* is known to exist in only one manuscript, British Museum Cotton Galba E. IV. The collection of scientific works of which it forms a part, presently bound after a fourteenth-century Register of Henry of Eastry, Prior of Christ Church, Canterbury, is one of the most important English scientific collections of the twelfth century. The script indicates that it was written in southeast England, possibly at Bury St. Edmunds, during the last quarter of the twelfth century,[9] most likely between 1190 and 1200. At any rate, it was in the Bury library in the late fourteenth century, when, as we have mentioned above, it was given the library's pressmark (M 21), *ex libris* and table of contents by Henry of Kirkestede. Kirkestede's table of contents is largely obliterated at the present time; all that can be made out is: "liber monachorum sancti Edmundi in quo continentur libri XXIIII de medicina, de herbis...." The book was acquired by Dr. John Dee after the dissolution of the monasteries, and the catalogue of his library provides us with twenty-six titles which once made up the

---

[9] Thomson, "*Liber Marii De Elementis*," pp. 180-181. In the following discussion of the manuscript, I am greatly indebted to Mr. Thomson both for sending me a copy of his article before it was published and for the helpful suggestions he has made both in conversation and correspondence. This generosity is all the more appreciated inasmuch as he put aside his own edition of Marii *De elementis* when he learned that I was working on it.

codex.[10] The manuscript has since been mutilated. Only nine items remain, and the two innermost folios of the first quire, including the beginning of Marius *On the Elements*, have been lost.

The collection begins on fol. 187r, according to the present foliation. The first item is an anonymous work on the elements, which presents an atomic view of the world, entertains the possibility of the earth's diurnal rotation, claims that the world and motion are eternal, and contains probably the earliest verifiable direct citations of Aristotle's *Physics* in Latin Europe.[11] Its ending is missing because of the loss of the inner two folios of the quire. The second work, Marii *Liber de elementis*, fol. 190r, is lacking the beginning for the same reason. Across the top margin of the first recto, originally page 2 of the work, is written "Liber Primus," and henceforth "Marii" on each verso and "Liber I" (or II) on each recto, except that fol. 192r has "Liber I De elementis." It was Thomson's supposition that the first folio, now lost, read "Marii Salernitani," which was subsequently shortened to "Marii" as "Liber Primus" was subsequently shortened to "Liber I."[12] The remaining works in our codex are: fol. 200v, an anonymous translation of the chapter on the elements from Nemesius of Emesa's *De natura hominis*;[13] fol. 201v, "Hippocrates" *Liber de aere et aquis*;[14] fol. 205r, Alfanus of Salerno's translation of Nemesius' *De*

---

[10] M.R. James, *Lists of Manuscripts Formerly Owned by Dr. John Dee. Transactions of the Bibliographical Society*, Supplement 1 (Oxford, 1921), pp. 29-30. The apparent discrepancy between Kirkestede's twenty-four books and Dee's twenty-six is no real problem, since Kirkestede often conflated similar works.

[11] Published by R.C. Dales, "Anonymi *De elementis*: From a Twelfth-Century Collection of Scientific Works in British Museum MS Cotton Galba E. IV," *Isis*, LVI (1965), 174-189.

[12] This completely plausible suggestion was made by Rodney Thomson, "*Liber Marii De Elementis*," p. 184.

[13] Published by R.C. Dales, "An Unnoticed Translation of Nemesius' *De natura hominis*," *Medievalia et Humanistica*, XVII (1966), 13-19.

[14] That is, the Hippocratic *Liber de aere, aqua et regionibus*; edited by H. Diller, *Philologus*, Supplement 23 (1932), 83-104. See Lynn Thorndike and Pearl Kibre, *A Catalogue of Incipits of Medieval Scientific Writings in Latin* (Revised and augmented edition; Cambridge, Mass., 1963), col. 1249.

natura hominis;[15] fol. 214r, Adelard of Bath's *Quaestiones naturales;*[16] fol. 228r, *Liber de phisiognomia secundum tres auctores,* a collection of alleged extracts from Aristotle, Loxus and Palemon;[17] fol. 233v, Constantine the African's translation of pseudo-Galen *De spermate;*[18] and finally, fol. 238v, pseudo-Soranus *Isagoge,* which is incomplete.[19]

The other works, now lost but known from Dr. Dee's catalogue, are: Constantine's *Liber de herbis,* Dioscorides' *De virtutibus herbarum,* Oribasius' *De virtutibus herbarum,* Odo of Meung's poem *Versus de virtutibus herbarum,* Isidore of Seville's *Etymologies* (probably only Book IV on medicine), Constantine's *Liber graduum,* six "Experimenta," one attributed to Eupho, one to Adamarius, one to Johannes Melancholicus, one to "the abbot," one to Wiscard and one to Picotus (probably both Englishmen), an anonymous *De urina mulieris,* "Hippocrates" *Expositio quinte incisionis epidemiarum,* Johannes Melancholicus' *Liber de substantia urine,* Palladius' *De agricultura,* and a *Liber de simplici medicina* probably by Platearius.[20]

The strongly Salernitan flavor of this collection is evident. Although, as the researches of Brian Lawn[21] and C.H. Talbot[22] have shown, the more primitive works of Salernitan medicine were known in England much earlier, the Cotton manuscript seems to be the earliest extant evidence for the penetration into England of the more advanced Salernitan writings. The transmission was remarkably rapid. The composition date of the

---

[15] Published by C. Burkhard, ed., *Nemesii Episcopi* Premnon Physicon *sive* ΠΕΡΙ ΦΥΣΕΩΣ ΑΝΘΡΩΠΟΥ *Liber a N. Alfano, Archiepiscopo Salerni in Latinum Translatus* (Leipzig, 1917).

[16] Edited by Martin Müller, *Die Quaestiones Naturales des Adelardus von Bath* (Münster i. W., 1934). *Beiträge zur Geschichte der Philosophie und Theologie des Mittelalters,* XXXI.2.

[17] These obscure works are unpublished. They are cited in the A version of the *Lumen animae* texts. See Mary A. Rouse and Richard H. Rouse, "The Texts Called *Lumen Anime,*" *Archivum Fratrum Praedicatorum,* XLI (1971), 5-113, especially p. 19.

[18] Printed in the Juntine edition of Galen's works (Venice, 1597), fols. 41 ff.

[19] Edited by V. Rose, *Anecdota Graeca et Graecolatina,* II (Berlin 1870), 243-274. See Brian Lawn, *The Salernitan Question* (Oxford, 1963), p. 9.

[20] On the attribution of this work to Platearius, see Lawn, *The Salernitan Questions,* p. 30.

[21] Lawn, *The Salernitan Questions.*

[22] C.H. Talbot, *Medicine in Medieval England* (London, 1967).

latest datable work in the collection is *ca.* 1170[23] and the script in which the text was copied in England cannot be later than *ca.* 1200 and is probably earlier.

Principal Teachings and Characteristics

De elementis is cast in the form of a dialogue between student and teacher.[24] The characters of the two participants are developed to some degree, as is the relationship between them. The student is much more than a foil and frequently asks some very sharp questions, points out inconsistencies in the teacher's explanations, or refuses to accept an unsatisfactory answer.

The purpose of the work is to investigate the material constitution and basic processes of the physical world. It consists of two books, the first treating the simple elements, earth, water, air and fire, and the second investigating the compound bodies that arise from them. The first two columns of the work are lost, as we have seen, and the extant portion begins with the student asking about the nature of water. One is struck immediately by the master's insistence on supporting every assertion by some sort of experimental evidence, ranging from appeals to everyday experience and "thought experiments" to experiments specifically contrived (and apparently performed) to test particular hypotheses. Marius observes closely and accurately over a wide range of phenomena. He places a wineskin, tied shut, below the surface of the water and notices the tendency of air to rise to its proper place above the water (p. 53). He separates the four elements out of milk (pp. 129-133). He tastes sal ammoniac to discover its "hot" nature (p. 153). He carefully observes and accurately describes the behavior of the flame of a candle (pp. 49, 51) and of firebrands in proving that air is the nourishment of fire (p. 55). He calls attention to the fact that the goldsmith's earthenware pot is turned to glass by intense heat (p. 141), and

---

[23]That is, the first work, Anonymi *De elementis.*

[24]This discussion appeared in much the same form in my "Marius *On the Elements.*" I am grateful to the editors of *Viator* for permission to use it here.

from this, he develops his theory of the formation of stones, holding that they are all kinds of glass. He notices the skin entering the tube when a physician places it on a patient's arm and sucks (p. 103). He stops up the pipe of a bellows to test the corporeity and compressibility of air (pp. 46, 101). Even though one must always beware of thinking that every experiment described by a medieval author was also performed by him (and to be sure some of Marius' came from literary sources, as the notes to the edition make clear), it must be conceded that the experimental habit of mind was one of Marius' most pronounced characteristics.

The heart of Marius' teaching is his doctrine of substance, which he calls "the key to the whole of philosophy." Its origin was God's creation. In itself it is three dimensional extension, devoid of all qualities. In fact, during the first part of Book I, Marius refers to it as "body" *(corpus)*. It occupies place, is spherical and is finite, for otherwise it could not be moved. This substance is analogous to what will at a later date be called *forma corporeitatis* or *prima materia,* but it is not simply a metaphysical principle. It is the physical foundation of the three-dimensional universe—extended substance. It is imperceptible to sense and can only be known by reason. Nevertheless, through the qualities imposed upon its four parts by the Creator, it ultimately causes all the sensible qualities which we perceive.

These sensible qualities, thought of "all together at one time, as though they were one thing," constitute the "form" of each element; they cannot exist independently of substance (he does not say "matter"), but once joined to substance they can be perceived, and they make it possible to know substance by reason even though it can never itself be sensed. This union of the formal parts, since it too can only be apprehended by reason, can be thought of in itself, and is not susceptible of corruption in thought, is also a kind of substance, and on the authority of "Aristotle" he calls it "secondary substance."

Marius' doctrine of substance is one of the most interesting and difficult parts of *De elementis.* If I am correct in my under-

standing of it, it is also an excellent example of the creative eclecticism of the best twelfth-century minds. Marius believed that he was giving the teaching of the ancients, and, although he picks and chooses somewhat, he certainly did not intend to be original. He seems to have read and had in mind a number of specific sources: Scotus Eriugena's *De divisione naturae,* Calcidius' commentary on the *Timaeus,* William of Conches' *Dragmaticon,* Algazel's *Metaphysics,* "Ibn Ḥasdāy's Neoplatonist," and probably some other Arabic sources which I have not identified. From these he borrowed several salient ideas, often conflating similar treatments by different authors and not infrequently misunderstanding the meaning of his authorities. Marius' resulting view is not without some vagueness and inconsistency, but it is based on some very difficult and complex sources.

Marius goes on to describe both the "nature" and "property" of each element. Earth's nature is cold and dryness; its property is heaviness. Water's nature is cold and moisture; its property is also heaviness. The nature of air is heat and moisture, its property is "to rise upward." Fire's nature is heat and dryness, and its property likewise is to rise upward. The tendency to move upward or downward does not depend on heat or cold, but rather on dryness and moisture. The pure elements do not have colors, tastes and odors; only composite bodies do. Each element can be changed into the one contiguous to it by an increase or decrease in one or more of the four qualities caused by the interaction of mixed bodies. Marius' elements are not, like those of William of Conches before him and Urso of Calabria after him, immaterial first principles, but are the actual physical constituents of the universe. The created things of the world all contain all four elements, and so no element ever actually exists in its pure state. However, everything that exists derives its being and its characteristics from the exact proportion of the four elements it contains.

At the beginning of Book II, Marius develops a quantitative theory showing the various ways in which the four elements could be mixed and presents this schematically in tables. He

begins with "just two elements at a time, so that we may understand better while we may gain some practice and become more accustomed to this sort of thing," and then goes on to specify the 145 possible mixtures of the four elements, assuming that they can be mixed either in equal or unequal proportions; in the latter case there may be either more or less, or, if there were more than two elements, there may be much, a moderate amount, or a small amount of each element. Of the 145 mathematically possible combinations, Marius says that "you will perceive some by a bodily sense, others you will understand only in your mind." Since everything which actually exists must be composed of all four elements, he must at least be excluding all combinations of fewer than four from things that actually exist; whether or not he also means that some combinations of all four are only theoretically possible is not clear. He also holds that any composite can be resolved into its constituent elements, and to illustrate his teaching he describes a qualitative analysis of milk.

At this point the student asks a key question: "How is it that there are in the world almost innumerable kinds of composite bodies, and yet you, in your analysis, have divided them into only 145 kinds?" But the teacher has a response: "If you multiply these 145 kinds either by increasing or decreasing the parts, you will undoubtedly find them innumerable. There are only seven in which you cannot either diminish or increase the elements: one, the mixture of all four elements in which they are all equal in the composite; the six others, the mixtures of two elements at a time in which the two similarly are equal in the composite."

The question now remains: In what way, if at all, do the elements persist in a compound? For even though a compound may be resolved into its elements, it is clearly something other than a simple mixture of them. Aristotle had attempted a solution,[25] and Marius may have had some sort of secondhand

---

[25]See H.H. Joachim, "Aristotle's Conception of Chemical Combination," *The Journal of Philo-*

knowledge of this. However, his own solution is much more thorough. Aristotle had ignored the question of *how* the process from element to compound occurs but had emphasized that the elements existed only potentially in a compound and that "only those agents are combinable which involve a contrary." He seems to have considered the resulting μίξις (usually rendered *mixtio* in Latin) as simply the mean established among the contraries involved. Marius, utilizing the concepts of "temperament" and "complexion" from post-Aristotelian medical literature, as well as adapting Aristotle's doctrine of potentiality, gives a much more satisfactory explanation. When any two elements are combined, the similar qualities will reinforce each other, but the contrary qualities will each try to destroy the other, and in the process each is altered from its own nature. This process must occur before the compound is formed and is something more than the establishment of a mean between the qualities, as Aristotle had it. Rather we have something occurring analogous to the modern notion of a chemical compound, with the result being actually different from the elements, although made by and from them, its characteristics depending on the proportions of the elements which constitute the compound. This preoccupation with process is one of the distinguishing characteristics of Marius' approach to nature. In four different places, he makes it explicit: "But *how* do you say this is done" (p. 67). "I do not know *how* it comes forth" (p. 159). "I wish you would reveal to me *by what means* this is done" (p. 137). "But I do not know *how* the elements come together to create the different tastes" (p. 169).

Next, after a discussion of the nine complexions, Marius explains the formation of stones and metals. Noting that a goldsmith's pot becomes transparent and is changed to glass when subjected to great heat, he concludes that all stones are formed this way in nature by heat enclosed in the interior of the earth. Their differences result from the different kinds of earth from

---

logy, XXIX (1904), 72-86; and Otto Apelt, "Die Schrift des Alexander von Aphrodisias über die Mischung," *Philologus,* XLV (1886), 82-99.

which they are made and from variations in the intensity of heat and the length of time the heat operates. He then quickly describes the composition of other minerals, using as examples sulphur, orpiment, petroleum, sal ammoniac and mercury. This is preparatory to his discussion of metals, which he says are compounded of sulphur and mercury.[26] The metals differ from each other because of variations in the purity of the sulphur or mercury or both and in the intensity and duration of the heat to which they are subjected in the earth's interior.

It is in connection with this discussion that Marius' naturalistic and mechanical approach becomes most apparent. In this regard, he may be compared with Adelard of Bath. In the *Natural Questions* Adelard had explained the fact that water would not run out of a tube open at the bottom so long as the top was closed by saying that "since the four elements make up this natural world, and they are joined together by a natural love in such a way that no one of them wishes to exist without the others, no place either is or can be empty of them."[27] Marius, on the other hand, after showing by experiments that two bodies cannot occupy the same place, simply asserts that "you cannot empty a place of a given body without another body's immediately entering it" (p. 103). The animism which had such a hold on even so naturalistic a thinker as Adelard is not to be found in Marius. On occasion during his treatise he had used metaphorical language, saying for example that fire flees from water, heat retreats into the earth's interior, and that contraries both flee from each other and seek to destroy each other. We can recognize these phrases as metaphors, since Marius provides us with a specific statement on the subject. The student asks: "How can one quality so abhor another that it seeks to demolish and destroy it, since a quality has no discretion nor

---

[26] This doctrine is Arabic. The only known source of it in Latin before Alfred Sareshel's translation of Avicenna's *De mineralibus* late in the twelfth century was the *Liber Apollonii* (or *Hermetis*) *de secretis naturae*, translated by Hugh of Santalla in or before 1143. See Lawn, *Salernitan Questions*, pp. 73-75 and below, note 40.

[27] *Ed. cit.*, p. 54 (see above, note 16).

does it know what it ought to do?" Marius answers that this is just a manner of speaking and gives as an example of what he means that waking is the contrary of sleeping and that one state may be said to flee as the other approaches. He also insists that only bodies act on other bodies and that qualities are efficacious only insofar as they inhere in bodies.

Marius' aversion to alchemical transmutation is clear in his discussion of the formation of metals. Metals, he says, are formed from sulphur and mercury of varying degrees of purity cooked by varying degrees of heat for longer or shorter times in the earth's interior. He never mentions the possibility of transmutation of metals, and he specifically denies the possibility of alteration of species (pp. 175-177).

The next topic to be discussed in detail is the vegetable kingdom. After spending a long time proving that plants possess local motion as a result of their growth, he argues that the principle of growth of a plant is contained in the seed, whence it is distended into all the growing parts. There are four powers of the "viridal soul," the appetitive, the digestive, the retentive and the expulsive. Growth takes place only as a result of increments of matter being changed into the nature of the plant and added to it. "These four powers always cause the grain to grow until it reaches the limit set for it, and then it makes innumerable plants completely similar to itself, just as each species of animal makes seeds not dissimilar to itself." Furthermore, a plant "will not stop growing so long as it is furnished the principle of growth by the seed. That seed will grow similarly if it is saved by man until the proper time and then placed in the ground.... For God commanded and bestowed the power upon the viridal soul to be able to preserve its own kind always in its own form and seed. The only reason that man plants trees is so he may enjoy the convenience of the fruit more quickly; for they grow in the same way from seed, only it takes a little more time" (p. 165).

From this point on, the quality of the book declines. In the last few columns, Marius depends completely on literary sources, which he has not subjected to the same rigorous

criticism and experimental testing which characterised most of the work up to this point. In explaining the tastes, he says that he found in a "philosophical book" a list of which elements cause which tastes, but he complains that his source does not tell him "how the elements come together to create these tastes," and he confesses to his student: "I do not have any lesson (*documentum*) to show you this."

The final subject of the book is the animal kingdom. It is quite brief and is confined mostly to investigating similarities and differences between animals and plants. Then, after putting off a number of his student's questions as inappropriate to the subject of his work and telling us that he has already written a book *De humano proficuo* and intends to write another on the five senses, Marius ends his work with a proof that man is the most wonderful of God's creatures and with praise of the Lord: "May He Who raised [man] above all the composite things of this world be blessed through all the ages."

Sources

It would be both pointless and misleading to try to trace every concept, formula and fact which one finds in the work of a twelfth-century scientist to a more ancient source, whether Latin, Greek, Hebrew or Arabic. The attitudes of men in the twelfth century led them to seize upon particular notions which they found in the works of other authors, to combine them in sometimes astonishing ways, to "misunderstand" them from our point of view, and to create novel works as a result. The authorities provided a wealth of fruitful suggestions, but these authorities were not merely recovered by scholars in the twelfth century; they were in fact transformed.

The willingness of twelfth-century writers to ignore what was not useful to them is also striking. An authority may be praised to the heavens when he is being followed, but then totally ignored when his work did not conform to the purposes of a twelfth-century scientist. This could be the result of naiveté, of stupidity, or of intellectual dishonesty. Or more likely it could

be the result of supreme confidence; a rejection, often though not always unconscious, of ancient views or habits of thought; and an intellectual climate where originality was not discouraged and where vitality of thought and stimulation virtually assured its occurrence. There is a strong element of continuity in the history of western science, and tracing the sources of our authors is a worthwhile enterprise. But even if we were completely successful in it, we should still not know the most important part of the story of twelfth-century science.

A. *Sources Marius Might Have Used But Did Not*. In evaluating a twelfth-century scientific treatise, it is often as important to establish what works an author did not use as those he did. This can aid us in dating and placing the work and in assessing its place in our intellectual history.

1. *Nemesius of Emesa*. If Marius were a Salernitan, he might be expected to have used Nemesius of Emesa's *De natura hominis*. This work had been translated in its entirety by Alfanus of Salerno in the eleventh century[28] (as well as by Burgundio of Pisa in the twelfth[29]), its chapter on the elements had been translated by an anonymous south Italian during the twelfth century,[30] the work was a favorite with Salernitan authors, and its subject matter was pertinent to Marius' treatise. But a detailed comparison between *De natura hominis* and *De elementis* on subjects which are common to both of them—the elements and their properties, tastes and smells—shows no trace of similarity. We may conclude that Marius did not use Nemesius.

2. *Avicenna*. Marius' treatment of the formation of metals and his denial of alchemical transmutation both suggest the possibility that he may have known Avicenna's *De mineralibus*,[31] often attributed to Aristotle in the Middle Ages. Since this work

---

[28]See above, note 15.

[29]Gregorii Nysseni (Nemesii Emenseni) περὶ φύσεως ἀνθρώπου *liber a Burgundione in Latinum Translatus*, ed. C. Burkhard, *Jahresberichte des k. k. Staats-gymnasiums* (Vienna, 1891-1902).

[30]Dales, "An Unnoticed Translation." See above, note 13.

[31]*Avicennae De congelatione et conglutinatione lapidum*, ed. E.J. Holmyard and D.C. Mandeville (Paris, 1927).

was translated by Alfred Sareshel late in the twelfth century,[32] if Marius used it we should have to date him much later than the 1160s. But a comparison of the details of their treatments of the formation of metals makes it clear that Marius did not know *De mineralibus.*[33]

3. *Aristotelian Works.* Since Marius frequently cites Aristotle, and there is undeniably some Aristotelian teaching in *De elementis*, it is important to determine with certainty whether or not he knew any of Aristotle's natural philosophy at first hand, and if not to discover, if possible, the sources of his knowledge. Enormous amounts of scholarly labor have been expended during the past 150 years on the matter of the translation and re-acquisition by Latin Europe of the natural philosophy of Aristotle, but even though great progress has been made, there are still many things about this process, especially in the twelfth century, of which we have an incomplete understanding.

Early in this century, Arthur Schneider and Martin Grabmann[34] realized that Aristotle often reached Latin authors during the twelfth century not exclusively by means of translations of his works, but also through intermediate sources. More recently Richard J. Lemay[35] has emphasized the role of Arabic astrological works, especially Abu Ma'shar's *Introductorium in astronomiam*, as a medium for the transmission of Aristotelianism. The history of both the translations of Aristotle's own writings and the penetration of his ideas through intermediate sources needs much more study.

---

[32] James K. Otte, "The Life and Writings of Alfredus Anglicus," *Viator*, III (1972), 290.

[33] I have published a detailed comparison of their treatments of metal formation in "Marius 'On the Elements,'" p. 210.

[34] Arthur Schneider, *Die abendländische Spekulation des zwölften Jahrhunderts in ihrem Verhältniss zu Aristotelischen und judischarabischen Philosophie* (Münster i. W., 1915). *Beiträge zur Geschichte der Philosophie des Mittelalters*, XVII. 4, pp. 36-40; Martin Grabmann, *Forschungen über die lateinischen Aristoteles Übersetzungen des XIII. Jahrhunderts* (Münster i. W., 1916). *Beiträge*, XVII. 5-6, p. 17; both in commenting on Pierre Duhem's assertion—"Du temps où la Scolastique latine a connu la Physique d'Aristote," *Revue de Philosophie*, XV (1909), 63-178—that the presence of certain Aristotelian doctrines in the works of several early twelfth-century writers indicated that they had direct access to his works. Both Schneider and Grabmann, however, looked only to the standard Latin handbooks.

[35] Richard J. Lemay, *Abu Ma'shar*. See note 5 above.

The broad outlines of this transmission are of course well known. Since late Antiquity there had been a group of Latin works which contained some Aristotelian doctrine: Pliny, Seneca, Aulus Gellius, Priscianus Lydus, Calcidius, Martianus Capella, Boethius, Cassiodorus, Eustathius' Latin paraphrase of Basil's *Hexameron*, the *De opificio hominis* of Gregory of Nyssa translated by Dionysius Exiguus in the sixth century, and the writings of many of the Latin Fathers, especially Ambrose and Augustine, who managed to transmit a good deal of handbook knowledge of Greek philosophy. A number of pseudo-Aristotelian works was also available in Latin.

Marius makes one lengthy quotation and two shorter citations of a work *De elementis*, which he ascribes to Aristotle. In discussing the original differentiation of first body (or substance, as he sometimes calls it) into the four elements, he quotes this work: "Indeed, it [the motion which causes the qualities of the elements] proceeds from the motion of the firmament, as Aristotle says in his book which treats the elements. For he spoke in these words: 'When the creation of the firmament and all things contained in it was finished, its creator moved it and it was mobile. But from the motion of the firmament, a part of the previously mentioned body, simple yet circumscribed by the six directions—that part, I say, which was most closely joined to the very firmament—began to move and to heat up violently; and this was fire. But the next part, which was a little farther away, was moved but not quite so violently. Therefore it became hot but not so hot as fire; and this is air. The third part, because it was far removed from the firmament, was neither moved nor heated, and therefore it remained cold; and this is water. But the fourth, because it is as far as possible away from the firmament, remained completely immobile. Therefore it too remained cold; and this was earth'" (below, p. 83). Several pages later he cites Aristotle as his authority for his doctrine of form: "On this we have the authority of Aristotle, who says that everything that can be thought of in itself, so that it is not susceptible of corruption in thought, must necessarily be substance. But the aforementioned parts of form cannot be

thought of separately as being without corruption. Therefore, you ought to give the name substance to that union of the formal parts as well as the first substance [i.e., first body], for Aristotle himself in his book *On the Elements* calls the first 'elemental substance,' the other 'formal substance'" (below, p. 93). Near the end of the work, there is another citation: "Nevertheless, colors sometimes deceive the sight, as Aristotle explains in his book" (below, p. 171). It is clear then that Marius had a book entitled *De elementis* which was ascribed to Aristotle. That this was not any authentic Aristotelian work is evident from its teaching of a creation *ex nihilo* and from its mentioning only four rather than five elements. But it seems equally clear that this book was based on genuine Aristotelian works. Much of what we have just quoted is quite similar to *Meteorology* I 3 (341a) and I 4 (341b), and the statement on colors sometimes deceiving the sight could have been based on *Meteorology* I 5 (342b) or possibly *De anima* II 6 (418a) or II 7 (419a). There are several other places where Marius does not always cite Aristotle but where his doctrine seems likely to have been based on an Aristotelian tradition. The assertion that Aristotle says that fire extends as far as the moon would apply to *Meteorology* I 3 (340b). That oil and fat are "airy" could have come from *Meteorology* IV 7 (383b) or *De longitudine et brevitate vitae* V (466a). The terms "of the physicists" *de medio* and *ad medium* are from *De caelo* I 3 (269b) and IV 1 (308a). From the same work, I 5 (271b-272a) and from *Physics* IV 8 (215b) are arguments similar to Marius' concerning the necessity of the spacial finitude of the universe if it is to be capable of motion.[36]

---

[36]In addition to the places mentioned in the text, Brian Lawn has pointed out to me the following correspondences: p. 53, wineskin experiment, cf. *Phys.* VIII 5 (255b), *Probl.* XXV 1 (937b) and *De caelo* IV 4 (311b); p. 55, fire descending to a wick, cf. *Meteor.* I 4 (342a); p. 65, earth is changed into other elements only over a very long time, cf. *De gen. et corr.* II 4 (331b); p. 71, that the three dimensions are unlimited but are not quantity, cf. *Phys.* III 5 (206a); p. 73, the different kinds of motion, cf. *De caelo* I 2 (268b); p. 100, compression of the elements and change in the volume of air, cf. *Phys.* IV 6-7 and *De gen. et corr.* I 5 (321a); p. 135, composites in which there is a preponderance of air and fire do not always rise, cf. *De caelo* IV 5 (312b); p. 145, a thing is potentially that into which it is changed, cf. *Phys.* IV 5 (213a) and *De caelo* III 2 (302a).

At this point we might seem ready to conclude that Marius possessed at least Aristotle's *Meteorology*, *De caelo* and *De generatione et corruptione*, but a close reading makes it clear that he could not possibly have known any of the "New Aristotle" at first hand. Even the closest correspondences between *De elementis* and Aristotle's works on natural philosophy are far from exact and appear to have been filtered through at least one intermediate source. And there are many discrepancies between Marius' views on a given subject and those of Aristotle. An essential part of Marius' teaching is that only bodies are capable of acting and being acted upon; qualities can be efficacious only insofar as they are attributes of bodies. Aristotle, on the other hand, has the contrary qualities acting on each other, and the elements themselves play only a minor role in his thought, especially in the *Meteorology*. Marius also insists that every created thing contains all four *elements* in some proportion. Aristotle insists only that all bodies are mixtures of the four elementary *qualities*. Also in his discussion of the formation of minerals, a very important section of *De elementis*, Marius seems to have been totally ignorant of Aristotle's teaching that minerals are formed "by vapors of smokey exhalations, developed within the earth's interior and brought by heat and dryness to their mineral condition" (*Meteorology* III 6 [383a-384a]). Their treatments of liquefying and congealing are also far apart. Marius holds fast to the doctrine that heat liquefies and cold congeals, whereas Aristotle, observing much more closely, notices that many substances can be either liquefied or congealed by heat or cold, and that olive oil is congealed by both (*Meteorology* IV 6-7 [383a-384a]). The conclusion seems inescapable that Marius did not have direct access to any of Aristotle's works on natural philosophy, but that he had acquired much Aristotelian teaching by way of intermediate works. We shall see below what some of these intermediate works were.

B. *Arabic Sources*. It is apparent that Marius had some acquaintance with Arabic works. At the beginning of Book II, he discusses those things "que vocant Sarraceni congelata." It

Introduction

is also clear that he has imbibed certain Arabic alchemical doctrines from some source. Even though Marius' attitude is completely naturalistic, his statements on page 79 that "a knowledge of this substance is the key to the whole of philosophy" and "through a knowledge of it, a man can rise to that lofty knowledge which is beyond nature," and on page 177: "You should know, therefore, that this is the foundation of this whole art," are unmistakable echoes of Arabic alchemical teachings. On page 93, Marius gives Al-Kindi's five "essences," although in different words from the Latin version usually attributed to Gerard of Cremona,[37] and, as we shall see below, he probably knew these through an intermediate source.

On page 179, his assertion that the rational soul is an incorporeal substance capable of taking on contrary qualities without being itself corrupted is very close to the wording of Costa ben Luca's *De animae et spiritus discrimine*, in the translation of John of Spain.[38] Marius had made a similar remark earlier (p. 93), based on Aristotle's *Categories* V (4a-b), but this was confined to substance in general and did not consider the rational soul. The examples of contrary qualities which Marius uses here are wisdom and foolishness. Costa ben Luca, however, uses virtues and vices. Calcidius (*In Timaeum*, 226), in a similar remark, mentions a series of pairs but not wisdom and foolishness. Marius' example is found in Gundissalinus' *De anima*,[39]

---

[37]The Latin version of Al-Kindi reads: "Res autem quae sunt in omnibus substantiis sunt quinque, quarum una est hyle, et secunda est forma, et tertia est locus, et quarta est motus, quinta autem tempus. In omni enim re in qua est substantia est hyle ex qua ipsa est, et forma qua videtur et qua distinguitur ab aliis rebus visione, et locus in quo ipsa existit in omni termino. Et illud ideo quoniam nullum corpus dirigitur ut sit nisi in loco et in termino. Et in ipsa etiam est motus quo ipsius constitutio existit, et hoc est ei essentia in loco et tempore" (*ed. cit.*, pp. 30-31). Marius says: "Modo ergo quinque esse cognoscimus que ad rerum creationem esse necessaria dicere valeamus: substantiam videlicet elementalem, et substantiam formalem, motum et locum quo aliquid moveatur, et tempus etiam quo mutus conficiatur" (below, p. 93). Since he took the distinction between "elemental" and "formal" substance from Isaac Israeli or the ps.-Aristotelian work on which he was commenting (see below, note 43), it seems that he knows of Al-Kindi's five essences from the same source.

[38]Edited by S. Barach (Innsbruck, 1878), p. 126.

[39]Edited by J.T. Muckle (Toronto, 1940), p. 37. For the date, see M.-Th. d'Alverny, "Notes sur les traductions médiévales d'Avicenne," *Archives d'histoire doctrinale et littéraire du Moyen Âge*, XIX (1952), 343.

so this work, rather than that of Costa ben Luca, is his probable source in this place.

An Arabic work which has much in common with Marius' *De elementis* is the *Liber Apollonii* (or *Hermetis*) *de secretis naturae*, which was translated by Hugh of Santalla in or before 1143.[40] It contains the doctrine of metal formation from sulphur and mercury (in fact, this work is the only presently known source for the doctrine among the Latins until Alfred Sareshel's translation of Avicenna's *De mineralibus* near the end of the twelfth century). It also contains material similar to the book in which Marius found an account of which elements cause which tastes (p. 169), and it mentions that green comes from yellow and black (p. 171). The *Liber Apollonii* also paraphrases Al-Kindi's five essences; Marius, however, seems to have taken them not from this work, but from the ps.-Aristotelian *De elementis*. In spite of these similarities, there are numerous places where Marius does not show any knowledge of the *Liber Apollonii* where its information was pertinent to his needs, and we must conclude that he did not know the *Liber Apollonii* but rather used another Arabic work or works which we have not identified.

By far the most interesting of Marius' Arabic sources is represented by the so-called "Chapter on the Elements" of Isaac Israeli, which survives only in a Hebrew translation of the Arabic original in Mantua, Bibliotheca comunale MS 28c, folios 16r-18r.[41] It is ascribed to Aristotle in the manuscript. The "Chapter on the Elements" is a commentary by Isaac on a lost pseudo-Aristotelian work, which has been reconstructed and

---

[40]Paris MS Bibliothèque nationale, lat. 13951, folios 1-31. This twelfth-century manuscript, formerly at St. Germaine-des-Près is entitled *Hermetis Trimegesti Liber de secretis naturae et occultis rerum causis ab Apolloni translatus*. A critical edition is being prepared by Mme. Hudry, an assistant of Mlle. Marie-Thérèse d'Alverny. I owe this reference to Mlle. d'Alverny. See also Lawn, *Salernitan Questions*, p. 73; C.H. Haskins, *Studies in the History of Mediaeval Science* (Cambridge, Mass., 1924; repr. 1960), pp. 79-80.

[41]The Hebrew text of this treatise, with an English translation, is published in Alexander Altmann, "Isaac Israeli's 'Chapter on the Elements' (Ms. Mantua)," *Journal of Jewish Studies*, VII (1956), 31-57. It is reprinted and provided with extensive notes by the same author in A. Altmann and S.M. Stern, *Isaac Israeli* (Oxford, 1958). *Scripta Judaica*, I. pp. 118-132.

given the title "Ibn Ḥasdāy's Neoplatonist" by Alexander Altmann.[42] Marius' long quotation from Aristotle *On the Elements* (below, p. 83) is very nearly the same as the beginning of the "Chapter on the Elements."[43] His views that plants and animals are composed of all four elements and if one is lacking the plant or animal will die (p. 131)[44] and the distinction between "elemental substance" and "formal substance" (p. 93)[45] are found in the "Chapter on the Elements," but his other citations of Aristotle *On the Elements* are not. It seems then that Marius was using a Latin version of "Ibn Hasdāy's Neoplatonist," which he knew as Aristotle *On the Elements*, and perhaps a Latin translation of Isaac's commentary as well. He probably derived his knowledge of Al-Kindi's five essences from one of these works rather than from the Latin version attributed to Gerard of Cremona.

Marius also knew other books of Isaac, which were available in Constantine's Latin translations. Marius' doctrine on seeds' attracting moisture (p. 163), the shapes of leaves (p. 171), and the withering of plants (p. 167) are all drawn from Isaac's *De dietis universalibus*, as is the experiment (p. 169) of cooking honey to produce salty and bitter tastes. Also, his remark, attributed to Aristotle, that "colors sometimes deceive the sight" (p. 171) could have come from this same work, although

---

[42]Altmann and Stern, *Isaac Israeli*, pp. 98-105.

[43]In Altmann's English translation, it reads: "When as a result of the motion of the sphere the nature of fire had come into being and the warmth moved away from its radiance and root, it diminished and dissipated. From this the nature of air came into being, the nature of fire being warm and dry, the nature of air being warm and moist. After the nature of air had come into being and after it had moved away from the root of fire, its warmth continued to diminish, dissipate and moisten, and from this the nature of water came into being. After the nature of water had come into being and after it had moved away from the air, its warmth and moisture diminished, cold befell it, and it lowered itself to the production of sediment, refuse and dry mud. From this the nature of earth came into being" ("Chapter on the Elements," p. 43; *Isaac Israeli*, p. 120).

[44]"Chapter on the Elements," pp. 45-46; *Isaac Israeli*, pp. 122-123. Eriugena, *De divisione naturae*, I, 54 (*PL*, CXXII, 498A), says something similar, but he is speaking only of the human body.

[45]"Aristotle the philosopher and master of wisdom of the Greeks said: "The beginnings of all roots are the two simple substances: one of them is first matter, which receives form and is known to the philosophers as the root of roots. It is the first substance which subsists in itself and is the substratum of diversity. The other is substantial form, which is ready to impregnate matter. It is perfect wisdom, pure radiance and clear splendor, by the conjunction of which with first matter the nature and form of intellect came into being, because it is composed of them." ("Chapter on the Elements," p. 41; *Isaac Israeli*, p. 119).

it is more likely that it came from "Ibn Ḥasdāy's Neoplatonist." Marius' experiment of separating the four elements out of milk (pp. 129-133) was probably suggested by Isaac's *De dietis particularibus*, although Isaac does not mention fire as a component of milk. During the course of this experiment, Marius says that the greasy part of milk is "airy," and that air is the nourishment of fire. This is based on *De dietis universalibus*, fol. XXXIXr. Marius' remark about the viridal soul in plants causing the various colors of flowers (p. 167) seems to be indebted to Isaac's *Book of Substances*.[46] There are several other doctrines in Marius which are also in the works of Isaac, but which exist elsewhere. Marius' observation that pepper is hot potentially (p. 145) is found in Isaac's *Liber de elementis* (not the same work as "Chapter on the Elements"), but it is also in Constantine's *Pantegni* (Theorice, I, 6-7), which Marius also used. The same two works share the teaching that man is the most temperate of all animals, and only the human skin is completely temperate (compare Marius, p. 179), but here Marius is much closer to Constantine than to Isaac. That fruit is composed of all four elements (p. 147) is asserted by Isaac in *De dietis universalibus*, but it is also in William of Conches' *Dragmaticon*.

Marius' use of these Arabic sources gives us a striking example of the tendency of twelfth-century writers to ignore the context from which they extracted what material was pertinent to their needs. The strength of Marius' naturalism is nowhere more evident than in his stripping Isaac's "Chapter on the Elements" and "Ibn Ḥasdāy's Neoplatonist" of their emanationist context in taking from these works what he considered to be their wisdom and useful information. The strength and integrity of his own world view, rather than the magic and Neoplatonism of his sources, are what stand out.

Another Arabic work which Marius used extensively is Algazel's *Metaphysics*,[47] in the translation of Gundissalinus. Many

---

[46] Altmann and Stern, *Isaac Israeli*, p. 94.
[47] Edited by J.T. Muckle (Toronto, 1933).

of his experiments were taken from this book: (p. 49) that wind is air in motion; (p. 53) the wineskin rising to the surface of water; (p. 51) the condensation of vapor on the lid of a jar; (p. 59) the color of a candle flame; (p. 67) pouring oil into a jar full of water (although Algazel uses vinegar and water); (p. 103) skin entering a tube when the physician sucks out the air; and (p. 103) whether a given volume of air can increase or decrease in size. Some of Marius' philosophical doctrines are also indebted to Algazel: (p. 73) the discussions of the different kinds of motion, (p. 73) of the impossibility of the infinite's being moved, and (p. 103) of the compression of the elements. Several other doctrines are contained in Algazel and other sources as well: (p. 59) that heaviness comes from cold, lightness from heat is also in Constantine's *Pantegni*, Theorice, IV, 2; (pp. 59-61) whether elements have color, taste and smell is similar to Isaac's *De dietis universalibus*, fol. XXXIIrv and to ps.-Aristotle *De coloribus* (791a), of which there may have existed an early twelfth-century Latin translation;[48] and (p. 71) Marius' rather confused statement concerning body and substance may have been derived from Algazel's doctrine that corporeal substance is composed of two other substances, matter and form, or from Eriugena's *De divisione naturae*, I, 20.

Among the Arabic sources should also be included the *Pantegni* of Constantine the African. The work which bore this title was a free translation of the *Kamil-As-Sinasa* of 'Ali Ibn 'Abbās,[49] completed by Constantine at Montecassino sometime before his death in 1087. It was used by William of Conches in his *Dragmaticon* during the second quarter of the twelfth cen-

---

[48]Cf. Lawn, *I Quesiti Salernitani*, tr. Alessandro Spagnuolo (Salerno, 1969), p. 79, n. 42 and note to question 21.

[49]Printed in Isaac Judaeus, *Opera omnia* (Lyons, 1515), folios 1-144. The first part of Book I has been edited and translated into Italian by Marco T. Malato and Umberto de Martini, Costantino l'Africano *L'Arte della Medicina (Pantegni)*, Parte I—Libro I (Rome, 1969). There is no satisfactory full-scale study of Constantine. For an excellent summary treatment and bibliography, see Heinrich Schipperges, *Die Assimilation der arabischen Medizin durch das lateinischen Mittelalter* (Wiesbaden, 1964), pp. 17-49. *Sudhoffs Archiv für Geschichte der Medizin und der Naturwissenschaften*, Beiheft 3. See also Boubaker ben Yahia, "Constantin l'Africain et l'école de Salerne," *Les Cahiers de Tunisie*, IX (1955), 49-59.

tury and after the middle of the century was used as a textbook for medicine at Salerno.[50] Apparently its antiquity and the ambiguity of its origins (it is, in fact, largely Galenic) had by this time removed its Arabic taint for the Salernitans.

Although in every case the material which Marius seems to have taken from Constantine could also have come from another source, the fact that there are so many correspondences between Marius and Constantine, that some of these are closer than is the case with the other possible source, and the probability that since Marius had access to Constantine's translations of Isaac and ps.-Galen he also had the better-known *Pantegni* lead us to place Constantine's *Pantegni* among the certain rather than the questionable sources of Marius' *De elementis*. Marius' knowledge of the nine "complexions" (pp. 133-135) seems clearly to have been based on *Pantegni*, Theorice, I, 6, although these are also discussed in ps.-Galen *De spermate*, which Constantine probably translated,[51] as well as Joannitius' *Isagoge*. His assertions that man is the most temperate of all animals and that only the human skin is completely temperate (p. 179) are probably based on *Pantegni*, Theorice, I, 7 and I, 9, but they can also be found in Isaac's *De dietis universalibus* and William of Conches' *Dragmaticon*. In both these cases, Marius is much closer to Constantine than to the other possible sources. He is also much indebted to *Pantegni*, Theorice, IV, 1-3 for his discussion of the natural powers of plants (pp. 157-165), although he augments the Constantinian material from other sources, especially Isaac's *Liber de elementis*,[52] *Book of Substances*,[53] *Book of Spirit and Soul*,[54] "Chapter on the Elements,"[55] and perhaps the lost work which he elsewhere refers to as Aristotle *De elementis*; and possibly from William of

---

[50]See Paul O. Kristeller, "The School of Salerno," *Bulletin of the History of Medicine*, XVII (1945), 154-155.

[51]M. Steinschneider, *Die europäischen Übersetzungen aus dem Arabischen* (Vienna, 1905-1906; repr. 1956), pp. 10-11.

[52]Isaac Judaeus, *Opera omnia* (Lyons, 1515), fol. Xra.

[53]Altmann and Stern, *Isaac Israeli*, p. 94.

[54]*Ibid.*, p. 109.

[55]*Ibid.*, pp. 124, 125.

Conches' *Dragmaticon*. But in none of these identified sources is there mention of a "viridal soul" in plants; this may have been original with Marius or it may have come from a source we have not yet discovered. On a number of other points, all noted in the edition, there is no way of telling whether Marius is depending on Constantine or one or more other possible sources.

C. *Latin Sources*. One would expect any twelfth-century author to have relied heavily on Calcidius' translation of and commentary on the *Timaeus*. Calcidius was clearly one of Marius' major sources for his doctrine of substance (pp. 71, 75, 77, 91) and his argument for the necessity of a Creator (p. 93).[56] Other correspondences with Calcidius can also be found in other sources.

Marius seems also to have known Macrobius, especially in the discussion (p. 75) of the qualities bestowed on the original substance to constitute each element. This teaching itself could have come from a number of other sources, but the manner of treatment strongly suggests Macrobius' *Commentary on the Dream of Scipio*, I, 6, 25-33.[57] In the same work are remarks similar to Marius' doctrine that composite bodies can be resolved into their elements and that the elements are never destroyed, but Marius probably used Constantine and Isaac on these points, as on the doctrine in the *Saturnalia* that fire is in perpetual need of nourishment.

Marius was also familiar with Eriugena's *De divisione naturae*. It was probably the model for the student-teacher dialogue form in which he cast his treatise, and like Eriugena he is at pains to account for all ten of Aristotle's categories in his analysis of physical nature. Portions of his account of matter (substance) and form (pp. 71-93), based in part on St. Gregory of Nyssa, also come from *De divisione naturae*.[58]

---

[56]Calcidius, *Comm. in Timaeum*, 304, 311; edited by J.H. Waszink (London, 1962), pp. 305-306, 311.

[57]Edited by James Willis (Leipzig, 1970), pp. 22-24.

[58]I am indebted to Marshall Clagett for suggesting to me the similarity between Marius' text and St. Gregory of Nyssa's *De opificio hominis* (*PG*, XLIV, 211-214; see also Pierre Duhem, *Le système*

D. *Problematical Sources.* In several cases, Marius used concepts or experiments which are found in the works of earlier authors, but either because the correspondence is not exact or because the same material can be found in several places, it is difficult to decide whether in fact he used a specific work. Costa ben Luca's *De animae et spiritus discrimine*, the *Liber Apollonii* and Al-Kindi's *De quinque essentiis* have already been discussed among the Arabic sources.

There are some similarities between Marius' *De elementis* and Nicolaus of Damascus' (ps.-Aristotle) *De plantis.* At the beginning of Book I, Nicolaus mentions that oysters have feelings like animals but grow like plants and do not move from place to place. Marius makes a similar comment on page 175. *De plantis* (II 1 [822a] of the Greek text, lacking in Alfred Sareshel's Latin version[59]) mentions that all four elements are in glass potentially. Although Marius makes a particular point of this (p. 145), it is completely consistent with the theory he has been developing that *all* composite bodies contain all four elements. *De plantis* (II 2 [838a], p. 8 of the Latin edition) also mentions in passing that air is present in glass, and that when fire is applied to glass, it breaks. But Nicolaus is talking here about earthquakes and other major movements of the earth, and he mentions glass and minerals as other examples of the same mechanism. Marius' discussion is much fuller. There are several other places where we can see a general similarity. Nicolaus mentions (I 4) that some people say plants have a soul (compare Marius, p.163), but he denies it; although later (I 7) he says that plants have "a part of a part of a soul." He also claims that plants get rid of superfluities (II 1, Latin ed. p. 27; compare Marius, p. 163), whereas Marius' other possible sources either deny this or do not mention it. And in fact Nicolaus had said earlier (I 2) that plants produce no excrement. Nicolaus also talks about

---

du monde, II [Paris, 1913], 429-430) and to Brian Lawn for pointing out that Marius probably derived it through Eriugena's *De divisione naturae*, I, 59-60 (*PL*, CXXII, 502-503).

[59]*Nicolai Damasceni De Plantis Libri Duo Aristoteli Vulgo Adscripti*, ed. E. H. F. Meyer (Leipzig, 1841).

gums and resins (I 8 and II 15), but unlike Marius (p. 163) does not cite them as evidence of the "expulsive power." Despite these similarities, it is doubtful, though not impossible, that Marius used *De plantis*. The main problem is one of chronology. We know of no Latin translation of *De plantis* before that of Alfred Sareshel, made about 1185-1190.[60] In order to have used Nicolaus' *De plantis* in Latin, Marius must either have had access to a translation now lost, or he must have written much later than all the other evidence indicates.

There are clearly some connections between *De elementis* and the Salernitan questions,[61] but it is unlikely that Marius actually used a collection of these questions. It is more probable that they shared common sources. Marius' treatment of fire descending from a lighted wick to an unlighted one (p. 55) is quite similar to the Salernitan question P 4 (Cambridge, Peterhouse MS 178, fol. 12)[62] and to Urso of Calabria's later work *De commixtionibus elementorum*, VII, k. A possible common source is William of Conches' *Dragmaticon*.[63] Marius' statement on page 65 that when two solid bodies are rubbed together or collide, the air in between ignites is treated similarly but more fully in the Salernitan question B 87 (Bodl., Auct. F. 3. 10, fol. 125). A possible common source could be Seneca, *Quaestiones naturales*, II, 22-23. The question of why in earth, water and air heat is sometimes found and sometimes cold, but in fire we always find heat and never cold is similar but not identical to two Salernitan questions, C 15 (Oxford, C.C.C. MS 233, fol. 26) and B 301 (fol. 150). The notion that fire cannot exist here below without the nourishment of air, found in Marius and C 15, is similar to Aristotle's *Meteorology* II 2 (355a) and IV 7 (383b), which I have shown above that Marius did not know,

---

[60] Otte, "Alfredus Anglicus," p. 290.
[61] For most of the information comparing *De elementis* and the Salernitan questions, and for the suggestions of possible common sources, I am indebted to Dr. Brian Lawn.
[62] I use Dr. Lawn's designation of the questions by manuscript and number. See his study of the prose questions soon to be published as volume III of the series *Auctores Britannici Medii Aevi*. At the first occurrence for each manuscript I give the complete citation, henceforth only the siglum.
[63] Edited by G. Gratarolus (Strassburg, 1567; repr. 1967), p. 40.

and to Macrobius, *Saturnalia*, 7, 13, 3, but both Marius and C 15 give more complete though different accounts than either of these two possible sources. Marius' treatment is undoubtedly based on Isaac's *De dietis universalibus*. Why well water is warm in winter and cold in summer is a very common physical question.[64] The answers given it in B 17 (fol. 128) and P 11 (fol. 3v) use the constriction and relaxation of the earth's pores as an explanatory principle, unlike Marius, who has heat fleeing from cold into the interior of the earth. William of Conches gives both explanations.[65] Finally, three questions having to do with leaves are common to Marius and the Salernitan questions. Why leaves fall in winter is given the same answer, different from Nicolaus' *De plantis*, by both Marius and one of the prose questions.[66] The common source, if there was one, is not known. The greenness of leaves is also the subject of question 15 (Lawn, *Salernitan Questions*, p. 170 and note p. 195) and is discussed in a similar but not identical manner in B 237 (fol. 144v) and N 39 (Paris, Bibl. nat. MS lat. 18081, fol. 219v). The shape of leaves, discussed very briefly by Marius, is treated more fully in B 60 (fol. 123). The source is Isaac's *De dietis universalibus*.

Whether Marius knew the works of William of Conches is more difficult to determine. There are many similarities, in addition to those we have mentioned in passing, between Marius' *De elementis* and William's *Dragmaticon* and *Glosses on the Timaeus*.[67] Marius' observation of fire descending to a wick, based ultimately on *Meteorology* I 4 (342a) and also contained in the Salernitan questions, probably comes from the *Dragmaticon* (p. 191). Brian Lawn suggests Priscianus Lydus' *Solutiones*[68] as a possible common source. Marius' discussion of matter also seems to be indebted to William on stripping

---

[64] See Brian Lawn, *The Salernitan Questions*, p. 198, note to question 44: *putei latices*.
[65] *Dragmaticon* (ed. cit.), pp. 204-205.
[66] B (fol. 156v), quoted in Lawn, *I Quesiti Salernitani*, p. 235.
[67] Guillaume de Conches *Glosae super Platonem*, ed. Edouard Jeauneau (Paris, 1965).
[68] Edited by I. Bywater (Berlin, 1886), p. 86.

three-dimensional body in place of all qualities (p. 69),[69] on the impossibility of moving an infinite body (p. 73),[70] on the transmutation of elements by alteration of qualities while substance remains unchanged (p. 77),[71] and on the doctrine that qualities are never found apart from substance (p. 77).[72] There are also similarities with Marius' discussion of the vegetable kingdom: that a fruit is composed of all four elements (p. 147);[73] and when fruit rots or is burned each element will be removed and exist actually, as it did before (p. 149);[74] and that since plants take from the earth only the nourishment appropriate to themselves, different kinds of plants can grow in the same soil (p. 161).[75] Finally, the thought-experiment of dropping a stone down a hole through the earth's center (p. 85) is also in William of Conches' *Glosses on the Timaeus*[76] as well as Adelard of Bath's *Natural Questions*, which Marius does not seem to have known. Even though it is not possible in any case to point to anything which Marius could only have got from William, it seems to me highly likely that he knew both the *Dragmaticon* and *Glosses on the Timaeus*.

All of this indicates that there was a large body of material concerning various aspects of *physica* which was used by the authors of the Salernitan questions, by William of Conches and by Marius. It is not yet possible to be specific about lines of influence among them.

E. *Unidentified Sources.* This account of sources is far from complete. We have not been able to identify the alchemical works mentioned above in the section on Arabic sources, nor are we sure which authors are meant by the "Sarraceni" who call minerals "congelata" at the beginning of Book II. Alfred Sareshel's translation of Nicolaus of Damascus' *De plantis* uses

---

[69] *Dragmaticon*, p. 29.
[70] *Glosae in Timaeum*, p. 143.
[71] *Op. cit.*, pp. 264, 275.
[72] *Op. cit.*, p. 258.
[73] *Dragmaticon*, p. 232.
[74] *Loc. cit.*
[75] *Op. cit.*, pp. 239-241.
[76] *Glosae in Timaeum*, pp. 60-61.

"minera" (not "congelata") for mineral; Hugh of Santalla's translation of the *Liber Apollonii* usually uses "mineria," although in at least one case (fol. 18r) it uses "congelata," and Hugh, unlike Marius, always uses the words "animal, nascens et mineria" for animal, vegetable and mineral. Marius also mentions a "Platonic book" which shows how tastes may be created artificially (p. 169). Although the single experiment of cooking honey to produce a bitter and salty taste is from Isaac Israeli, the remainder of Marius' material is not.

Certain conclusions emerge from this study of Marius' sources. The Latin Neoplatonic tradition was still very strong, as is evidenced by Marius' dependence on Calcidius, Eriugena and William of Conches. It is apparent that Marius did not know any of Aristotle's *libri naturales* at first hand and that most of the Aristotelian material in his book (except for that from the standard Latin works) came by way of recently translated works of Arabic authors, both the Spanish translations of Algazel's *Metaphysics* by Gundissalinus and the Constantinian translations of 'Ali Ibn 'Abbās, Isaac Israeli and ps.-Galen. The most unexpected sources are "Ibn Ḥasdāy's Neoplatonist," which Marius calls Aristotle *On the Elements*, and Isaac's commentary on this work, the so-called "Chapter on the Elements." The former is now completely lost, and the latter exists only in a single manuscript, a Hebrew translation of the Arabic original. Marius' citations may aid somewhat in reconstructing "Ibn Ḥasdāy's Neoplatonist," and his use of this work and of Isaac's commentary shows that there once were Latin translations of both, since Marius apparently did not know either Greek or Arabic. There also seems to be a bare possibility that there may have existed a Latin version of Nicolaus' *De plantis* earlier than Alfred Sareshel's. If it were not for the chronological problem, Nicolaus could be considered among Marius' highly probable sources.

This study has added a little more definite information to our knowledge of twelfth-century intellectual currents, and it has also raised new questions. Much remains to be done in this area. To appreciate adequately the scientific works of the twelfth

century, it is necessary to know what books our authors read. We are still far from being in a position to do this.

Conclusion

Marius' *De elementis* presents us with a piece of twelfth-century scientific investigation of a high order. The general rigor of its arguments, the sophisticated, if not completely developed, experimental technique, the attempt to devise a quantitative explanation for the variety of compound bodies made up of only four elements, and the explanation offered for the way elements persist in a compound are most impressive and do not square with the commonly-expressed characterizations of twelfth-century science. *De elementis* is also a study of what we would call chemical substances and processes which is completely naturalistic and materialistic and free of any magical or animistic notions. It therefore represents a kind of early Latin chemistry whose existence has not previously been taken into account in histories of chemistry.

It is important to know whether Marius was unique or whether he was one of a group of naturalistic students of matter in the twelfth century; and further, whether his work had any influence on subsequent chemical investigation or lay ignored in the Bury library. To answer the former question, one need not look beyond Chartres and Salerno. Both the collections of medical and physical questions associated with the schools of Salerno and the writings of its two most renowned physicians, Maurus and Urso, exhibit the same attitudes, as do the works of Thierry of Chartres and William of Conches in northern France.

To answer the latter is more difficult, but there is some evidence to indicate that Marius' influence was not negligible. We have already mentioned two late twelfth- and early thirteenth-century authors, both anonymous, who used his *De elementis*. One of these wrote an untitled work, largely on astronomy, contained in Paris MS Bibl. nat. lat. 15015, folios 200r-223v, which

borrowed considerable material from Marius. Using *De elementis* even more extensively was the early thirteenth-century author of the *Compendiosus tractatus de philosophia et eius secretis*, which appropriates, among other things, Marius' tables of the elements. This work is now contained in Vatican MS Barb. lat. 283, which was written in northern France in the early fourteenth century, thus showing that well over a century after its composition, *De elementis* was exerting some influence in a major intellectual center through its use in the *Compendiosus tractatus*. And in the third quarter of the thirteenth century, Roger Bacon mentions that there are 145 mixtures of the elements.[77] Where would he have got this particular number if not from Marius, either directly or indirectly? This would indicate that there are probably other yet unnoticed thirteenth-century examples of its influence.

This brings us to a consideration of what *De elementis* tells us about the nature of twelfth-century science. First of all, there is a high degree of coherence both in Marius' world view and in his treatise. Marius' world consisted of the elements with their properties behaving according to the necessities of their natures. There is no room in his conception for spontaneity or caprice. The world of nature obeyed laws, and these laws were accessible to human reason. His presentation of this world does not consist of a string of *ad hoc* explanations, but rather of a carefully worked out, internally consistent, naturalistic scheme, based on a careful and accurate observation of nature and handled with considerable dialectical skill.

We conclude then that at least a part of twelfth-century science was far from being naive, animistic and *ad hoc*. It was also much more than a revival of Antiquity, important though this was. It was bold, original, imaginative and daring. At its best it was rigorous in its arguments and precise in its observations. The world that it investigated was regular and knowable,

---

[77]"Post hec sequitur sciencia de omnibus rebus inanimatis que fiunt primo ex elementis, et hec est Alkimia, que docet quomodo centum quadraginta quinque sunt mixtiones elementorum...." *Liber Primus Communium Naturalium*, ed. Robert Steele (Oxford, 1909), I, 2. Opera hactenus inedita Rogeri Baconi, Fasc. II, p. 6.

and man by virtue of his reason was the most wonderful of God's creatures.

The Edition

Editing a text from a unique manuscript is mechanically simple, but it has its own problems. For example, if something seems to be wrong or if a given word is difficult to read, there are no other manuscripts to turn to. Fortunately, our text is quite good and has been corrected both by a contemporary reader and by a later hand. These corrections are noted in the apparatus. It has also been necessary occasionally to make conjectural emendations, but I have been quite conservative in this regard and have only departed from the text when grammar or sense made it necessary. There are two omissions in the manuscript. The first (below, p. 63) occurs in the midst of a series of clauses in parallel construction, so supplying at least the sense of the omitted words was no problem. The second (below, p. 169) omits the words "quedam pingua" from a list of the tastes. In one other place (below, p. 151) the binder has cut off three words which the corrector had added in the margin, but the context makes it clear what these words were. I have supplied them in parentheses.

The hand of the principal corrector is contemporary with, and nearly identical to, the hand of the text. There is no evidence that the corrections were made from a second manuscript; they simply correct slips made by the scribe. Transpositions of words are indicated by the corrector by placing the first two (or three or four) letters of the alphabet above the misplaced words to indicate the correct order, except in one place (p. 141) where " is placed above the transposed words. When more than two words are involved, the apparatus gives the orignal order. In several places, a later hand (designated *manus recentior* in the apparatus) has made minor changes. The authority for these corrections was undoubtedly nothing more than grammatical or contextual necessity.

In order that the notes might be as clear and simple as possible, the apparatus to the manuscript itself is keyed to the Latin text by means of line number references on each page. All other notes are keyed to the translation by a consecutive numbering throughout the work. Two devices used in the apparatus require explanation: eam] ea *cod*. indicates that "ea" of the codex has been emended to "eam" by the editor; *tr*. indicates that the corrector has transposed the order of words in the manner described above. The others are self evident.

The spelling of the codex has been maintained in the edition, even when it is unusual (i.e., diversic*u*lor, su*g*gente, me*n*brorum), except that I have used "v" for the consonant sound and "u" for the vowel. The cedilla under the "e" to indicate the "ae" diphthong is used quite whimsically by the scribe. I have reproduced his usage.

Since the meaning of the text sometimes varies considerably with the punctuation and one of an editor's responsibilities is to make clear the meaning of his text, I have adopted modern punctuation and capitalization. The text itself is highly punctuated, using the inverted semicolon for a minor pause and the point for a major pause, and this has been very useful to me in determining the meaning in many places, but as in all medieval texts punctuation is based on sound rather than grammar.

A word of caution is in order concerning the manner in which the *fontes* are listed in the notes. I indicate works which Marius probably actually used by an asterisk. Where possible, I indicate the ultimate source, even though Marius did not know it. Next I list similar material in earlier or contemporary works, without any implication that Marius necessarily used them. And finally I give later texts containing similar material, but without implying that it was derived from Marius.

Making a graceful and accurate translation is a difficult task. I have tried to preserve the tone and feeling of the original, but I have considered my primary responsibility to be accuracy. When a literal translation resulted in good English, I kept it. Sometimes, however, it was necessary to exercise some license either to achieve acceptable English or to make the meaning

Introduction

clear. In those few places where the meaning was not clear, I have added notes to the translation.

I suppose that no one is really satisfied with a translation. Still, making this one has been a pleasure. It is my hope that those with a little Latin may, with the help of the facing translation, improve their feeling for the Latin language at a time when it was a flexible, natural and sensible vehicle for human communication, as it usually was in the twelfth century.

Some Observations on the Milieu of Marius' De Elementis: *An Extract from a Personal Correspondence to the Editor*

by
Brian Lawn

So far, the evidence seems to point more and more away from Salerno. In addition to the objections which you have made in *Viator*, III (1972), 210 ff., one might point out that Salerno was nourished on Greek thought, not Arab, hence its ancient title, 'Civitas Hippocratica.' The masters there followed Aristotle, not Plato, and made use for the most part of translations from the Greek, not from Arabic, as Birkenmajer has shown. Because of this, the penetration of the translations of Constantinus, made from the Arabic, into Salernitan medical and scientific thought was very slow, as Daremberg was the first to notice (see C. Vieillard, *Gilles de Corbeil* [Paris, 1909], pp. 166, 182), and Kristeller also drew attention to this fact (see his "School of Salerno," *B.H.M.*, XVII [1945], 154 and my *Salernitan Questions* [1963], p. 20). Again, the Salernitans also seemed to show extremely little interest in mineralogy (see *Sal. Quest.*, p. 48), a lack of interest reflected earlier by Adelard, who devoted none of his questions to this subject, and later by Alexander Neckam, who was much influenced by Urso and the Salernitans. It would seem inevitable therefore that in spite of the designation of the author of the treatise as 'Marius Salernitanus,' the work itself cannot be called, in any sense of the word, a Salernitan text, written in Salerno and transmitting Salernitan ideas. We must look much further north for the intellectual climate in which it took shape, a climate in fact quite the opposite of that which prevailed in Salerno, one permeated by Arab though and a very definite interest in practical mineralogy, and one in which Neoplatonism prevailed over Aristotelianism.

I had at first thought that perhaps Chartres could be a pos-

sibility (cf. Haskins, *Studies in the History of Mediaeval Science*, pp. 88 ff.), with its prevailing Neoplatonism and contact with Spanish translators from Arabic. By about the third decade of the eleventh century (not later than *ca.* 1135) William of Conches was using the *Pantegni* of Constantinus, but there is no evidence that he knew the translations of Isaac's *De dietis* so much used by Marius, nor is there any evidence, as far as I know, that these other translations of Constantinus had reached Chartres before the end of the century. Also, mineralogy and the more practical part of the work do not fit in with Chartres at all. Similar remarks apply to England, where in the twelfth century Arab learning imported from Spain and Lorraine was more concerned with mathematics and astronomy than with mineralogy and chemistry, and there is no evidence of the Constantinian translations being used there before the end of the century (see *Sal. Quest.*, p. 58). At the end of the century, Neckam's natural philosophy was much more Salernitan in tone than the *De elementis* of Marius. In Paris, it is probable that scientific and medical studies developed later still (see *Sal. Quest.*, pp. 67 ff.).

Finally, one ought, I think, to consider Montpellier. John of Salisbury, in his *Metalogicon*, written 1159-60, classes Montpellier along with Salerno as a centre for medical teaching, and the French city soon rivalled and later surpassed the Italian one in its reputation for learning. About 1140, after the invasion of Spain by the Almohad sect, there was a persecution of the Jews, causing many of them to flee and settle in Languedoc and Provence. Many Jewish translators from Arabic, philosophers and physicians seem to have come to Montpellier after this date, and this, combined with the already existing communications with the Arabs of Spain, produced an intellectual climate much more orientated towards Arab philosophy, science and medicine than was the case in Salerno. S. d'Irsay draws attention to the fact that it was often through the intermediary of Hebrew that such Arab texts passed into Latin in the twelfth century, just as earlier on, in the ninth century, Syriac formed the bridge connecting Greek texts with Arabic (*Histoire des Universités* [Paris,

1933], I, 112, and see pp. 110-120 for a discussion about Montpellier). Of the earlier writings of Isaac Israeli which may have been known to Marius, the surviving fragments of the *Book of Substances* are in Arabic, the *Book on Spirit and Soul* and the "Chapter on the Elements," also both fragmentary, are in Hebrew. It is also extremely likely that other works of Isaac, including the Constantinian translation of his book on diets, would be studied at Montpellier long before they were accepted at Salerno, for the reasons given above. In Montpellier, therefore, it seems to me that we have exactly the combination of Spanish-Arab-Hebrew learning that we are looking for in connection with Marius. There is evidence too of inter-relations between Montpellier and Salerno during the twelfth century and of the migration of students from the latter city to the former (see d'Irsay, *op. cit.*, p. 117 and the authorities there quoted), so that there would be nothing unusual in Marius' coming from Salerno to work and study in Montpellier, and there absorbing and using in his writings the newer Arabic learning. Towards the end of the century, when the reputation of Montpellier was firmly established, Gilles of Corbeil stayed for a time at Montpellier on his way from Salerno to Paris (see my *Sal. Quest.*, pp. 69 ff.). This might account too for the traces of Salernitan influence which are still apparent in Marius' treatise. As for the Neoplatonic tendencies in the *De elementis*, in the words of Klibansky: "Through the Arabs the Neoplatonic current was transmitted to medieval Jewish thought" (*The Continuity of the Platonic Tradition* [1950], p. 17), and I have no doubt that Neoplatonism was prevalent in any philosophic teaching which may have taken place during the second half of the twelfth century in Montpellier. This is born out by the writings of Alain de Lille, who taught in Montpellier towards the end of the century and who was probably only reflecting a tendency which was already well established. (On him see M.-Th. d'Alverny, *Alain de Lille, textes inédits* [Paris, 1965], and for his Neoplatonism and connections with the school of Chartres, *ibid.*, pp. 21-22 and Baumgartner, "Die Philosophie des Alanus de Insulis," *Beiträge*, II.4 [1896].) Whilst in Montpellier he evidently got to

know a considerable section of the prose Salernitan questions, and it is possible that he even contributed some of the questions himself, since a group of one hundred forty-one found in a Paris manuscript (Bibl. nat. lat. 18081, *ca.* 1230) bears the title "Questiones Alani." M.-Th. d'Alverny has shown that we find ideas from two of these questions in works known to be by Alain, i.e., *Parabola*, *Distinctiones*, and a sermon by him (*op. cit.*, p. 56). Rather more than half of these questions, seventy-three to be exact, are found in other manuscripts containing these prose questions, thus leaving us with sixty-eight which are found in no other manuscript. Perhaps it would not be too fanciful to suggest that these particular questions originated in Montpellier through the influence of Urso and the Salernitans. That by this time this influence was pretty strong we can gather from the commentary of Alain's pupil, Raoul de Longchamp, on the *Anticlaudianus* of his former master at Montpellier. In this commentary, he makes considerable use of Urso's *Aphorisms* and accompanying *Gloss*, as C. Matthaes was the first to show (see his *Der Salernitaner Artz Urso* [Leipzig, 1918], pp. 6-7, where he lists five borrowings). Also in this work, and in a little philosophic Summa entitled *Cornicula*, probably written earlier, Raoul shows his dependence on the *De philosophia* of William of Conches (see M. Grabmann, *Handschriftliche Forschungen und Mitteilungen zum Schrifttum des Wilhelm von Conches* in *Sitzungsberichte der Bayerischen Akademie*, Heft 10 [München, 1935], pp. 31-39, where he lists parallel passages), thus showing the continuing influence of Chartrian Neoplatonism in Montpellier. Finally, first B. Hauréau (*Notices et Extraits*, I [Paris, 1890], pp. 325-333) and then A. Birkenmajer (*Le Rôle* [1930], pp. 8 ff.) drew attention to Raoul's use of translations from Arabic of the Aristotelian *libri naturales* with the commentaries of Averroes, and of works by Avicenna and Ptolemy, as well as of medical writings by Hippocrates, Galen, Rhazes and Isaac Israeli (on Raoul, see also R. Bossuat's edition of Alain's *Anticlaudianus* [Paris, 1955], esp. p. 43, and the work by M.-Th. d'Alverny already quoted).

It is quite true that the writings of both Alain and his pupil

only represent the state of affairs in the schools at Montpellier during about the last quarter of the twelfth century, when the full tide of Arab learning had begun to flow pretty strongly in the Latin West, when the influence from Salerno was much greater, and possibly that of Chartrian philosophic thinking had increased. Nevertheless, as I have tried to show, these movements do not suddenly appear. There is a gradual advance along preconceived lines, and tendencies which are already there slowly develop. It seems to me that Marius' *De elementis* could be a milestone along this route, pointing rather towards the beginning of these tendencies than marking out the middle of the way or the end.

In conclusion perhaps it should be pointed out that, if the Montpellier origin is accepted, the original text could have been copied out by an English student resident there during the last quarter of the twelfth century. Dr. Richard Hunt tells me that he dates the MS well before 1200. It could, of course, as you say, equally well have been copied in Paris, which had just as good communications with Montpellier. That it was known and used in north France you have already discovered. My feeling is that there is now no need to bring in Salerno in any part of its transmission.

THE ELEMENTS by Marius, BOOK ONE

[D.]...And what is the nature of water?

M. It is cold and moist; and similarly we have two arguments. One argument is that the bodies of those people who drink a lot of water or who are around it all the time, such as fisherman and sailors and many others, although they are not composed of water, are nevertheless always cold and moist. Another argument is: concerning its coldness, although you heat water until it boils, if you take the heat away it will little by little return to its natural coldness; concerning its moistness, all things which arise from the earth dry out and die without water, even those things which are in the earth.

D. And what is its property?

M. Undoubtedly the same as earth's, namely heaviness. For although you lift water as high as you can, still when you let it go it will immediately return to a lower place. And this heaviness, along with its moistness, forces it to liquefy, that is to flow from a higher place to a lower one unless it encounters some obstacle. This heaviness also makes both earth and water move toward the center; the physicists call this motion "motion toward the center." Therefore earth and water have in common coldness and weight, although these are greater in earth. But water differs from earth in being moist; for this reason it is also liquid and earth is not.

D. And what is the nature of air?

M. The nature of air is heat along with moistness, although you ought to inquire first if air exists or not. For many have denied and still deny that such a thing as air can be found in the world.

D. And so what arguments will you offer to prove that it can be found?

M. What better argument can you seek than the inflation of a bellows? For unless some body entered it, it could surely never be filled up. Likewise, if you take a jar and place it mouth

LIBER PRIMUS Marii DE ELEMENTIS

...[190^A] aque quę est?

M. Frigida utique est et humida, et in duo similiter habemus argumenta. Unum quidem eorum corpora qui aquam bibunt assidue vel eam frequentant, ut piscatores et naute ac multi alii, etsi non sint de aqua, algentia tamen sunt semper et humectantia. Aliud autem de frigiditate quidem quia, licet aquam calefaceris usque ad fervorem, tamen si ignem subtraxeris, ad naturalem paulatim redibit algorem. De humiditate vero, quia omnia que nascuntur de terra, si aqua eis defecerit, siccantur atque moriuntur ęciam quę sunt in terra.

D. Et que eius proprietas?

M. Procul dubio que et terrę, videlicet ponderositas. Nam licet aquam in altum quam potes efferas, cum tamen dimissa fuerit, statim in inferius remeabit. Et hec ponderositas cum humiditate cogit eam liquescere, hoc est de loco altiori ad inferiorem, si nullum inveniat obstaculum, elabi. Quę eciam ponderositas et terram et aquam moveri facit ad centrum; quem motum vocant phisici "motum ad medium." Conveniunt igitur terra et aqua in frigiditate et pondere, licet maius sit in tellure. Differt autem aqua in humiditate a terra, unde et liquida est et non terra.

D. Et que est natura aeris?

M. Natura aeris est calor cum humiditate, licet prius debeas inquirere si existat aer necne. Negarunt enim multi atque adhuc negant illum in mundo inveniri posse.

D. Quod igitur dabis argumentum quo approbes inveniri posse illum?

M. Quod melius queris argumentum quam de inflatione follium? Quippe qui nisi corpus aliquod subingrederetur, nequaquam utique implerentur. Item: Si amphoram accipias et

---

2. utique *add.*   3. Unum quidem] Unumquodque *cod.*   4. sint *add.*   15. hoc *corr. ex.* hec   21. et non terra *add.*   28. inflatione *corr. ex* inflamatione

downward in water, you will see that no water entered it. This would not happen unless it was already full of air.[1]

D. From the things you have said and many other things of the same sort, I understand that air can be found. But what is the difference between air and that vapor which rises from water when it is heated by fire?

M. The same as between one loaf of bread well cooked and another not well cooked.

D. Therefore, according to you, that vapor is a kind of air.

M. Yes indeed, that is what I say it is. And from this scientists prove that water is changed into air, because if you take a kettle full of water and heat it until all the water has boiled away, you must not believe that the water has completely perished, but rather that all of it has changed into vapor. But that vapor becomes gradually more rare, and thus it is finally completely mixed with air.

D. Indeed I understand this well, but what is the difference between air and wind?

M. The truth is that there is the same difference between these two things as there is between air before it has entered a bellows and the same air when it is being forced out of the bellows.

D. It is completely clear from what you have said that wind is air, but air moved, not at rest.[2]

M. I believe that this is so beyond doubt, and those people whose business it is to investigate nature also assert it to be thus.

D. It has been proved sufficiently that air does exist, and that there are three kinds of air, namely vapor, air at rest, and air in motion. But how can you prove that air is hot and moist?

M. I can give you two arguments concerning its heat. One is that vapor only rises from water when the water is heated by the sun or by fire. Another is that air itself is the nourishment of fire, because fire cannot remain very long when air cannot get at it. If you want visible evidence of this, take a lighted candle and

---

[1] *Cf.* Philo, *De ingeniis spiritualibus* (ed. V. Rose in *Anecdota Graeca et Graecolatina*, II, 300)
[2] *Cf.* Algazel, *Metaph.* * (ed. J. T. Muckle, p. 159)

directe eam ore subterius in aquam mittas, videbis quia de hac aqua nichil subintrabit; sed hoc nisi quia aere plena est non evenit.

D. Ex his sane quę dixisti et aliis multis huiusmodi, intelligo ego aerem posse inveniri; sed que est differentia inter aerem et eum qui ex aqua igni calefacta consurgit vaporem?

M. Eadem que est inter panem bene coctum et panem alium non bene coctum.

D. Ergo secundum te genus est aeris vapor ille.

M. Nempe. Sic dico ego esse. Et ex hoc probant magistri aquam in aerem commutari. Quia si lebetem plenam aquę acceperis et usque ad aquę totius decoctionem calefeceris, non est credendum quod aqua omnino perierit, sed in vaporem tota exit. Vapor autem ille paulatim subtiliatur, ac sic tandem aeri commiscetur.

D. Hoc ecce intelligo ego bene, sed inter aerem et ventum quid est distantię?

M. Revera idem distantie est et inter eos quod est inter aerem antequam in folles intraverit et eundem cum vi follium expulsus exierit.

D. Patet certe ex tuis sermonibus quia ventus est aer, sed aer motus, non quietus.

M. Ita proculdu-[190B]-bio credo ego esse, et sic esse asserunt, qui dant operam naturę investigande.

D. Aerem posse inveniri satis est probatum, et trium generum esse ipsum: vaporem videlicet, ac quietum aerem, atque aerem motum. Sed quomodo poteris probare aerem calidum et humidum esse?

M. Utique de calore possum ego argumenta duo dare: unum quidem quod non consurgit vapor aque nisi vel ex solis vel ex ignis calore; aliud vero quod dieta ignis extat aer ipse. Quia nusquam potest ignis diu stare, ubi aerem moveri non sit

---

1. hac *add.*   2. quia] + de *del.*   5. ego *add.*   13. omnino] + non *del.*
19. follium *corr. ex* folium

put it in a large jar. Then stop up the mouth so that no air can get in or out, and immediately you will see that the fire goes out.[3] Another proof that air is the nourishment of fire is that the fire which appears in a brazier does not rise from the wood or oil or wax or any other fuel whatsoever until after that fuel is turned into a vapor. Whence also no one doubts that flame is nothing other than air heated by fire. And that flame comes into being from vapor, I can show you thus. For if you have a fire of burning wax or pitch or some other fatty matter, and then you throw some water into the fire, but not so much that it could put out the fire, you will see that the flame will suddenly increase and leap upward. But no body is increased unless another is added to it; and so the body by which the flame was thus increased was doubtlessly the vapor of water. Therefore you see and understand clearly that air is the nourishment of fire. But nothing is the nourishment of anything to which it is not similar in some way. But since fire is hot, air which is its nourishment is also hot, since it is not similar to it in any quality other than heat.

D. It has indeed been sufficiently proved that air is hot. But why is it not so hot as fire?

M. It cannot be so hot; for if it were, it would be fire itself, and not just its nourishment.

D. The arguments you have put forth suffice to establish that air is hot. But can you offer some argument concerning its humidity?

M. Indeed, I can give you two. One is that the vapor which rises from water rises only until it reaches a cold place. Then it cannot rise any higher but is changed again into water and quickly falls to a lower place. In the same way, vapor in a jar, when it strikes the lid by which the jar is covered, cannot rise any higher and is turned again into water and falls again into the jar.[4] For unless heat were the only difference between vapor

---

[3] *Cf.* Philo, *De ingeniis spiritualibus* (*ed. cit.*, pp. 308-309) and Constantine the African, *Pantegni,* * Theorice, IV, 6-7. Urso of Salerno describes a similar experiment in his *Glossas*, 8, 51 and 72

[4] *Cf.* Algazel, *Metaph.* * (*ed. cit.*, p. 158)

possibile. Quod si visibiliter velis inspicere, accipe candelam atque illam accensam in dolium mitte, atque ita foramina cuncta claude quod aer nec intrare possit nec exire, statimque videbis quoniam extinguetur ignis. Item quod aer dieta sit ignis, flamma enim que apparet in foco non fit nisi vel ex lignis vel ex oleo vel ex cera, vel ex alio quolibet ignis postquam in vaporem vertitur nutrimento. Unde eciam dubitat nullus quia flamma nichil est aliud quam aer igni calefactus. Et quod flamma fiat ex vapore, possum tibi ita ostendere. Igni siquidem, cere vel pici vel cuilibet alii pingui materię adherenti, si tunc in ignem proicias aliquid aquę, non tantum tamen quod ignem possit extinguere, videbis utique flammam subito multipliciter crescere et sursum altissime emicare. Sed nullum corpus augmentatur nisi ei aliud adiungatur, corpus autem quo flama ita crevit procul dubio vapor aque fuit. Vides igitur et intelligis perpatenter quia ignis dieta est aer. Sed nichil est dieta alicuius rei quod in aliquo simile non sit ei. Cum vero ignis sit calidus, calidus est et aer, qui est dieta illius, cum in aliqua qualitate alia quam calore similis non sit eius.

D. Calidum sane esse aerem probatum est satis, sed quare non est tam calidus quam et ignis?

M. Non potest esse tam calidus. Si enim ita esset, iam aer ignis esset et non dieta illius.

D. Argumentatum est quod sufficit de calore aeris, sed de eius humiditate nunquid aliquod argumentum dabis?

M. Etiam certe duo. Unum quidem quod vapor ille qui ex aqua surgit cum tantum usque conscendit, quod locum frigidum repperit, superius emicare non potest; immo iterum in aquam conversus, in inferius repente recidit quemadmodum et vapor urcei, cum operimentum quo urceus est opertus offendit, ulterius nequit transcendere, et rursus in aquam vertitur et in

---

2. illam accensam *tr.*   14. flama ita *tr.*   17. calidus] + esse *del.*   24-25. de eius humiditate nunquid *tr. ex* nunquid de eius humiditate   31. rursus in aquam vertitur *tr. ex* vertitur rursus in aquam

and water, when heat was removed the vapor would not be turned again into water. Therefore, it is clear that air is humid, just as water is. Another argument concerning the humidity of air is that it is empty and loose and does not prevent men from penetrating it in going from place to place as the solidity of earth does. For this reason, some people have said that it does not exist.

D. You have shown well by your arguments that air is hot and moist. But what is its property?

M. To rise upward. One proof of this is that whenever a kettle of water is heated by fire, you will always see a vapor rising upward. Another proof is that if you take a wineskin and fill it full of air and then tie the mouth closed tightly; if you then force it down into the depths of water, as soon as you let it go you will see it spring up to the surface of the water, that is, to the place of the other air.[5]

D. Therefore I see that the property of air is to fly upward, that it is empty and loose, penetrable, hot and moist; and that air and water differ in that air is hot and water is cold, but that they are alike in that they are both penetrable, but we can penetrate air more easily. They also are alike in being moist and in receiving heat or cold quickly, depending on whether the sun or fire is near or far away.

M. You have spoken well and shown that you have understood well. And therefore I do not doubt that you also understand what the difference is between air and earth, or between earth and water.

D. I assure you it has not escaped me. But what is the nature of fire, or what is its property?

M. It is hot, of course, and dry. There is no need to prove that it is hot since everyone knows this by experience. But an argument for its dryness is that it dries out all moist things to the point that they utterly dissolve. Its property is to fly upward, in the same manner we have said air does, but it does so

---

[5] *Cf.* Algazel, *Metaph.* * (*ed. cit.*, pp. 99, 135 and 143); also Aristotle, *Physica* VIII 5 (255b) and *De caelo* IV 4 (311b)

Liber Primus

urceum redescendit. Quod nisi nulla preter calorem esset differentia inter vaporem et aquam, deficiente calore, non verteretur vapor in aquam, patit igitur aerem esse humidum, sicut et aquam. Aliud autem de aeris humiditate argumentum est quia ipse inanis et laxus est, nec prohibet hominem de loco ad locum penetrare per se, sicut facit soliditas terrę. Unde non nulli illum non posse dixerunt inveniri. [190 C]

D. Bene argumentis tuis ostendisti de aere quia calidus est et humidus. Sed que est proprietas illius?

M. Conscendere in altum, et inde est argumentum unum quia lebete aquę plena calefacta est igne, semper vaporem videbis sursum emigrare. Alterum, quia si utrem acceperis, et aere illum impleveris, atque firmissime os ligaveris, et ad aquam profundam veniens usque in fundum aquę vi demiseris, si tamen ibidem dimiseris statim usque ad aquę superficiem emicare videbis, ad locum videlicet alterius aeris.

D. Video igitur proprietatem esse aeris evolare sursum, eumdemque esse inanem sive laxum, penetrabilem, calidum atque humidum, et quia differunt aer et aqua in eo quod aer est calidus et aqua est frigida; in eo vero conveniunt, quod penetrabilis est uterque quamvis aerem facilius valeamus penetrare. Conveniunt ęciam in humiditate et in recipiendo velociter calore vel frigore, sole vel igne prope existente seu longe.

M. Bene dixisti et bene intellexisse te monstrasti; et inde non dubito ego te etiam intelligere inter aerem et terram vel inter terram et aquam quid sit distantię.

D. Non est absconditum michi scias, sed que est ignis natura vel eiusdem proprietas?

M. Calidus nempe est et siccus. Sed ad calorem ostendendum nullum est necessarium argumentum, cum nemini sit incompertum. Argumentum autem est ad eius comprobandam siccitatem quod humida omnia desiccat usque ad ipsorum dissolutionem. Proprietas vero eius est sursum evolare, quemad-

---

4. aeris humiditate *tr. corr. ex* esse   14. fundum *corr. ex* profundum   16. ad locum *add.*   29. ad

more quickly and more obviously than air. For we see that flame always rises upward rapidly, while a vapor only does so slowly when forced by the power of some heat. Physicists call this sort of motion "motion from the center."

D. I am considering carefully what you have said about the property of fire, but there is still one thing that makes me doubt. For if you take a lighted wick, and you blow it out quickly with your breath; if nevertheless you quickly, before the charred portion is burned up, place it close underneath a flame, you will see the flame descend and the wick begin burning again.[6]

M. You ought not to doubt on this account. For many before you have also had this doubt. The ancient teachers solved the problem this way: They said that the vapor which arises from the wick is the nourishment of fire and that fire turns itself in whatever direction it finds its nourishment. But I myself solve this problem in another way. For I say that when a flame is put near a wick which has just been blown out, fire arises in the wick because of the heat of the flame itself, which is greater above, but is present, even though slightly, below [that is, near the wick]. The vapor which rises from the wick and is common to both is heated up and illuminated, and thus the wick to which the vapor adheres is set on fire. And thence it is argued that unless some amount of fire were remaining in the wick, the vapor could not be heated or illuminated, nor could the wick then be lighted. Similarly when some fire adheres to two firebrands which are nearly touching, the air which touches them both is heated and illuminated, and the air itself is flame. But if there were no fire in the other, the air would not be set on fire.

D. I understand well and without doubt that the property of fire is to fly upward. But is it impenetrable like earth, or can it be penetrated like air?

M. Since we can only find three kinds of fire, therefore we assert that there are three species of it. For it is found either in

---

[6] *Cf.* William of Conches, *Dragmaticon** (ed. Gratarolus, pp. 40, 191); also Salernitan question P 46 (Cambridge, Peterhouse MS 178, fol. 12), Priscianus Lydus, *Solutiones* (ed. I. Bywater, p. 86), Urso, *De commixtionibus elementorum*, VII, k (ed. Stürner), and Arist. *Meteor.* I 4 (342a)

Liber Primus 55

modum diximus et de aere, sed citius tamen atque apertius evolat aere. Videmus namque flammam semper atque festinanter sursum conscendere, vaporem vero, non nisi paulatim alicuius caloris vigore cogente. De motu autem isto, dicunt phisici, quia est "motus de medio."

D. Intueor aperte quod de ignis dixisti proprietate sed unum est quod me adhuc facit dubitare. Si enim lichinum accensum acceperis, et illum flatu tuo repente extinxeris, si tamen statim antequam consumatur carbo, prope aliquam flammam subtus adhibueris, flammam quidem descendere et lichinum reaccendere videbis.

M. Non debes equidem inde dubitare. Multi enim ante te hanc dubitationem habuere, et antiqui doctores hoc modo eam persolvere. Dixerunt quippe vaporem illum qui de lichino surgit dietam ignis esse, ipsumque ignem ubicumque dietam suam invenerit illuc se vertere. Sed ipse ego dubitationem illam aliter persolvo. Dico enim de lichino illo flatu subito extincto, cum flamme adhibetur, ex ipsius flamme calore superiori et inferiori, licet minimus ignis fit lichino. Vapor qui ex hoc consurgit et medius est utriusque calefit et illuminatur, et ita lichinus cui vapor adheret accenditur, et inde argumentum est quia nisi in lichino aliqua ignis plenitudo remansisset [190^D] nec vapor calefieri aut illuminari, nec lichinus iam accendi posset. Quemadmodum duobus ticionibus quibus aliquid ignis adheret prope adiunctis, aer qui est medius calefit et illuminatur, et ipsa est flamma. Quod si in altero ignis non esset, nec aer accenderetur.

D. Bene et absque dubitatione intelligo proprietatem ignis esse sursum evolare, sed numquid eum penetrari non posse ut tellurem vel posse penetrari dicam ut aerem?

M. Quoniam ignem nisi tribus modis invenire non possumus, ideo tres eius species esse asserimus. Aut enim invenitur in aliqua solida et spissa materia, ipso igni calefacta et accensa,

some solid and dense matter, which is heated up and set aflame by the fire itself, such as wood or iron or other similar things; or it will be found in flame; or it will be found in air, illuminated by the gleaming of the fire itself. The fire which adheres to the solid and dense matter cannot be penetrated because of the solidity of the matter itself. Indeed flame cannot be traversed by an animal without injury, but it can be penetrated by an inanimate body. However, air illuminated by the gleaming of fire can easily be penetrated by any sort of body.

D. You have shown adequately above that its property is to rise upward; but nevertheless you have intimated that it stops when it arrives at its natural place, just as you pointed out similarly about the wineskin full of air. But what is that place in which the burning fire is contained, and where it rests when it arrives there?

M. According to Plato, all the way to the sun;[7] but according to Aristotle and others who study natural phenomena, as far as the upper limit of the air.[8] For they say that the whole place as far as the circle of the moon is fire, since because that place exists close to the motion of the firmament, it is heated up by that motion and receives the qualities of fire.

D. I see well what you have said about fire, and I understand clearly from your words in what respect air and fire are different, namely that in the one (that is, fire) there is dryness, and in the other, moistness. And that they are alike in being hot, although the heat is greater, stronger, and burning in fire, while in air it is less and weaker and does not burn things up; and that they both also fly upward, although fire does so much more rapidly. I have also read in ancient books on the elements that their first qualities were heat and cold, dryness and moistness, and that from coldness came the heaviness of earth and water, while from heat came the lightness of air and fire.[9] But I do not understand either why earth falls more rapidly than

---

[7] secundum Platonem] Cf. *Tim.* 40 A-B
[8] secundum Aristotelem] *Cf. Meteor.* I 3 (340b)
[9] *Cf.* Constantine, *Pantegni,*° Theorice, IV 2 and Algazel *Metaph.*° (*ed. cit.*, p. 143)

Liber Primus

ut in ligno vel ferro seu qualibet alia; vel invenietur in flamma; vel invenietur in aere, ipsius ignis illuminato splendore. Sed qui solide ac spisse materiei adheret, propter ipsius materiei soliditatem penetrari non valet. Flamma vero animali quidem sine lesione pervia non est, sed inanimato corpori penetrabilis est. Aer autem splendore ignis illuminatus a quolibet corpore facillime penetrari potest.

D. Satis supra ostendisti de aere quia proprietas eius est sursum conscendere, sed tamen cum ad suum naturalem locum pervenerit, eum insinuasti pausare, sicut per simile ostendisti de utre pleno aere. Sed quis est ille locus in quo terminatur ignis accensus, et ad quem cum venerit requiescit?

M. Secundum Platonem quidem usque ad solem, sed secundum Aristotilem et alios qui de naturalibus agunt, usque ad finem aeris superiorem. Dicunt enim exinde locum totum usque ad lunę circulum esse ignem, quia enim motui firmamenti locus ille vicinus extitit, ex ipso motu concaluit atque ignis qualitates recepit.

D. Bene quod dixisti de igne video, et bene ex verbis tuis in quo differant aer atque ignis cognosco, videlicet quod in altero, hoc est igne, siccitas est atque humiditas in altero. Et quod conveniunt in calore, licet in igne maior sit calor fortiorque et concremans; in aere vero minor atque debilior et non cremans; et quod evolant eciam sursum ambo, licet ignis multo magis properet evolando. Legi quoque in antiquis voluminibus de elementis quod prime eorum fuerunt qualitates calor atque frigiditas, siccitas atque humiditas, et quod ex frigiditate supervenit terrę et aquę ponderositas, ex calore vero aeri atque igni levitas. Sed non percipio quare vel terra in inferius descendat velocius

---
2. illuminato *corr. ex* illuminatio

water—since both are cold—or why fire flies upward more rapidly than air, since both fire and air are hot. For if I should say that fire has a greater upward speed because it is hotter than air, what shall I say about earth, which has a greater downward velocity than water even though water is much colder than earth?

M. Do not think, my son, that heat or moistness confers that velocity; rather it is dryness which makes fire fly upward more quickly and earth descend swiftly downward.

D. I understand well what you have said, and I also understand this from the force of your words, that slowness comes forth from moistness and affects water so that it descends more slowly than earth, but affects air so that it flies upward more slowly than fire. But I ask myself this: show by a strict argument whether or not colors, tastes, and odors exist in the elements in the same manner they do in things composed of the elements.

M. Indeed they seem to have colors, for in some places earth is seen to be white, in others black, in others red, and in others even yellow.[10] But water, when someone sees it from afar, looks somewhat green, and when it falls into the depths from on high, it appears nearly white. Air is also variously colored, depending on whether it is close to the sun, the moon, or fire. Fire too, when it is in dense matter, is reddish, but in a flame it is yellowish; while in sunlight it is nearly white. They appear, I say, to have colors of this sort; but the truth of the matter is that they have no color, as is evident in the case of the earth. Indeed, I say, true earth in its simplest state ought to be thoroughly dry and cold and completely one. And if it were colored, it ought to have only one color. But since it seems to have not one, but rather innumerable, colors, these colors are not its own but belong rather to those things which are associated with it. And similarly with tastes and odors. Also, true water ought to be cold and moist and similarly completely one,

---

[10] *Cf.* Calcidius, *Comm. in Tim.* * 331-333 (ed. Waszink, pp. 325-327), Algazel, *Metaph.* * (*ed. cit.*, p. 143), Isaac, *De dietis universalibus* * (*Opera omnia*, Lyons, 1515, fol. XXXIIr-v) and ps.-Arist., *De coloribus* (791a).

quam aqua, cum utraque sit frigida, vel ignis cicius evolet superius quam aer, cum calidus sit et ignis et aer. Si enim dixero quod illa ad superna velocitas sit in igne propter hoc quod calidior est aere, quid de terra dicam, cui maior inest velocitas in infima plusquam aquę cum multo sit maior aquę frigiditas quam terrę?

M. Ne reputes, fili, quia velocitatem illam [191^A] conferat calor sive humiditas; immo siccitas quę et ignem sursum cicius evolare, et terram facit ad ima properanter descendere.

D. Bene quod dixisti intelligo, et hoc etiam ex sermonis tui vigore percipio, quod ex humiditate provenit tarditas, aquę quidem ut tardius quam terra descendat ad infima, aeri vero ut igne tardius evolet ad suprema. Sed hoc michi queso: recto argumento ostende si colores, sapores et odores sint in elementis, quemadmodum in his quę ex eis composita sunt necne.

M. Colores quidem habere videntur, sicut terra alias alba, alias nigra, alias rubra, alias etiam crocea esse conspicitur. Aqua vero cum quis eam delonge videt, quodammodo viridis apparet, et cum de sublimi in ima decidit, paret quoniam candida sit. Aer quoque est diversiculor secundum quod vel soli vel lunę vel igni est proprior. Ignis etiam in spissa materia est, quasi rubeus; in flamma vero, quasi croceus; in splendore autem est quasi candidus. Videntur, inquam, huiusmodi colores habere, sed in rei veritate, nullo participant colore, sicut patens est in tellure. Quippe quę vera, dico, atque simplissima sicca penitus debet esse et frigida et omnino una; et si colorata esset unum tantummodo colorem habere deberet. Cum vero non unum sed innumerabiles habere colores videatur, non sunt utique eius illi colores; immo eorum quę ipsi associantur, et similiter de saporibus et odoribus. Aqua vero vera frigida et humida et omnino similiter una esse debet, et unum solummodo habere colorem si haberet, sed ipsam quam plurimos habere apparet. Viridis enim, ut supra dictum est, esse videtur cum procul conspicitur;

---

20. soli] solis *cod.*   25. penitus] + non *del. man. rec.*   27. colorem *corr. ex* calorem
28-29. illi colores *tr.*

and if it had color, to have only one. But it appears that it has a great many. For it seems to be green, as we have said above, when it is seen from a distance. But when the person who saw green from a distance comes near, it is evident that there is no green in it. Also, when it is falling from above, water appears to be white, but that whiteness is not in it. Rather it is an appearance caused by the clarity of the air and the tenuity of the water itself. But the other colors too which appear in waters, as for instance in flame or in a stream stirred up by a storm, or in many other things, indeed these are not the colors of the water but rather of things joined with the water.[11] And thus with tastes and odors. But in water which is used for drinking, neither color nor taste nor odor is found. Concerning air, however, it is not necessary to prove that it does not have color, for it is because of the fact that it is colorless that it is reputed by some people not to exist. Because if it had color, they say, it would be known from its color. Also as in the previous case, if it is going to have color, since it itself is only one thing, namely hot and moist, it ought to have only one color. But it has one color when the sun is rising or setting and another at midday. It appears to be alternately of various colors around the moon, sometimes red, sometimes yellow, and sometimes green. And if fire is without doubt completely one, namely hot and dry, if it had color it ought all to be a single color. But it appears to us to have many, and this is because of the matter to which it adheres, as we see concerning flame in dense matter. For if it adheres to pitch, the color verges on black; if to waxy matter, on yellow; and if to sulphur—depending on which kind of sulphur it is—it will verge either on blue or between green and yellow. A coal also, if it is of solid or wet wood, takes on a red color; if of porous or dry wood, white. Therefore, if an odor is found in air or fire, it is not the odor of these elements themselves, but of things which are joined to them. No taste, however, is perceived to be in them.

D. You have shown sufficiently that neither color nor taste

---

[11] *Cf.* Algazel, *Metaph.** (*ed. cit.*, p. 156)

Liber Primus

sed cum qui delonge viridem videbat prope est, nullam sibi viriditatem inesse comperit. Videtur etiam cum de alto elabitur, alba esse, sed albedo illa in ea non est, immo apparet ex aeris claritate et ipsius aquę tenuitate. Sed et alii colores qui apparent in aquis, sicuti in flamma vel rivis ymbrę conturbatis, vel aliis multis, aquę quidem non sunt, immo ex adiunctis; et sic de saporibus atque odoribus. In aqua vero quę bibitur, nec color nec sapor nec odor invenitur. De aere autem quod colorem non habeat, non est necesse probare. Propter hoc enim quod non habet, reputatum est a quibusdam eum inveniri non posse. Quod si, inquiunt, haberet, et cognosceretur ex colore. Rursum quoque si colorem habiturus esset cum ipse tantum sit unus, calidus scilicet et humidus, unum tantum habere deberet. Habet autem alium sole oriente sive occidente et alium in meridie. Est etiam circa lunam vicissim varii coloris, aliquando rubeus quidem, aliquando vero croceus, et aliquando viridis. [191^B] Si et ignis cum absque dubio omnino sit unus, calidus videlicet atque siccus, si colorem haberet, unicolor deberet esse totus. Multos vero secundum quod videtur nobis habet et hoc secundum materiam cui ipse adheret, quemadmodum de flamma videmus in pingui materia; si enim pici adheret, vergit color in nigrum; si cereręi, in croceum; si vero sulphuri, secundum quod sulphur est, vel in lividum, vel inter viridem et croceum. Carbo etiam, si solidi est ligni vel madidi, trahit in rubeum; si inanis aut sicci, in candidum. Quod si vel in aere vel in igne odor invenitur, non ex ipsis est, sed ex his quę ipsis adiunguntur. Sapor autem nullus in eis esse percipitur.

   D. Sufficienter ostendisti nec colorem, nec saporem, nec

---

14. autem *add*.   17. cum *add*.   17. omnino] + cum *del*.   23. inter *corr. ex* in
24. solidi *corr. ex* solida

nor odor can be found in the elements. For if they had color—as for example some people have said that earth is black, water white, air yellow, and fire red—then that ought to show up in things composed of the elements, so that, for example, if something has a large amount of earth in its composition, it should have a corresponding amount of blackness; that which has more water, of whiteness; that which has more air should share in the color of air; and that which has more fire ought to be more red. But we do not see it to be thus.

M. Beyond a doubt, you have argued well, and I say to you now in confirmation of your argument that the wise men of old, when they gave a description of each one of the elements, never made any mention of color. They said about fire that it was hot and dry; [about air that it was hot and moist. Water, they said, was moist,] porous and cold, and allowed sight to pass through it; but earth was cold and dry, solid and dark, and blocked sight. If these men had known colors to be in the elements, they would surely have described them with respect to their colors.

D. There still remains one thing which I wish you to pursue now, namely what you promised you were going to show us in what follows about how one element is converted into another.

M. It is known that vapor rises from water and that vapor is made from water. But since it was proved above that vapor is a kind of air, it ought not to be doubted that water is turned into air. But just the opposite also happens, that is, air is turned into water. For when air—that is, a vapor which arises from a kettle—arrives at a cold place, it comes together in drops and thus falls downward. The case is similar with rain. For when vapor rises upward from water because of the sun's heat, first it makes a mist, and then clouds. But clouds always rise upward until they encounter something cold. Therefore, because they cannot rise any higher, they are pressed into drops, and thus they fall back down. Also, concerning dew, I say that during spring and fall nights when the air becomes colder, its humidity makes very tiny drops from itself and combines them into that which we see appear as dew on plants at daybreak. It is also

odorem in elementis posse inveniri. Si enim haberent colorem, sicut quidam dixerunt terram nigram, aquam albam, croceum aerem, atque rubeum esse ignem, iam illud in compositis deberet patescere, videlicet ut in quo plus est de terra, magis esset et de nigredine; quo magis de aqua, magis et de albedine; quo magis de aere, magis aeris participaret colore; quo magis de igne, et plus deberet rubere. Sed non ita videmus nos esse.

M. Bene procul dubio argumentasti, et ego adhuc dico tibi ad tui confirmationem argumenti quia sapientes antiqui cum uniuscuiusque elementi dederunt descriptionem, nullam de colore fecerunt unquam mentionem; dixerunt namque de igne quia calidus et siccus, et [de aere quia calidus et humidus; de aqua autem quia humida] inanis et frigida esset, et quia visum aperiret; terra vero, frigida et sicca, solida et obscura, et quod visum constringeret. Qui si colores in eis esse scirent, et per colores utique ea describerent.

D. Adhuc restat unum quod iam ecce volo exequaris, videlicet quod promisisti de elementis te in sequentibus ostensurum quomodo unum converti in aliud videre nos dixeris.

M. Notum est quia vapor ex aqua consurgit et vapor aqua fit. Sed cum vaporem aeris esse speciem supra probatum sit, non debet dubitari aquam in aerem commutari. Sed e regione, aer in aquam convertitur; cum enim aer, vapor videlicet qui ex lebete consurgit, frigidum locum reperit, concrescit in guttas, et ita inferius recidit. Similiter et de pluviis. Cum enim solis calore vapor ex aquis consurgit, prius quidem nebulas, ac nubes demum conficit. Nubes autem semper ascendunt quousque frigoris aliquid offendunt; unde, quia ultra transcendere nequeunt, glomerantur in guttas atque ita infra redescendunt. De rore etiam dico quia vernis noctibus vel estivis aere frigescente, humiditas eius minutissimas ex se [191^C] guttas conficit, atque in illum quem diluculo in erbis apparere conspicimus rorem coit. Notum est etiam aerem converti in ignem. Neque enim dicta esset ignis, nisi mutaretur in ignem; et cum videmus ignem

---

2. terram *add.*   6. magis^1 *add.*   12-13. de aere...autem quia *supplevi; om. cod.*
13. frigida] frigidus *cod.*

known that air is changed into fire. For it would not be the nourishment of fire unless it were changed into fire. And when we see fire increase because of some vapor which has joined itself to it, since the vapor is air, there is no doubt that air is converted into fire. Likewise, we know plainly that when two solid bodies are rubbed together or collide, the air which is between them becomes fire and begins to burn,[12] as for example we see in millhouses that fire frequently springs forth because of the constant grinding together of the mill wheels, or when we whack two stones together we see little sparks of fire come forth from them. And that fire is turned into air we see clearly when a candle is extinguished,[13] for its fire is then visibly mixed with air and disappears for good. For the humidity of air is so great and the dryness of its fire is so small that the dryness is annihilated by the humidity, and thus all of the fire is changed completely into air. But it cannot be said that the fire utterly perishes. Indeed there is no body which consists of these three visible dimensions which we can say is ever completely annihilated. Rather it is changed into another body.[14] And what is it more proper that fire be changed into than that which is so close to fire in both place and qualities? Therefore, because it has been proved that water is converted into air and air into fire, it has also been proved that water is changed into fire. And going in the opposite direction, since fire is turned into air and air into water, it follows also that fire too is changed into water. But concerning earth, it is known to many people that it is not changed into the other three elements or they into earth except over a very long span of time.[15] Just as water congeals when it is cooled to a certain point, indeed that which it has in common with earth, namely cold and dryness, turns it into ice, and it

---

[12] *Cf.* Salernitan question B 87 (Oxford, Bodl. MS Auct. F. 3. 10, fol. 125) and Seneca, *Quaest. nat.* II 22-23

[13] See above, p. 48

[14] *Cf.* Plato, *Tim.* 33C, cited by Adelard of Bath, *Quaest. Nat.*, cap. IV; also Ovid, *Metam.* XV 254 seqq., Macrobius, *In somnium Scipionis* II 12, and Constantine, *Pantegni*, Theorice, I 5

[15] *Cf.* Calcidius, *Comm. in Tim.* ° 323 (ed. cit., p. 318), William of Conches, *Glosae in Tim.* ° (ed. Jeauneau, p. 270), Algazel, *Metaph.* ° (ed. cit., p. 149), Urso, *Glossae* 51, and Arist. *De gen. et corr.* II 4 (331b)

crescere propter aliquem qui se ei adiungit vaporem, cum vapor aer sit, dubium non est aerem converti in ignem. Item plane intuemur quia cum duo solida corpora invicem fricantur sive colliduntur, aer qui in medio est ignis fit atque accenditur, sicut videmus in molendinis quod ex molarum attritu assiduo multociens consurgit ignis, vel duo saxa collidimus, ignis scintillulas inde prosilire conspicimus. Quod autem ignis in aere commutetur ex candela cum extinguitur patenter percipitur; nam eius ignis visibiliter aeri commiscetur et nusquam ulterius invenitur. Est enim aeris humiditas tanta et siccitas ignis illius tam exigua, quod ex humiditate siccitas adnullatur; et sic ignis ille totus aer efficitur. Neque enim potest esse quod omnino perierit ignis ille. Nullum quippe est corpus de his visibilibus quod tribus constat dimensionibus quod omnino adnichilari dicere valeamus; immo in aliud commutatur corpus. Ignis vero in quod magis debeat commutari quam in illud quod et loco [et] qualitatibus iunctius extat igni? Quia ergo probatum est aquam in aerem et aerem in ignem converti, probatum est etiam aquam in ignem commutari. Rursus cum ignis in aerem et aer vertatur in amnem, sequitur etiam quod et ignis mutetur in amnem. De terra autem quod in alia tria commutetur elementa, sive in terram ea ipsa, notum quidem multis est sed non fit, nisi in tempora longa. Sicut aqua cum usque adeo frigescit quod congelatur. sane unum quid quod idem est terrę efficitur glacies, videlicet frigida et sicca, et meatum sustinet hominum sicut terra. Et sunt loca in mundo multa ubi comburi dicitur aqua illa quemadmodum et terra. Rursus aqua mutatur in terram. Sole quippe longo tempore terram calefaciente, aqua quidem exsiccata conficit salis petram, quam siquis infra terram demiserit atque diutius ibidem dimiserit, videbit quia et salem remittet et vertetur in solidam. Quod

---

16. et² *om. cod.*

sustains the passage of men just as earth does. And there are many places in the world where that kind of water is said to be consumed, just as earth is. Again, water is turned into earth. When the sun has been heating the earth for a long time, the water extracted from it forms a rock of salt. If anyone should place this rock of salt under the earth and leave it in the same place for a long time, he will see that it both yields up the salt and is turned into a solid. If you want to try this, take a rock of salt, put it into an oven, and leave it there for a long time. After you take it out, you will find that it has become solidified, and even if you place it in water you will not be able to liquefy it again. I shall tell you how it may easily be perceived that earth is changed into water. If you take salt which originates inside the earth, either nitron or sal ammoniac, and you place it inside the intestine of an animal with a weight and place this under water for a long time, you will see that it is all changed into water, but the weight is nevertheless not increased. Now, since, as we have shown, earth is changed into water, and water into air, and air into fire, therefore earth is changed into both air and fire, and the other way around.

D. You have shown by an unassailable argument that each one of the elements is changed into the others. But how do you say this is done? Do only the qualities change, or does their substance change also?

M. Do you know what natural bodies are?

D. Of course I know: the elements and all things composed of them.

M. Do you also know that each one of these bodies occupies its own place in such a way that while it remains in it, another cannot enter.

D. Indeed, I have heard this. But I wish that you would make me understand it more clearly.

M. Very well then. Of the elements take (for example) water, and completely fill a pitcher with it. Now of the composite bodies take oil and pour it on top of the water, and see if any

si temptare velis, accipe petram salis atque, in clibanum mittens, si eam longo tempore ibidem dimiseris, cum postea emittes, ita quidem demum solidatam invenies; quod licet in aquam demerseris, in secundum tamen liquefacere non valebis. Quod autem in aquam terra commutetur dicam tibi qualiter facile percipiatur. Si enim sal quod intra terram nascitur sive nitrum seu sal amoniacum accipias, et in aliquod animalis intestinum cum pondere illud mittas, et ita longo tempore in aquam dimittas, videbis quia totum in aqua mutabitur, et pondus tamen non augmentabitur. [191^D] Cum vero, ut dictum est, et terra in amnem, et aqua in aerem, et aer mutetur in ignem, ergo terra et in aerem vertitur et in ignem. Et converso.

D. Inexpugnabili argumento ostendisti elementorum unumquodque in aliud converti. Sed quomodo dicis hoc fieri? Nunquid enim qualitates solummodo, [vel] etiam substantiam eorum commutari?

M. Et scis tu quę sint corpora naturalia?

D. Quidni scirem? Elementa utique et que ex eis composita sunt cuncta.

M. Scis tu etiam quia eorum corporum unumquodque ita occupat locum suum quod dum in eo consistit aliud non potest subintrare?

D. Audivi nempe, sed volo ut me planius facias intelligere.

M. Accipe igitur, verbi gratia, de elementis aquam et urceum imple. De compositis vero accipe oleum ac superinfunde, et vide si quid olei poterit subintrare donec tantundem exierit aquę.

---

3. emittes *corr. ex* emittens   15. vel *om. cod.*   16. eorum] astrium *cod.*   26. exierit *corr. ex* exient

of the oil can enter the jar until an equal amount of water has left it.[16]

D. No, it cannot.

M. So now you understand clearly that water occupies the jar with its own body, but the oil which you poured in also seeks to occupy the place in a similar manner. But it will never be able to do so unless it has first forced out an equal quantity of water.

D. Indeed, I understand most clearly, and I understand that it is the same with all bodies; as, for example, if a certain man wished to enter a vessel full of water, there is no doubt that he couldn't until a volume of water equal to him had been removed from the vessel.

M. Since, as you say, you understand with complete clarity that each one of the natural bodies occupies its own place in such a manner that as long as it is in it, it cannot give its place to another, and if another enters, the natural body must be driven out, therefore when I say to you in what follows that each natural body occupies a place, or that whatever occupies a place is a natural body, you won't contradict me further.

D. Since this is so very evident, I don't see how I could contradict you.

M. Think now about one body which occupies a place; but no such body exists which does not consist of three dimensions. And think of this body as devoid of heat or cold, humidity or dryness, and completely lacking every quality.[17]

D. I am thinking of it.

M. Indeed, such a body the ancients called substance, stripped of all quality and quantity and relation;[18] and similarly I might have called it substance. But I have rather called it "body"[19] so that I might make you understand better what I meant.

---

[16]*Cf.* Algazel, *Metaph.* * (*ed. cit.*, p. 135)
[17]*Cf.* William of Conches, *Dragmaticon** (*ed. cit.*, p. 29)
[18]*Cf.* Arist. *De caelo* III 7 (305b)
[19]*Cf.* Algazel, *Metaph.* * (*ed. cit.*, p. 19) et John Scotus Eriugena, *De divisione naturae** I 20 (*PL*, CXXII, 467D)

D. Non utique.

M. Modo igitur intelligis aperte quia aqua urceum occupat suo corpore, sed et oleum subinfusum locum similiter querit occupare; quod nequaquam potest facere, nisi prius tantundem quantum ipsum est expulerit aquę.

D. Lucidissime certe intelligo, et in cunctis corporibus idem conspicio, quemadmodum si in vas aquę plenum introire voluerit quidam homo, procul dubio non poterit, nisi prius quantus ipse est tantundem exierit aquę de vase illo.

M. Cum, ut dicis, evidentissime intelligis quia unumquodque corporum naturalium ita occupat locum suum quod quamdiu in eo est, non potest alii dare locum, et si aliud subintrat necesse est illud fore pulsum, igitur cum dixero tibi in sequentibus quia locum occupat unumquodque naturale corpus, vel quia quodcumque locum occupat est naturale corpus, contradicere nolis ulterius.

D. Cum adeo evidens sit, non video quomodo contradici possit.

M. Cogita itaque modo unum corpus quod locum occupet; sed nullum tale est quod tribus dimensionibus non constet; et cogita illud nudum calore et frigore, humiditate atque siccitate, et inmune pęnitus omni qualitate.

D. Iam ecce cogitavi.

M. Corpus profecto tale substantiam antiqui appellavere, nudam omni qualitate et quantitate et relatione, et ego similiter substantiam appellassem; sed ideo corpus appellavi, ut quod dicere volebam melius te intelligere facerem.

D. You may call it body or substance; I don't much care about the names if I understand the meaning. But what is that thing which you say both consists of three dimensions and nevertheless lacks every quality or even quantity or relation, since it is generally agreed that these three dimensions, sc. length, width and height, are quantities?

M. As to my having assigned three dimensions to substance, I meant that it is diffused in six directions,[20] namely up and down, right and left, before and after, but I have not understood the length, breadth and width to be limited.[21] I am well aware that those dimensions are quantities and that every quantity is an accident, and I have said that this is devoid of all quality, quantity and relation, which whole thing is an accident. Whence, through this whole thing, I have pointed out that I mean this is a substance existing through itself, to be sure, but nevertheless occupying a place.

D. It still remains to be discussed whether this diffusion is terminated by a limit or exists without limit.

M. As long as you think about this substance with your reason,[22] you will not be able to say that its diffusion is either without a limit or with a limit.[23] And so I ask you to think about it as both something which occupies a place and as devoid of all accidents. But if you were to think of it as something which receives some mobile quality, you would know that it cannot be such a thing, without being limited by the three dimensions of bodies.

D. I should very much like you to give me an argument for this.

M. Indeed, I shall give you an argument concerning that, but none other than that which the illustrious philosopher who, before me, provided about the same body. For he has said:

---

[20] *Cf.* Eriugena, *De divisione naturae** I 39, 40, 45 (*ed. cit.*, 481C, 482A, 487A) and Calcidius, *Comm. in Tim.** 348 (*ed. cit.*, pp. 339-340).

[21] *Cf.* Apuleius, *De dogmate Platonis* I 5 (ed. P. Thomas, p. 87), J.C.M. van Winden, *Calcidius on Matter* (Leiden, 1959), pp. 155-156, and Eriugena, *De divisione naturae* I 56 (*ed. cit.*, 499D).

[22] *Cf.* Calcidius, *Comm. in Tim.** 312 (*ed. cit.*, pp. 311-312).

[23] *Cf.* Calcidius, *Comm. in Tim.** 319-320 (*ed. cit.*, pp. 314-316).

D. Sive corpus appelles sive substantiam, non multum curo de nominibus cum sententiam intelligam. Sed quid est quod et illud tribus dimensionibus constare, et tamen omni qualitate quam etiam quantitate vel relatione dixeris nudum esse cum tres illas dimensiones, longitudinem scilicet, latitudinem et altitudinem, quantitates constet esse.

M. Sane quod illi tres dimensiones assignavi, dicere volui quod sex partibus diffusum sit, sursum videlicet et deorsum, ad dextrum et ad sinistrum, ante et post, sed neque longitu-[192^A]-dinem neque latitudinem neque altitudinem terminatas intellexi. Quippe et illas dimensiones quantitates et omnem quantitatem accidens esse novi, et illud omni qualitate, quantitate et relatione, quod omne est accidens, nudum esse dixi. Unde per hoc totum, illud esse substantiam per se quidem existentem, sed tamen locum occupantem, innuere me ostendi.

D. Adhuc restat dicendum de illa diffusione si fine terminatur, vel existit sine fine.

M. Quamdiu substantiam illam ratione cogitabis, nec sine fine nec cum fine esse eius diffusionem dicere poteris. Et ego quidem te illam rogo ita cogitare quod et locum occupet et sit nuda omni accidente. Quod si ad recipiendum aliquam qualitatem mobilem excogites esse, scias quia talis esse non potest quin trina etiam sit terminata corporum dimensione.

D. Hoc certe volo michi ostendi argumentum.

M. Argumentum quidem dabo tibi inde, sed non aliud quam dedit philosophus ille, qui ante me argumentum dedit de eodem corpore. Dixit autem ille: Omnis corporis motus vel est

---

2. curo *corr. ex* circo illi *et i.m.*   4. quantitate] qualitate *cod.*   7. *Illegibiliter corr. man. rec. supra*

Every motion of a body is either from place to place, and this is called motion in a straight line; or it is circular; or it is from the center toward the outside; or it is from the outside toward the center. And it is known that everything which is not circumscribed with respect to the six directions occupies all place. But that which fills up everything cannot move in a straight line. For anything to be moved thus, it is necessary that the place which is full of it be emptied so that another which was empty of it may be filled up.[24] Therefore, as we have said, that thing by which all place is filled up is not moved in a straight line. Likewise, that which is not terminated with respect to the six directions does not move circularly. For every circular motion is accomplished in a definite determined time. But it must also have a center around which it turns. However, whatever is moved in this way, the farther its parts are removed from the center, the greater its circles become. Therefore, if something lacking a limit were moved in this way, it would have infinitely large circles. But that which is not terminated by a limit cannot be moved in a finite time. Also, there is no such thing as "from the center towards the outside," of "from the outside towards the center" in something which is not terminated by a limit. For whatever has a motion of this sort is moved either from the center to the circumference of a circle or from the circumference toward the center. But since that which lacks a limit would not have a finite circle or circumference, how could it possibly be moved by motions such as these? Therefore, because that which is not circumscribed by the six directions is not moveable according to any of the kinds of motion, it is clear to all that whatever is moveable is also terminated by the triple dimension of body.[25]

D. It is indicated by what you say that quantity was the first thing that was added to substance itself.

---

[24]*Cf.* Algazel, *Metaph.* (*ed. cit.*, p. 135) and Arist. *De caelo* I 2 (268b) and I 5 (272a)

[25]*Cf.* Algazel, *Metaph.* * (*ed. cit.*, p. 139), Eriugena, *De divisione naturae* * I 46, 49, 71 (*ed. cit.*, 488A, 491B, 516A-B), William of Conches, *Glosae in Tim.* * (*ed. cit.*, p. 143), and Arist. *Phys.* IV 8 215b)

de loco ad locum, et hic dicitur directus motus; vel est circularis; vel est de centro foras; vel est de foris ad centrum. Et notum est quia omne quod VI partibus non est circumscriptum occupat omnem locum. Sed quod omnem implet, recto motu moveri non valet. Quicquid enim sic movetur, plenus eo locus necesse est deseratur, ut alius qui eodem vacuus erat impleatur. Quare, ut dictum est, illud a quo locus omnis impletur recto motu non movetur. Item quod VI partibus non terminatur, circulariter non movetur. Omnis siquidem circularis motus tempore certo conficitur. Sed et centrum habeat necesse est circa quod versetur. Quicquid autem sic movetur, quanto magis partes eius a centro longius removentur, tanto magis etiam circuli augmentantur. Quare si ita moveretur illud quod fine caret, circulos etiam infinitos haberet. Sed quod fine terminatum non est terminato moveri tempore impossibile est. Item quod fine non est terminatum, de centro foras non est vel de foris ad centrum. Quodcumque enim huiusmodi habet motum vel de centro ad extremum circulum vel de extremo circulo movetur ad centrum. Cum vero quod fine caret circulum finitum vel extremum non habeat, quonam modo motibus istis moveri valeat? Quia ergo quod VI partibus circumscriptum non est nullo omnium motu mobile est, patet omnibus quia quod mobile est et trina corporum dimensione terminatum est.

D. Ecce innuitur ex hoc tuo sermone quod quantitas primum fuit quod ipsi supervenit substantię.

---

12. removentur] removetur *cod.* 17. enim *add.* 20. quonam modo *corr. ex* quomodo

M. That is also true, and I ask you to remember it. For I am sure you know we have already found two of the ten categories which were named by Aristotle, namely substance and quantity. Therefore, fasten your mind now on that substance with quantity, and you will find it bounded by the triple dimension, namely length, width and depth. Therefore it can also be moved if its creator should wish to move it.

D. That is true.

M. Therefore, since that substance is now terminated, you can also think of it as being divisible; wherefore I propose to divide it into four parts.

D. So be it.

M. If, then, one of its four parts should be heated until it is as hot as it can possibly get, and the same part is dried out until it is almost completely dry, could you not call that part fire?

D. In my opinion there is no doubt about it.

M. But if another of the four is also heated, but receives a great deal of humidity, will this not become air? And if you rendered the third part utterly cold and somewhat moist, will it not be water? And if you also make the fourth cold and completely dry, will you not find earth?

D. Indeed, this is thoroughly evident to everyone and indisputable.

M. Now, therefore, if you truly have any discretion at all, you can understand and see that there is one common substance of the four elements. And from this, let your discretion also perceive that unless this substance (or body, if you prefer) of the elements occupied place, neither could any of the elements occupy place.[26] But you should also know from what we have said that the difference among the elements lies not in the diversity of their substance (or body), but rather among the qualities themselves.[27]

D. I understand each of these things clearly as you say

---

[26] *Cf.* Eriugena, *De divisione naturae* * I 53 (*ed. cit.*, 496A) et Macrobius, *In somnium Scipionis* * I 6 25-33 (ed. Willis, pp. 22-24)

[27] *Cf.* Calcidius, *Comm. in Tim.* * 309, 325 (*ed. cit.*, pp. 310, 319-320)

Liber Primus

M. Verum est etiam illud quod rogo memoriter tene. Scias enim quia iam ecce invenimus duo de X predicamentis quę dicta sunt ab Aristotile, substantiam videlicet quantitatemque. Cogita itaque modo substantiam illam cum quantitate, inveniesque eam [192^B] trina terminatam dimensione, longitudine scilicet, latitudine atque altitudine. Quare etiam moveri potis est, si voluerit eam suus creator movere.

D. Verum est.

M. Cum ergo iam terminata sit illa substantia, et divisibilem potes cogitare; quare rogo in IIII^or eandem partire.

D. Fiat.

M. Si igitur una de IIII^or illius partibus calefiat usque ad maiorem qui potest esse fervorem, et siccetur eadem usque ad precipuam siccitatem, nunquid non illam dicere potes ignem?

D. Nullam in eo considero dubietatem.

M. Quod si alia de IIII^or etiam calefiet sed humiditatem infinitam recipiet, nunquid non aer fiet? Terciam vero si omnino frigidam eandemque etiam humidam reddideris, nunquid non erit amnis? Sed et quartam siquidem frigidam et omnino efficies siccam, nunquid non invenies terram?

D. Cunctis sane perpatens est et indubitabile.

M. Nunc igitur revera si sit tibi prudentia aliqua potes intelligere et videre quia IIII^or elementorum una est communis substantia. Unde et illud percipiat discrecio tua quia illa elementorum substantia, seu mavis corpus, nisi locum occuparet, nec aliquod etiam elementorum locum occupare posset. Sed et inde differentiam elementorum cognoscas quia non est in substantię seu corporis diversitate, immo inter qualitates ipsas.

D. Bene intelligo quę dicis singula, sed apertius velim edisseras quare premiseris talia et ad quid tendant cuncta ista.

---

1. quod *om. cod.*   18. humidam] humiditatem *cod.*   21. indubitabile] dubitabile *cod.*

them, but I wish you would set forth more fully the principles on which you base your arguments and toward what all these things tend.

M. Indeed, everything I say tends towards this: that in the beginning God created a certain body, and He created it simple and devoid of any accident, but nevertheless such that it would also occupy a place, and He attributed quantity to it and circumscribed it by three dimensions; and He also wished it to be moved, and behold, it received motion. But He also divided this same body into four parts, of which He completely heated up and dried out one, and from this He made fire; the second He also heated up and made completely wet—this was air. From the third, which He made completely cold as well as wet, He made water. The fourth was made cold and utterly dry—this is earth. There was therefore this one and simple substance for the four elements, much as a ball of wax is to four diverse forms made from it,[28] one of a man, another of an ox, the third of a fish, and the fourth of a bird. For, just as, although the form of a man might be destroyed and the form of an ox take its place, or the form of an ox be replaced by that of a fish, or that of a fish by that of a bird, and the other way around, nevertheless the wax will always be one thing; in the same way, although earth may be changed into water, water into air, and air into fire, and the other way around, nevertheless substance will always remain exactly the same. Also, just as the forms which were in the wax will not be found existing by themselves but only in wax or in another body, similarly howsoever the qualities of the elements are changed or destroyed, you will never be able to find them apart from substance.[29] For just as, if someone says to you: "Make the form of a man for me," you will only be able to accomplish this in some body, so if he says to you: "Show me heat," you can never do this unless you heat up

---

[28] *Cf.* Calcidius, *Comm. in Tim.* * 309 (*ed. cit.*, p. 310), *Liber Apollonii de secretis naturae* (Bibl. nat. MS lat. 13951, fol. 12r) and William of Conches, *Glosae in Tim.* * (*ed. cit.*, pp. 264, 275)

[29] *Cf.* William of Conches, *Glosae in Tim.* * (*ed. cit.*, p. 258) and Eriugena, *De divisione naturae* * I 53 (*ed. cit.*, 496A)

Liber Primus

M. Sane ad hoc tendit sermo meus iste totus: quia in principio creavit Deus quoddam corpus, et creavit illud simplum et omni accidente nudum, sed tale tamen necnon occuparet locum, eique quantitatem attribuit ac tribus dimensionibus circumscripsit; moveri quoque ipsum voluit, et ecce motum recepit. Sed et idem corpus in IIII^{or} partes divisit, quarum unam quidem omnino calefecit et siccavit, et inde ignem fecit; aliam quoque calefactam et omnino humidam fecit aerem. De tertia vero, quam omnino frigidam egit et humidam, fecit aquam. Quarta autem frigida facta est atque omnino sicca, hec est terra. Fuit igitur illa una ac simpla substantia ad IIII^{or} elementa, quemadmodum cere massa ad IIII formas diversas ex eadem confectas, unam hominis, aliam bovis, terciam piscis, et quartam volucris. Quemadmodum enim, licet forma hominis deleatur et fiat forma bovis, bovis vero forma piscis et piscis forma volucris et econverso, cera tamen semper una erit, ita licet terra mutetur in amnem, aqua in aerem et aer in ignem, et econverso, substantia tamen prorsus eadem remanebit. Quemadmodum etiam formę quę in cera erant non invenientur per se, nisi vel in cera vel in alio corpore, ita et elementorum qualitates quo-[192^C]-quomodo commutentur sive deleantur, sine substantia nequaquam poteris invenire. Sicut enim si dicet tibi aliquis: "Fac michi formam hominis," non poteris illam efficere, nisi in aliquo corpore; ita si dicet tibi: "Ostende michi calorem," nequaquam poteris, nisi aliquod corpus calefeceris. Est etiam de eadem substantia et eius qualitatibus, quemadmodum de aliquo homine et eiusdem actionibus. Sicut enim ille sedens non est similis sibi stanti, vel dormiens vigilanti, licet semper homo idem sit; ita etiam substantia illa, cum calida est, sibi ipsi

---

5. ecce *add.* quedam   8. humidam] humiditatem *cod.*   12. quemadmodum *corr. i.m. ex* quod
12. massa *corr. ex* massam *man. rec.*   22. dicet *corr. i.m. ex* dicitur *man. rec.*

some body. We can also compare substance and its qualities to a man and his actions. For just as a man sitting is not similar to himself standing, or the same man sleeping is not similar to himself when he is awake, although he always remains the same man; just so, substance, when it is hot, is not similar to itself when it is cold, and when it is wet is not similar to itself when it is dry, although it always remains the same thing. And just as the state of a man's being seated perishes and is annihilated when he stands up, thus also the heat of substance completely perishes and is annihilated when that substance becomes cold. Therefore, it is clear concerning the qualities of these four elements that when one of any two diverse qualities impresses itself on substance, the other quality recedes and completely perishes. But substance always continues to exist and will remain the same as long as it continues to be the sort of thing it is. And in this way the elements are changed into each other, as we can easily see in water, which is one part of that substance, namely cold and moist. If heat is added to it, the cold will completely perish; but the humidity will remain, and without a doubt it will become air. And thus with the others.

D. Thank you, dear teacher, who have deigned to open up these things to me and to confer so great a good on both me and on all those who might chance to read this book.

M. Now, then, remember henceforth that substance is a thing of this sort: you should know, that is, that it is something which exists by itself and is bounded by the triple dimension of bodies, and that it occupies a place, and that it underlies qualities, which can both accrue to it and depart from it. It is also completely unchangeable in itself. You should also know that a knowledge of this substance is the key to the whole of philosophy, and he who does not understand it well cannot acquire much philosophy. But through a knowledge of it, a man can rise to that lofty knowledge which is beyond nature. But you are not ignorant of the qualities: that they do not exist by themselves but rather always adhere to substance, and that they come and go; neither are they found by themselves nor do they come from far away. Instead, when substance is moved, it heats

frigide similis non est, idem sibi humide cum sicca est, quamvis ipsa semper eadem est; et sicut sessio hominis, cum exurgit, perit atque annullatur, ita et calor substantię, cum frigessit, omnino perit et annichilatur. Patet igitur de his IIII^{or} elementorum qualitatibus quod cum duarum quarumlibet diversarum altera substantię supervenit, altera sane recedit et omnino perit. Substantia vero semper eadem existit et erit, quamdiu secundum istud stabit; et hoc modo commutantur elementa, sicut facile possumus videre nos in aqua que illius substantię pars est una, frigida atque humida. Cui si superveniente calore frigiditas omnino peribit; humiditas autem remanebit, procul dubio aer erit; et sic de ceteris.

D. Gratias tibi doctor care, qui hec michi dignatus es aperire et tantum boni conferre tam michi quam omnibus illis quibus istum librum contingat perlegere.

(M.) Iam ergo a modo substantiam illam talem esse memoriter recordare: scias videlicet quia est existens per se et trina corporum terminata dimensione et eandem locum occupare, et quia qualitatibus subdita est cui advenire valeant et abire; ipsa autem omnino incommutabilis in se. Scias etiam quia huius noticia substantie totius est clavis philosophię, et qui bene eam non intelligit nec ad multam potest philosophiam pertingere; per eius vero cognitionem, ad illam excellentem quę preter naturam est scientiam potest homo ascendere. De qualitatibus autem non ignoras, quia non existunt per se, immo ipsi semper adherent substantię, sed adveniunt et recedunt, nec inveniuntur per se, nec tamen adveniunt de longe; sed cum movetur substantia, calescit ex motione; cum vero quiescit, frigescit ex requie; cum vero calescit, laxatur atque diffunditur, et cum laxatur,

---

15. quibus *corr. ex* qui   15. contingat] contingent *cod.*   16. M. *om. cod.*

up because of the motion; but when it comes to rest, it grows cold as a result of its stillness. But when it is heated up, it becomes loose and diffuse, and when it is loose, it is made humid and penetrable. And when it grows cold, it becomes solid and compressed; but when it is compressed, it once again becomes dry and cannot be penetrated by anything. Wherefore, diffusion comes about as a result of motion, and solidity as a result of rest.

D. Whoever diligently looks into the subtlety of your teaching will see that humidity comes forth from heat, and dryness from cold.

M. Indeed, such is the opinion of the best philosophers.

D. I see clearly all you have said, and I have firmly committed to memory both what substance is and what quality is, both because they can be perceived visibly and because you yourself have explained them to me most clearly. But now, if you please, I wish you would show me how heat results from motion.

M. Surely. You can perceive this clearly from the grinding of a millstone, or from a man running fast and from this motion heating up not a little. But fire itself is also an argument: if you move it, you will see it suddenly increase.

D. This is sufficient concerning heat and motion; and so the other question—how substance becomes cold when it is at rest—is now clear.

M. Without a doubt, anyone can grasp that with his reason. For, since heat comes about as the result of motion, reason demands that rest should make cold, since rest is the contrary of motion and cold the contrary of heat. But if you wish a further example of the same thing, you can learn this visibly from horseback riders on the road. For when a man rides, he gets cold because of his state of rest; but if he walks, he is warmed by the motion of his body.

D. Now I see this most clearly, but I wish to inquire about another thing. What did you mean when you said that substance is loosened up and diffused by heat, and made moist, but is solidified and compressed by cold, and is dry?

humida et penetrabilis efficitur; et cum frigescit, solidatur et stringitur; cum vero stringitur, sicca ac nulli pervia redditur. Quare et ex motu provenit illa diffusio et ex quiete solidatio.

D. Qui sermonis tui subtilitatem diligenter inquirit videt quia ex calore humiditas et ex frigore siccitas provenit.

M. Ista quidem optimorum sententia est philosophorum.

D. Bene quidem video cuncta que dixisti, et quid sit substantia, quid qualitas, firmiter memorie [192^D] commendavi, tum quia visibiliter possunt agnosci, tum quia ipse lucidissime intelligere me fecisti; sed quomodo ex motu calor proveniat, vellem michi libenter ostendi.

M. Hoc certe ex molis molendini patenter potes percipere, vel ex aliquo homine velociter currente, et ex illo motu non minimum calescente; sed et argumentum est ignis ipse, quem si commoveris, subito videbis concrescere.

D. De calore quidem et motu sufficit, quare de alia parte iam aperi, quonam modo videlicet frigescat substantia cum quiescit.

M. Procul dubio ratione potest illud quivis percipere. Cum enim ex motu calor proveniat, ratio exigit quod et quies frigus conficiat, cum et quies motui et frigus calori contrarium existat. Sed et idem si voles, ex equitantibus in via visibiliter agnoscere potes. Cum enim equitat homo ex quiete frigescit, cum vero pede ambulat, ex corporis motu calescit.

D. Iam istud evidentissime video, sed aliud volo inquirere: quomodo dixisti quia ex calore laxatur atque diffunditur illa substantia et efficitur humida, ex frigore vero solidatur et constringitur, et est sicca?

---

24. pede *corr. ex* pes

M. All philosophy agrees on this, and it is illustrated visibly by gold, silver, and all metals, wax, oil, fat, or any other greasy substance, pitch, frankincense, myrrh, and the rest of the gums, all of which, when they are heated, are loose and spread out, and become moist. But when they are cooled, they become solid and compressed, and are dry once again.

D. What you have said is truly evident. But, I ask, where does the motion come from by which fire and air are made hot, or the rest by which water and earth are made cold?

M. Indeed, it proceeds from the motion of the firmament, as Aristotle says in his book which treats the elements. For he spoke in these words: "When the creation of the firmament and all things contained within it was finished, its creator moved it and it was mobile. But from the motion of the firmament, a part of the previously mentioned body, simple yet circumscribed by the six directions—that part, I say, which was most closely joined to the very firmament—began to move and to heat up violently; and this was fire. But the next part, which was a little farther away, was moved but not quite so violently. Therefore, it became hot, but not so hot as fire; and this is air. The third part, because it was far removed from the firmament, was neither moved nor heated, and therefore it remained cold; and this is water. But the fourth, because it was as far as possible away from the firmament, remained completely immobile. Therefore, it too remained cold; and this was earth."[30]

D. Behold! I understand well whence motion came to substance, and that heat proceeds from motion and cold from rest.

M. Since, therefore, by the common agreement of all the philosophers, heat is a quality, and so is cold, we have now discovered in substance a third category, namely quality.

D. I concede that heat is a quality, but I do not see that cold is.

---

[30]*Cf.* A. Altmann, "Isaac Israeli's 'Chapter on the Elements' (Ms Mantua)," *Journal of Jewish Studies*, VII (1956), 43 and A. Altmann and S.M. Stern, *Isaac Israeli* (Oxford, 1958), p. 120.* See above, "Introduction," p. 24

M. In eo nempe tota concordat philosophia, et id ostendit visibiliter aurum, argentum, et metalla cuncta, cera, oleum, saginum, vel quelibet pinguedo alia, pix, thus, mirra, et gummi reliqua, que omnia cum calefiunt, laxantur, diffunduntur, et fiunt humida. Cum vero frigescunt, solidantur, constringuntur, et redduntur sicca.

D. Vere evidens est quod dixisti, sed unde queso advenit vel motus igni et aeri quo concaluerunt, vel quies aque et telluri unde frigere facte sunt?

M. Hoc quidem ex firmamenti motu procedit, sicut dicit Aristoteles in eo quem de elementis libro agit. Ait enim his verbis: "Completa creatione firmamenti omniumque que ipsum in se comprehendit, movit illud creator suus et mobile fuit. Ex motu vero firmamenti, pars illa predicti corporis, simpli et tamen VI partibus circumscripti, pars inquam illa que ipsi firmamento iunctissima fuit, moveri cepit et vehementer concaluit, atque ignis fuit. Pars vero alia, que fuit remotior paulisper, mota quidem est sed non adeo vehementer; quare et calefacta est sed nequaquam tam ardens, et ipsa est aer. Tercia autem quia multum fuit a firmamento remota, neque mota est neque calefacta, et ideo remansit frigida, et hęc est aqua. Sed et quarta quoniam omnino recessit, omnino immobilis extitit; quare et similiter frigida remansit, et ea terra fuit."

D. Ecce bene intellexi unde substantię illi venit motus, et quod ex motu calor et ex requie procedit frigus.

M. Cum ergo omnium assensu philosophorum qualitas sit calor atque frigiditas, iam ecce in substantia tercium invenitur predicamentum, [193^A] videlicet qualitas.

D. Calorem quidem qualitatem esse concedo; de frigore quod qualitas sit non video.

---

17. ignis] facta *cod.*   19. ardens] ardantem *cod.*   29. Calorem *corr. ex* Calor *man. rec.*
29. qualitatem *corr. ex* quantitatem *man. rec.*

M. And what is it, friend, that causes you to have doubts about this?

D. Because you said that heat arose in substance as the result of motion and cold as the result of rest; and you had asserted that in the beginning, substance was devoid of any quality. But the implication of what you have just said is that substance was at rest before it received any quality. But if it was at rest, it must necessarily also have been cold. Therefore, either, if cold is a quality, we will say that substance possessed quality in the beginning; or, if it did not possess quality, we will not call cold a quality.

M. And do you doubt that everything heats up when it moves and becomes cold when it rests from motion?

D. I have no doubt whatsoever about this, nor do I think anyone has ever doubted it; for whoever wishes can see this for himself.

M. Therefore, store this away in the treasure chest of your memory, so that you won't say you have forgotten it when I return to this subject after having talked about other things.

D. I shall do as you ask.

M. And so, say this: If you dig a shaft ten fathoms deep, and you make a very narrow opening at its top, say one palm's width across, then, taking a stone, you throw it into the air as high as you wish, and you let the stone, which you have thrown upward as straight as you can, fall back into the opening of the shaft, do you think it will fall all the way to the bottom of the shaft, even though this is far away, or will it turn aside at the surface of the earth because this is closer?[31]

D. It will very definitely descend to the bottom.

M. It is clear, therefore, that all heavy things seek not just the earth, but rather its center, which is also the center of the whole universe; and it is just the opposite with light things.

D. This is clear.

M. And so, beyond any doubt, those philosophers have

---

[31] *Cf.* William of Conches, *Dragmaticon* (ed. cit., pp. 60-61), Adelard, *Quaest. nat.*, cap. XLVIII and Oresme, *Quaestiones in De caelo et mundo* I 17 (ed. Menut and Denomy, p. 230)

M. Et quid est, amice, quod te inde facit dubitare?

D. Quia dixisti quod illi substantię et ex motu calor et frigus advenit ex requie, et tu quidem proposueras illam omni qualitate in principio nudam extitisse; sed et ex sermonis tui innuitur vigore, eandem priusquam quantitatem receperit, quietam fuisse. Quod si quieta fuit, frigida etiam necesse est fuerit. Unde vel si frigus qualitas est illam in principio habuisse dicemus qualitatem; vel si qualitatem non habuit, nec frigus appellabimus qualitatem.

M. Et de hoc dubitas tu quod omne cum movetur calescit, et cum a motu quiescit, frigescit?

D. Nec ego inde dubito, nec aliquis reor unquam dubitavit; hoc enim visibiliter quilibet inspicit.

M. Reconde ergo illud memoriter in cordis armario, ne quia alia interseram, mente te dicas excidisse, cum ad idem rediero.

D. Sic faciam ego.

M. Dic itaque: Si puteum X ulnarum effoderis, et os eius valde artum palmo uno verbi gratia effeceris, demum lapidem accipiens in altum efferes quantum volueris, et elatum quanto rectius poteris in os putei recidere dimiseris, cadetne in fundum putei, licet longius existentem, vel divertet se extra in terrę superficiem quia propinquior est, sicut reris?

D. Immo revera putei descendet in ima.

M. Patet ergo de ponderosis omnibus quia non terram tantum quęrunt, immo etiam centrum eius, quod est centrum orbis tocius; et econtrario de levibus.

D. Patet.

M. Itaque procul dubio veridici sunt quicumque ex philosophis illud dicunt quod terrę particulę universę undique ad centrum tendunt.

---

7. illam in principio *tr. ex* in principio illam   12. ego *add.*   20. efferes *corr. ex* efferis
27. orbis tocius *tr.*

spoken truly who have said that particles of earth always tend toward the center from every direction.

D. This also is absolutely true.

M. Therefore, stones which are on the earth, even though they do not seem to move by themselves, are nevertheless potentially mobile; for unless the soil were blocking the way, they would encounter no resistance this side of the center.

D. Indeed, it ought to be thus; and you have forced me very subtly to concede something I did not think I was going to concede.

M. And what is that, dear son?

D. Just this: that cold comes about in substance as the result of motion; but that motion seems to us to be rest; and that the part of that substance which heats up is the part which is moved upward from the center; but the other part, which descends toward the center, becomes cold. But there still seems to me to be a contradiction. For if, as you have said, all parts of the earth demand to come to the center from every direction, then the center itself must be immobile. But in that case, some immobile thing is cold.

M. Don't you know that the center is nothing but a certain indivisible geometrical point and that one can only perceive it in thought? Thus it is described by philosophers. Therefore, you cannot say that there is in the earth any immobile place.

D. You have completely dispelled the doubt which I had.

M. Therefore, what we touched on above is also true, that we have now discovered three of the categories, namely substance, quality, and quantity.

D. That is true.

M. But this should also be known, that of the four elements, earth is the coarsest and heaviest; fire is the lightest and most fine; water is light and fine with respect to earth but coarse and heavy with respect to air; air similarly is fine and light with respect to water, but coarse and heavy with respect to fire.

D. That is true.

M. Therefore, because substance shares in the qualities, we

D. Et hoc quidem verissimum.

M. Igitur lapides qui super terram consistunt, etsi per se moveri non videntur, in potentia tamen mobiles sunt, nisi enim obstaret solum, nusquam prorsus resisterent citra centrum.

D. Ita utique esse est debitum, et subtiliter quidem me coegisti ut tale quid concedam quod me concessurum fore non putavi.

M. Et quid est illud, care fili?

D. Hoc videlicet, quod illi substantię ex motu frigus exoritur; sed motus ille quies nobis esse videtur. Et quod illius substantię ea quidem pars calescit quę de centro movetur sursum; frigescit vero illa que descendit ad centrum, sed tamen adhuc restat michi quoddam contrarium. Si enim, ut dixisti, omnes terrę partes undique expostulant venire ad centrum, ipsum esse immobile est necessarium. Verum igitur quoddam immobile est frigidum.

M. Nunquid non nosti quia centrum nichil est aliud quam quidam geometricalis punctus indivisibilis et qui non percipitur nisi cogitatione tantum? Sic quippe a philosophis est descriptum; unde etiam dicere non potes aliquem in terra immobilem esse locum.

D. Bene profecto meam explicasti dubitationem quam habeam.

M. Ergo et [193^B] verum est quod supra tetigimus, quia iam de predicamentis tria, substantiam videlicet, quantitatem atque qualitatem invenimus.

D. Verum est.

M. Sed et hoc sciendum, quia horum IIII^{or} elementorum terra quidem grossissima est atque ponderosissima; ignis vero subtilissimus atque levissimus; aqua autem respectu terrę levis et subtilis, sed grossa et ponderosa respectu aeris; aer etiam similiter respectu aquę subtilis est et levis, grossus vero atque ponderosus respectu ignis.

D. Verum est.

M. Quia ergo substantia participavit qualitatibus, iam ecce

---

18. indivisibilis] indivisibiles *cod.*   18. qui *corr. ex* quis *man. rec.*   30. aqua *corr. ex* aque

have now discovered among its parts the fourth category, namely relation.

D. Since you have now pointed out four of the categories, I wish you would similarly show me where the six others may be found.

M. These four categories, which are simple, we have been able to find in the elements, which are also simple. But because the six others are composite, they can only be found in those things which are composed of the elements.

D. Would it be possible to discover that substance—which in fact we discovered by reason—by means of any of our bodily senses before it had taken on the three categories?

M. Absolutely not. For by sight we perceive a thing in only three ways, either by its colors, or by its quantities, or that it exists nearer or farther away. But substance then had neither color nor quantity, nor was it near or far. And by our hearing, we hear only voices or sounds, but substance then had neither voices nor sounds. By smell, one discerns good and bad odors, but substance then smelled neither good nor bad. By taste we discover flavors, but at that time there was no flavor to substance. By touch it is possible to know about something if it is hot or cold, wet or dry, soft or hard, or something of this sort. But then there was neither heat or cold, nor moisture or dryness, nor softness or hardness, nor, truly, any quality to it. And since this is so, it could be perceived only by reason.[32] And it is right that all those things with which substance is invested, up until fire is brought into being, all gathered together, should be called form.

D. And let us call them that now.

M. However, all those things by which substance is comprehended in form, if separated from substance, will not be perceived by a bodily sense.

---

[32] *Cf.* Eriugena, *De divisione naturae* I 59-60 (*ed. cit.*, pp. 502-503). Eriugena's source is Gregory of Nyssa, *De opificio hominis* 24 (*PG*, XLIV, 211-214; see P. Duhem, *Le Système du monde*, II, 429-431). *Cf.* also Plotinus, *Enn.* II 4 12

inter partes eius predicamentum quartum, relationem videlicet, reperimus.

D. Quoniam iam IIII^{or} ostendisti predicamenta, ostendas velim similiter ubi reperiri possunt sex reliqua.

M. Hec nempe IIII^{or} quę simpla sunt potuimus reperire in elementis quę sunt similiter simpla; sex vero alia quia composita sunt inveniri non poterunt, nisi in his quę sunt ex elementis composita.

D. Et illam substantiam quam ratione invenimus, nunquid aliquo de corporeis sensibus ante trium predicamentorum susceptionem invenire possemus?

M. Sane nullatenus. Visu enim tribus tantum modis aliquid percipimus, vel per colores, vel per quantitates, vel quia propius existat aut longius. Sed illa substantia neque colorem neque quantitatem tunc habebat, neque prope seu longe erat. Auditu autem audimus tantum vocalia vel sonora, sed tunc neque vocem neque sonum habebat illa substantia. Olfactu vero bonos et malos odores discernit aliquis. Sed illa substantia neque boni neque mali fuerat tunc odoris. Gustu quoque sapores discernimus, sed illi substantię tunc temporis sapor erat nullus. Tactu vero de aliquo potest dinosci, si calidum sit aut frigidum, humidum sive siccum, molle seu durum, vel aliquid huiusmodi; sed tunc neque calor sive frigus, neque humiditas sive siccitas, neque mollicies seu duricies, neque aliqua prorsus qualitas erat illi. Et cum ita sit, nullatenus nisi ratione percipi potuit. Et rectum est quia omnia illa quibus substantia investitur usquequo ignis efficitur, simul collecta, forma appelletur.

D. Et iam sic esse dicamus.

M. Veruntamen cuncta illa quibus substantia in forma, si a substantia separata accipiantur, sensu corporeo non percipientur.

---

7. inveniri] invenire *cod.*   15. habebat] habeat *cod.*   17. habebat *corr. ex* habeat
22. molle *corr. ex* mole

D. Indeed, not only could they not be sensed, they could not even be found.

M. Similarly also, we have already said above about substance that we cannot discover it until it has taken on qualities.

D. That is true.

M. Therefore, the form of fire was one part of it, and the other part was substance. And when these two parts came together in equal measure, they brought about sensible fire.[33]

D. This is clear.

M. And so he who called form substance did well in a certain sense. For, as in the case of substance, form also helps something to become perceptible to the bodily senses.

D. Surely, as you say, he spoke well who called form substance. But form does not assist something to be perceived by a sense of the body in the same way that substance does.[34]

M. Truly, it is as you say. But I ask that you do willingly one thing that I say. If you do this, you shall be called a good student.

D. What is that?

M. Think now about the parts by which the form of fire was made; think, I say, about all these together as though they were one thing, and think about the forementioned substance of that thing, comprehensible only to reason, being invested with these parts at one stroke. And at the same moment, think of such a body's being made that it can be perceived by the five senses of the body.

D. I have thought of it.

M. What therefore is that thing now with which you have invested substance? For since it can be discovered in itself by reason, just as substance can, can it not rightly be called substance?

D. You have forced me to concede that it ought to be called substance, but substance of a different kind than first

---

[33]*Cf.* Plato, *Tim.* 49-52 and Calcidius, *Comm. in Tim.* * 312, 331, 332 (*ed. cit.*, pp. 311-312, 325-327)

[34]*Cf.* Eriugena, *De divisione naturae* * I 63 (*ed. cit.*, 507A, 508A)

D. Sane non solum non possent sentiri, sed nec etiam inveniri.

M. Similiter quoque iam superius de substantia prediximus quia ante qualitatum susceptionem eam invenire nequivimus.

D. Verum est.

M. Ergo forma ignis illa pars fuit eius una, et pars alia substantia. Quę duę partes, cum pariter convenerunt, ignem sensibilem effecerunt.

D. Patet.

M. Itaque qui formam substantiam appellavit, quodammodo bene fecit; quemadmodum enim substantia, ita quoque et forma adiutorium tribuit, ut sensibus corporeis aliquid subiacere possit.

D. Utique, ut dicis, bene dixit qui formam substantiam appellavit, non tamen forma eo [193^C] modo adiuvat quo substantia ut sensu corporis percipi valeat aliquid.

M. Profecto itaque est, ut tu dicis, sed unum queso quod dicam efficere velis. Si enim feceris, et bonus discipulus appellaberis.

D. Quid est illud?

M. Cogita modo particulas quibus forma ignis confecta fuit; cogita, inquam, illas omnes simul quasi unum quid illiusque predictam substantiam, ratione quidem tantum comprehensibilem uno ictu investiri; eodemque momento, cogita corpus tale effici quod V corporis sensibus valeat persentiri.

D. Iam cogitavi.

M. Quid est ergo modo illud unde substantiam investisti? Cum enim ratione valeat per se quemadmodum et substantia reperiri, nunquid non iure substantia potest appellari?

D. Bene me coegisti ut illud concedam debere substantiam nuncupari, sed substantiam alterius generis quam prima sub-

---

4. invenire] inveniri *cod.*   17. ut *corr. ex* quod

substance is, because first substance is simple, but that substance is joined by many accidents. Therefore, there is some doubt as to whether it is substance or not.

M. If you consider separately by itself each one of the parts by which substance is clothed according to the five senses, and if you consider them as coming and going, you will not indeed rightly be able to call them substance. But when you consider them all together at the same time and whether they produce what can be understood in itself by reason, you will be able to call them substance. On this we have the authority of Aristotle, who says that everything which can be thought of in itself, so that it is not susceptible of corruption in thought, must necessarily be substance.[35] But the aforementioned parts of form cannot be thought of separately as being without corruption. Therefore you ought to give the name substance to that union of the formal parts as well as to first substance, for Aristotle himself in his book *On the Elements* calls the first 'elemental substance,' the other 'formal substance.'[36] Remember that well, so that you will not later say you are ignorant of it when I treat this same matter again. Now, therefore, we have learned that there are five prerequisites which we can say are necessary for the creation of things: elemental substance, formal substance, motion and a place in which something may be moved, and also time in which the motion might be accomplished.[37] But there was a time when these five prerequisites did not exist. Therefore of necessity they had a creator who made them.[38]

D. This is likely.

M. And now, I think, we have investigated the elements sufficiently. I do not think you have any further questions, except about that which is composed of the elements.

D. No. There still remain a few things I should like to discuss with you concerning the elements, namely why in earth,

---

[35] *Cf.* Arist. *Categ.** V (4a-b). See below, p. 180

[36] *Cf.* Isaac "Chapter on the Elements,"* p. 41; *Isaac Israeli*, p. 119

[37] *Cf.* Al-Kindi *De quinque essentiis* (ed. Nagy, p. 30) and *Liber Apollonii de secretis naturae* (MS cit., fol. 18r)

[38] *Cf.* Calcidius, *Comm. in Tim.** 304, 311 (*ed. cit.*, pp. 305-306, 311)

stantia est, quia illa simpla, sed illud ex multis accidentibus adiunctum est; unde substantia sit an non, dubitatum est.

M. Si particulas illius unde investitur substantia unamquamque per se secundum V sensus consideres easque etiam sicut abeuntes et advenientes, non quidem substantiam iure poteris appellare. Cum vero simul omnes uno ictu cogitabis et nunquid illas efficere quod per se intelligi valeat ratione, substantiam poteris dicere, testante Aristotile. Qui omne inquit quod potest cogitari per se, ita quod in cogitacione corruptionis non sit susceptibile, esse substantiam necesse est. Sed predictę particulę forme per se nequeunt unaqueque cogitari sine corruptione. Debes itaque illam formalium partium unionem, quodammodo sicut et primam, substantiam appellare, ipse enim Aristotiles in suo libro *De elementis* primam quidem elementalem appellat substantiam, istam vero formalem substantiam. Tene autem illam memoriter, ne postea te ignarum eius dicas cum de ipsa agam. Modo ergo quinque esse cognoscimus quę ad rerum creationem esse necessaria dicere valeamus: substantiam videlicet elementalem, et substantiam formalem, motum et locum quo aliquid moveatur, et tempus ętiam quo motus conficiatur. Sed et hec quinque fuit aliquando quando non fuerunt; quare et creatorem necessario qui ea condiderit habuerunt.

D. Verisimile est.

M. Igitur de elementis, sicut reor, sufficienter actum est; nec puto quod amplius aliquid questionis habeas, nisi de eo quod ex elementis compositum est.

D. Immo adhuc restant aliqua de elementis, de quibus queso respondere atque disserere velis, quare videlicet in terra et

---

1. illa *corr. ex* illud   15. istam] ista *cod.*

water, and air heat is sometimes found, and sometimes cold, but in fire we always find heat and never cold.[39]

M. And do you concede that fire here below is a sort of visitor and stranger, because, as we have said before, its place is above, and because unless it found some nourishment down here it could not remain among us as long as it takes to blink your eye?[40]

D. Yes, this can be seen.

M. Likewise, when it comes upon appropriate nourishment, it heats it up violently, and having been nourished by it, it turns it completely to its own nature.

D. There is no doubt about this.

M. What if heat were lacking to this same fire? Would it then be able to be nourished?

D. No.

M. Now therefore you can understand that if heat were lacking, it would not be able to nourish itself, and if it could not be nourished it could not remain here for one moment. But earth, water, and air remain in their proper places here among us. Therefore, they do not lack nourishment, nor do they need it in order to persevere in their qualities. But when they receive accidental qualities, when these depart, earth, water, and air then return to their own natures.

D. I should still like you to answer me one more thing: For what reasons do the philosophers say that there is more of heat in fire, more of humidity in air, more of coldness in water, and more of dryness in earth, when the natural order of the world requires something different? For since heat and cold are contraries, then just as heat is preeminent in the highest element, so also cold ought to be greatest in the lowest.[41]

M. Indeed, it ought to be the way you have reasoned it out. But more cold is said to be in water because cold is perceived in it more quickly as a result of its softness, whereas in earth we do

---

[39] *Cf.* Salernitan question C 15 (Oxford, C.C.C. MS 233, fol. 26) and B 301 (fol. 150)

[40] *Cf.* Macrobius *Sat.* * 7 13 3 (ed. Willis, p. 444), Salernitan question C 15 (fol. 26), and Arist. *Meteor.* II 2 (355a) and IV 7 (383b)

[41] *Cf.* Constantine, *Pantegni,* * Theorice, I 5

aqua et aere aliquando invenitur calor et aliquando frigus; in igne vero semper calor et nunquam frigus.

M. Et concedis tu quod ignis hic infra quasi advena est et peregrinus, quia, ut supradiximus, sursum est locus eius, et quia ipse nisi hic dietam suam inveniret uno ictu oculi apud nos non remaneret? [193D]

D. Hoc etiam visui subiacet.

M. Item cum ad suam dietam accidit, utique eam vehementer calefacit, et inde dietatus, in suam ipsius naturam eam omnino convertit.

D. Et hoc quoque in dubium nulli venit.

M. Quod si eidem igni calor defecerit; nunquid nam dietari iam poterit?

D. Non.

M. Nunc ergo potes agnoscere quia si calor defecerit, nec se poterit dietare, et si dietari nequiverit, nec uno hic momento poterit remanere. Terra vero, aqua et aer in suis locis propriis hic apud nos permanent; quare et dieta non indigent, nec necesse est ut in suis qualitatibus perseverent. Sed quandoque accidentales qualitates recipiunt, quibus recedentibus, ad naturam suam iam redeunt.

D. Item etiam michi aliud volo responderi: Quare enim dicunt philosophi plus caloris esse igni, plus humiditatis aeri, plus frigiditatis aque, plus siccitatis telluri, cum econtrario exigat naturalis ordo mundi? Cum enim contraria sint calor atque frigiditas, sicut in superiori elemento precipuus calor est, ita etiam in inferiori maxima deberet inesse frigiditas.

M. Sane ita esse deberet ut iudicas, sed ideo aquę maior frigiditas inesse dicitur, quia in ea propter suam mollitiem citius persentitur quod in terra propter soliditatem suam atque

---

2. nunquam] nuquam *cod. rep.* 9. calefacit *corr. ex* calefecit 18. hic *add.* 19. necesse 22. enim *add.*

not sense cold so quickly, because of its solidity and hardness. What they say about there being more heat in fire than in air does not require an explanation, because no one is ignorant of the fact. Air and water, however, are in some respects equal in humidity, and in some respects they differ. We can say there is equality in them in this respect, because they both moisten a body equally; but they differ in that water moistens it more in one sense, although it enters the body more slowly, because it adheres to it more and stays for a longer time. But air moistens it more in another sense, because it enters more swiftly but nevertheless immediately passes beyond. It was for this reason that the philosophers ascribed greater humidity to air than to water, because it is both swifter and more gentle in moistening than water, and it penetrates better. Finally, about dryness: We know that whatever is more solid and closely joined together, and which has a greater desire for this, is drier. But because earth is such a thing, it is therefore drier. But fire is neither solid nor closely joined together, but it has a desire for this. Therefore, it has dryness, but not so much as earth.

D. I wish you would now clarify for me what the physicists say, namely that these four qualities are the first to come to every body, and no others can come about unless these have come first.

M. Indeed, they have perceived this by sight. For it is seen that when much cold comes upon water, it is congealed and then it becomes hard. But later, when heat enters it, it dissolves and liquefies, and thus it recovers its softness. And the same thing is apparent visibly in gold and silver and all the metals to which softness comes about from heat and hardness from cold. Similarly, lightness and slipperiness to the touch occur to human bodies and to many other things as a result of moisture. But they are somewhat roughened by dryness and are not slippery when they are touched. It is therefore most evident that heat and cold, dryness and moisture are the cause of the other qualities.

D. This gives rise to another question. For we see that dryness sometimes is joined to heat as in fire, and sometimes mois-

duritiem prohibetur. Quod autem dicunt plus caloris esse igni quam aeri, non est necesse causam reddi, cum incompertum sit nemini. Aer vero et aqua quodammodo in humiditate sunt paria et quodammodo diversa. Et in eo quidem est paritas quod ambo equaliter aliquod humectant corpus; in eo autem diversitas quod aqua quodammodo plus humectat, licet ingrediatur tardius, quia circa illud magis adheret et moratur diutius; aer vero alio modo plus, quia intrat velocius, sed statim tamen transit ulterius. Sed ideo philosophi maiorem aeri ascripserunt humiditatem quam amni, quia et in humectando velocior et mollitior est quam aqua et penetrabilior. De siccitate vero scimus quod omne illud quod solidius est atque adiunctius et cui est maior appetitus, idem est et siccius, et econverso. Sed quia terra talis est, ideo et magis sicca est. Ignis vero nec solidus est nec adiunctus, sed est ei appetitus; et ideo siccitatem habet, sed non quantum tellus.

  D. Item volo ostendas michi quod dicunt phisici, quia hę IIII^{or} qualitates primę adveniunt omni corpori, et nullę alię possunt subvenire nisi illę primo advenerint.

  M. Hoc quippe ex visu perceperunt ipsi. Videtur enim quod cum multa frigiditas aquę supervenit, congelatur atque tunc demum durescit. Postea vero, calore accedente, resolvitur ac liquescit, atque ita suam molliciem recipit. Sed et idem [194^A] visibiliter apparet in auro et argento atque omnibus metallis quibus ex calore mollicies, et ex frigiditate accedit duricies. Similiter humanis corporibus atque aliis multis ex humiditate accidit levitas atque in tangendo lubricositas; ex siccitate vero parum exasperantur, nec sunt lubricosa cum tanguntur. Est igitur evidentissimum quia calor atque frigiditas, siccitas atque humiditas cęterarum causa existunt qualitatum.

  D. Item aliud subiit inquirere. Videmus namque quod calori quando siccitas se adiunxit, ut in igne, atque humiditas

ture is. But I wonder at this junction of dryness and heat, since dryness does not come forth from heat. Similarly, dryness is sometimes coupled with coldness, and sometimes moisture is, as in water. But I similarly wonder about the coupling of moisture with cold, since moisture does not come forth from it.

M. Dryness, as we have said above, produces a desire for things. Whence also it necessarily acts upon fire, which by its natural heat consumes the entire thing to which it adheres until it has changed it completely to its own substance. For unless fire were necessarily dry, it would be moist, in the same way that air is; since fire itself is loose and penetrable and flies upward and quickly enters a body, just as air does. However, it happens that humidity is joined to cold in water not naturally, but by accident. For water is naturally cold, but accidentally it has a little heat, which is apparent because of its mobility. And when it loses a little bit of its heat, the humidity also diminishes, for when the heat diminishes it becomes cold and congealed; indeed, it is turned into cold, dry ice. So now you need not wonder any more why humidity is present along with cold, and dryness with heat.

D. There still remains one question about the elements. How can it be that sometimes they are so condensed and compressed that they seem to be in a smaller place, but sometimes they are so diffused and loosened that they seem to occupy a larger place? From this fact, it would seem that they are composed of very small particles which are sometimes united and sometimes moved apart.[42] Either those particles are like dough, which rises and becomes loose when it is fermented, but when it was unleavened was smaller and solidified; or, when they increase, they take on something from the bodies which are nearby, and when they give this up they also decrease in size. But if neither of these is the case, then this increase was from nothing. But the philosophers deny that something can be made from nothing, except in the beginning of the world.

M. If an element were a substance made up of very small

---

[42]*Cf.* Algazel, *Metaph.* * (*ed. cit.*, pp. 149-150) and Arist. *Phys.* IV 6-7 (213a-214b)

Liber Primus 99

quandoque; sed de siccitatis et caloris miror adiunctione, cum non proveniat siccitas ex calore; frigiditati vero similiter aliquando siccitas et aliquando copulatur humiditas, ut in aqua; sed de copula humiditatis cum frigore similiter admiror, cum ex eo non procedat humiditas.

M. Siccitas quidem, ut a nobis est supradictum, rebus suggerit appetitum; unde et necessario igni advenit, qui ex naturali calore illud cui adheret totum consumit quousque in sui ipsius substantiam convertit. Quod nisi ignis necessario siccus esset, esset utique humidus quemadmodum est et aer; cum ipse laxus sit et penetrabilis sursumque evolet ac statim ingrediatur in corpora, sicut aer. Quod autem in aqua frigiditati humiditas se adiungit, non naturaliter sed ex accidenti contingit. Est enim aqua naturaliter frigida, sed accidentaliter parum caloris habet, quod ex eius mobilitate apparet. Et cum illud tantillum caloris amittit, etiam humiditas recedit. Cum enim, recedente calore, frigescit et congelatur, glacies quidem frigida et sicca efficitur. Iam itaque ulterius non debes admirari quare vel humiditas frigori vel siccitas adhibuerit se calori.

D. Item de elementis restat in questionem. Quomodo enim potest hoc esse quod usque adeo densantur ac constringuntur quandoque ut in minori videantur loco esse, quandoque vero adeo diffunduntur ac laxantur quod maiorem locum videntur optinere? Ex hoc namque diminutissimis particulis composita esse videntur, quę aliquando adunantur et aliquando a se invicem elongantur. Vel sunt illę particulę admodum paste, quę cum fermentatur, crescit et laxatur Azima autem minor erat et solidabatur. Vel cum crescunt, de corporibus quę prope sunt aliquid assumunt, quod cum remittunt, et decrescunt. Si vero horum neutrum est, ergo de nichilo illud incrementum est. Sed aliquid de nichilo potuisse fieri, nisi in mundi principio, negant [194^B] philosophi.

M. Si elementum substantia ex minutis, ut dicis, composita

---

5. procedat *corr. ex* procedit   15. mobilitate *corr. ex* humiditate   21. densantur *corr. ex* densatur

parts, as you say, then by a joining together of the parts, it would make only very dense earth. But water or air or fire would never come forth except by the diffusion and loosening of the parts.

D. I wish you would clarify this statement for me and produce a stronger argument.

M. Have you never squeezed a wineskin or a bellows full of air hard between your hands?[43]

D. Yes, I have often done this.

M. And did you see that the air which was inside was squeezed closer together or that it repelled your hands and remained in the same condition?

D. Yes I have seen this, because I have done absolutely nothing to it.

M. And what does it seem to you about that air? For if it were made up of very small particles set somewhat apart from each other, wouldn't they join together when you squeezed them, and wouldn't that air arrive at its own nature and, if you had squeezed more and more, approach the nature of earth?

D. Beyond a doubt, it must be thus according to reason.

M. And do you know what emptiness is?

D. No. What is it?

M. Emptiness is called a place which one body has left and another has not yet entered.

D. Indeed, you have described it well.

M. Therefore, if the body of man were composed of very small particles at a distance from each other, shouldn't there be emptiness between them? But if this were true, why would a man, when he was pricked in one part of his body, hurt in his whole body? Or, if this were true, how could the power of the soul pass through into every part of the body? Therefore, the substance of the elements (or any body at all) is not composed of parts at a distance from each other. But neither do some parts exist as fermented dough—that is to say, that sometimes there is a hole in them and in other places they are adjoined.

---

[43]*Cf.* Arist., *Probl.* XXV 1 (937b)

partibus esset, ex partium adiunctione densissimam terram tantum conficeret. Aqua vero vel aer vel ignis nequaquam nisi ex diffusione et laxatione partium proveniret.

D. Hunc certe vellem michi sermonem reserares atque argumentum fortius attraheres.

M. Nunquid nunquam utrem vento plenum sive follem inter manus tuas cohartasti vehementer?

D. Feci utique iam frequenter.

M. Et vidisti quod aer qui intus erat se cohartaverit vel quod manus tuas reppulerit et in statu suo remanserit?

D. Hoc quidem vidi, quia nichil omnino ei feci.

M. Et quid tibi videtur de illo aere? Si enim esset ex minutis particulis a se invicem elongatis, nonne cum stringeres adunarentur et ad naturam suam deveniret aer ille et, si magis magisque coarteres, ad naturam terrę?

D. Procul dubio sic exigitur a ratione.

M. Item nosti vacuitas quid sit?

D. Quidni?

M. Vacuitas quippe locus dicitur qui ab aliquo corpore deseritur et aliud non subingreditur.

D. Sane bene descripsisti.

M. Si ergo corpus hominis de minutis esset compositum particulis a se invicem remotis, nunquid inter ipsas non deberet esse vacuitas? Si vero ita esset, quare in aliqua menbrorum particula punctus homo toto corpore perdoleret? Vel, si ita esset, quomodo virtus animę in omnes corporis particulas pertransiret? Itaque substantia elementorum nec aliquid omnino corpus ex partibus a se invicem distantibus extat compositum. Sed neque admodum paste fermentate existunt alie particulę, videlicet quod alicubi sit in eis concavitas, atque alias sint

---

11. ei *add.*   16. a *add.*

And I can give you an argument for this, if you wish, which is crude but nevertheless intelligible.

D. I very much wish to hear the argument.

M. When a tube is put against a man's flesh, and air is removed from the tube by the mouth of a physician, why does the flesh enter the tube?[44]

D. Indeed, I don't know, but I think it is because when the mouth sucks the air, the flesh follows it.

M. And why should the flesh follow the air?

D. I don't know what answer to give you except that in this world, you cannot empty any place of a given body without another body's immediately entering it.

M. Beyond a doubt, you have answered well. You could also prove it to be true by other philosophical devices, that the world does not have an empty place, but there is not room here. And this is the opinion of all the philosophers, except for a few.

D. Now that you have shown that no emptiness exists in any body, and that elemental substance fills up all space, and that its parts are closely joined without any interval, how would you be able to show that air sometimes increases and is made larger, but sometimes decreases and is made smaller?

M. On this point, the opinions of the philosophers vary. Some of them say that no body can be made larger or increase unless another is joined to it. But others say that all bodies have the power to become large up to a certain limit under some conditions, and to become small under other conditions. And when they reach one limit, they cannot become any larger, but when they reach the other they cannot be smaller.[45]

D. And which of the two opinions seems to you to be sounder?

M. That which holds that no body is increased unless another is added to it. Indeed, I think that nothing more re-

---

[44]*Cf.* Algazel, *Metaph.** (*ed. cit.*, p 140) and Urso, *Aphor. Gloss.* 26

[45]*Cf.* Algazel, *Metaph.** (*ed. cit.*, pp 149-150), Arist., *Probl.* XXV 1 (937b), *Phys.* IV 6-7 (213a-214b) and *De gen. et corr.* I 5 (321a)

Liber Primus

adiuncte; et inde argumentum tibi si velis possim dare, grossum quidem sed tamen intelligible.

D. Argumentum sane volo libenter audire.

M. Cum itaque carni hominis ventosa adhibetur, et per phistulam ore medici aer educitur, quare in ventosam caro ingreditur?

D. Nescio sane, sed puto quia ore suggente aerem, subsequitur eum caro.

M. Et que cura est carni aerem subsequi?

D. Aliud certe tibi nescio dare responsum, nisi quia in hoc mundo non poteris quodam corpore vacuare locum ullum quin aliud statim subingrediatur in illum.

M. Bene procul dubio respondisti. Verum etiam aliis philosophicis instrumentis (sed hic non habet locum) probare posses id ipsum quia non habet mundus locum vacuum; et hęc est omnium sententia philosophorum, preter quam paucorum.

D. Postquam ostensum est in nullo omnium corporum vacuitatem existere, et illam elementalem substantiam omnem locum implere, eiusque particulas sine aliquo intervallo iunctissimas esse, quomodo illud poteris ostendere quare aer quandoque crescit atque augmentatur, descrescit autem et minor efficitur quandoque?

M. In hoc sane philosophorum sententia variatur. [194^C] Dicunt enim quidam quod nullum corpus augmentari potest vel crescere, nisi aliud ei adiungatur. Alii vero dicunt quod omnia corpora ad quandam usque ad certam metam potentia sunt immensa, ad quandam vero aliam sunt parva. Et cum ad alteram pervenerint, maiora esse non possunt; cum vero ad alteram, iam ulterius non decrescunt.

D. Et utra duarum sententiarum tibi potior esse videtur?

M. Illa profecto qua dicitur quia nullum corpus augmentatur nisi sibi aliud adiciatur. Nichil sane de ipsis elementis arbi-

---

12. subingrediatur *corr. ex* ingreditur 14. aliis philosophicis *tr.* 14. habet] habent *cod.*
16. omnium sententia *tr.* 16. quam *i.m., a.m.* 18. elementalem *corr. ex* ementabilem
21. augmentatur *corr. ex* argumentatur 23. M] D *cod.* 23. sententia *corr. ex* sentia
25. aliud ei *tr.* 26. certam *corr. ex* certissimam

mains which we need to inquire about the elements. Therefore, let us make an end to the first chapter, and in the second let us inquire about those things which are composed of the elements.

D. It is a good idea, if it please you, to rest for awhile. But I don't want you to delay long, for I know that after we have begun, if we take up the discussion again anew, you will be able to question me better, and I shall be able to answer more subtly.

Here ends the first book.

tror iam restare, de quo necesse habeam inquirere. Primo ergo capitulo finem faciamus, ut in secundo de his que ex elementis sunt composita inquiramus.

D. Bonum quidem est, si placet paululum respirare, sed moram longam nolo te facere, scio enim quia postquam cepimus si recenter institerimus, et tu melius querere, et ego subtilius potero respondere. Explicit liber primus, incipit secundus.

HERE BEGINS THE SECOND BOOK

D. Now I wish you would give me some arguments concerning the fact that animals and plants and those things which the Saracens call 'congelata' (minerals),[46] such as quicksilver, sulphur, and all of the metals, are all composed of the four elements.

M. I shall be glad to. And now, for example, let us compose some one thing from the four elements and see what results. If we shall be able to find something similar to it among animals or plants, or among minerals, then we shall already have given you a partial argument.

D. This is satisfactory to me.

M. Well, then, let us mix cold and heat in equal portions. That which comes forth from this mixture will in fact be neither hotter nor colder, just as we can see by experience in hot and cold water mixed together in equal parts.

D. I think it ought to be thus.

M. Likewise, in a similar mixture made up of equal parts of dryness and moisture: If earth, which is dry, is joined to an equal quantity of water, which is wet, and they are both mashed up until they are a paste, the composite will be neither so dry as earth nor so wet as water.

D. Certainly it ought to be this way.

M. What if we could mix these two composites together; what sort of thing would result from both of them?

D. Indeed, if we should touch it, we ought to find a thing which is temperate with respect to heat and cold, dryness and moisture.

M. Now keep that composite in mind, while we see if we can find anything similar to it among the created things of the world which we have enumerated.

D. I shall keep it well in mind.

M. Let us think of this same process of mixing occurring in

---

[46] *Cf. Liber Apollonii de secretis naturae* (MS cit., fol. 184)

II

D. Iam igitur michi vellem dari argumenta quod animalia atque virentia et ea quę vocant Sarraceni congelata, sicut vivum argentum, sulphur, et metalla cuncta, composita sunt de IIII^{or} elementis cuncta.

M. Placet. Et iam, verbi gratia, ex IIII^{or} elementis aliquid unum componamus, et quid illud devenerit videamus; quod si illi simile sive in animalibus sive in virentibus, sive in congelatis invenire poterimus, iam tibi argumentum pro parte dederimus.

D. Et hoc michi placet.

M. Commisceamus igitur equaliter calorem et frigus, et quod ex illa commixtione proveniet revera neque calidum magis erit neque frigidius, quemadmodum in calida aqua et frigida equali pondere commixta experiri valemus.

D. Sic censeo esse debet.

M. Item: siccitate pariter et humiditate conmixta simile, si terra quę est sicca cum aqua quę humida est equali mensura sit adiuncta, si macerentur simul ambe usque dum fiat pasta una, illud utique compositum neque adeo siccum erit ut est terra neque humidum sicut aqua.

D. Sed et hoc sic esse oportet.

M. Quod si illa duo ita composita possemus commiscere, quale esset illud quod fieret ex utroque?

D. Sane si attactu illud contingeret nos temptare, calore et frigore, siccitate et humiditate temperatum deberemus invenire.

M. Observa modo illud compositum memori mente, donec videamus si in illis mundi quas enumeravimus creaturis reperiri valeat simile.

D. Observabo bene.

M. Modo hanc eandem commixtionem in elementis fieri

---

1. D *om. cod.*   23. attactu *corr. ex* attractu   26. reperiri *corr. ex* reperire

the elements, at first just two elements at a time, so that we may understand better, while we gain some practice and become more accustomed to this sort of thing; and afterwards we can take them three at a time; then finally let us do the same thing with all four elements. And let us begin first with the two extremes, and let us mix earth and fire in equal portions. The heat of the fire will drive out the coldness of earth, and therefore the composite will be neither too hot nor too cold, but temperate in both respects. But because both fire and earth have dryness in common, therefore the mixture is going to be extremely dry. Also, because fire is fine and earth is coarse, the composite will be neither fine nor coarse, but midway between. However, since the 'appetite' of earth is joined with the 'appetite' of fire, the composite will be made violently 'appetitive.' Likewise, earth compresses sight, and fire opens it up;[47] therefore the composite will have neither of these powers completely, but it will go half-way between. But since the lightness of fire goes against the heaviness of earth, therefore also the mixture will be neither heavy nor light, but temperate in both qualities. And since earth is not nourished, but fire is nourished violently, therefore the composite will also seek to be nourished, but never so violently as fire. Therefore, that composite which comes forth from fire and earth will be temperate with respect to heat and cold, between fine and coarse, temperate also in compressing or opening up sight, between light and heavy; but it will be extremely dry, have a moderate 'appetite,' and wish to be nourished a little bit. In a similar manner, if you should mix the elements two by two in equal proportions, only six composites will come forth from the mixture, thus:

        Fire   Air
        Fire   Water
        Fire   Earth

---

[47] In twelfth-century visual theory, sight was often considered to be caused by a beam of visual force going forth from the eye. This beam was compressed by darkness and allowed to become diffuse by light.

cogitemus, ac primum in binis et binis, ut facilius intelligamus, donec exerceamur in illis et usitemus, et postea in ternis et ternis; denique in ipsis IIII^{or} idem faciamus. Atque in primis de duobus extremis incipiamus, terram [194^D] videlicet et ignem equaliter commisceamus. Repugnabit itaque calor ignis frigiditati terre, quare et compositum nec frigidum nec calidum erit nimium, sed temperatum in utroque. Quia vero et ignis et terra conveniunt in siccitate, ideo commixtum necesse est siccissimum futurum esse; quia etiam et ignis subtilis et terra grossa existit, compositum quidem nec subtile nec grossum sed medium inter utrumque erit. Quoniam autem terrę appetitus cum appetitu ignis adiungitur, commixtum quoque vehementer appetitum efficietur. Item terra visum constringit, et ignis aperit; unde et compositum nec alteram omnino virtutem habebit nec alteram, sed inter medium abibit. Sed quoniam levitas ignis ponderositati contraibit terrę, ideo et commixtum nec ponderosum erit nec leve, sed temperatum utrinque. Quoniam vero non dietatur terra, sed dietatur vehementer ignis, ideo et compositum dietari quidem queret, sed nequaquam quantum ignis. Erit igitur illud quod ex igne et terra proveniet compositum calore et frigiditate temperatum inter subtile et grossum, temperatum quoque in constringendo et aperiendo visum, inter leve et ponderosum; sed erit vehementer siccum, nimium habet appetitum, ac dietari volet paulum. Simili autem modo si elementa bina ac bina equaliter miscueris VI tantum composita provenient ex adiunctis, hoc modo:

        Ignis   Aer
        Ignis   Aqua
        Ignis   Terra

---

9. grossa] sicca *cod*.   15. medium *add. i.m.*

Air	Water
Air	Earth
Water	Earth

You will consider each one of these mixtures carefully in the same manner as was pointed out about that composite which the mixing of earth and fire could make. Next, mix the elements in equal portions three at a time; and you can have only four such mixtures, thus:

Fire	Air	Water	Fire	Water	Earth
Fire	Air	Earth	Air	Water	Earth

First consider carefully the mixture that results from these elements, and afterwards mix all four of the elements in equal portions, and consider carefully the make-up of the composite. See whether it is similar to the make-up of that composite which you were instructed above to commit to memory.

D. Indeed, I shall both mix them up and consider the resulting mixture; and after I have considered it, I shall explain it to you if you wish.

M. See. We have now discovered that twelve kinds of composites can be made by mixing together equal portions of the elements. But only one of these exists in actuality; the other eleven exist only in thought. And by mixing two elements at a time in unequal proportions, we can find twelve; by mixing three at a time, forty-eight—twenty-four when each one of the elements is unequal to any of the others and twenty-four when two of them are equal and one unequal. In all four of these together, there are seventy-four. In eight of these, three of the elements are equal in the mixture and the fourth is unequal. But there are six others in which two of the elements are equal to each other and the other two are equal to each other, but there is inequality between the pairs. There are thirty-six others in

ILLUSTRATIONS
British Museum Cotton Galba E. IV,
Fols. 190r-200r, Marius: *De elementis*

Fol. 194v: includes the beginning of Book Two (see p. 107)

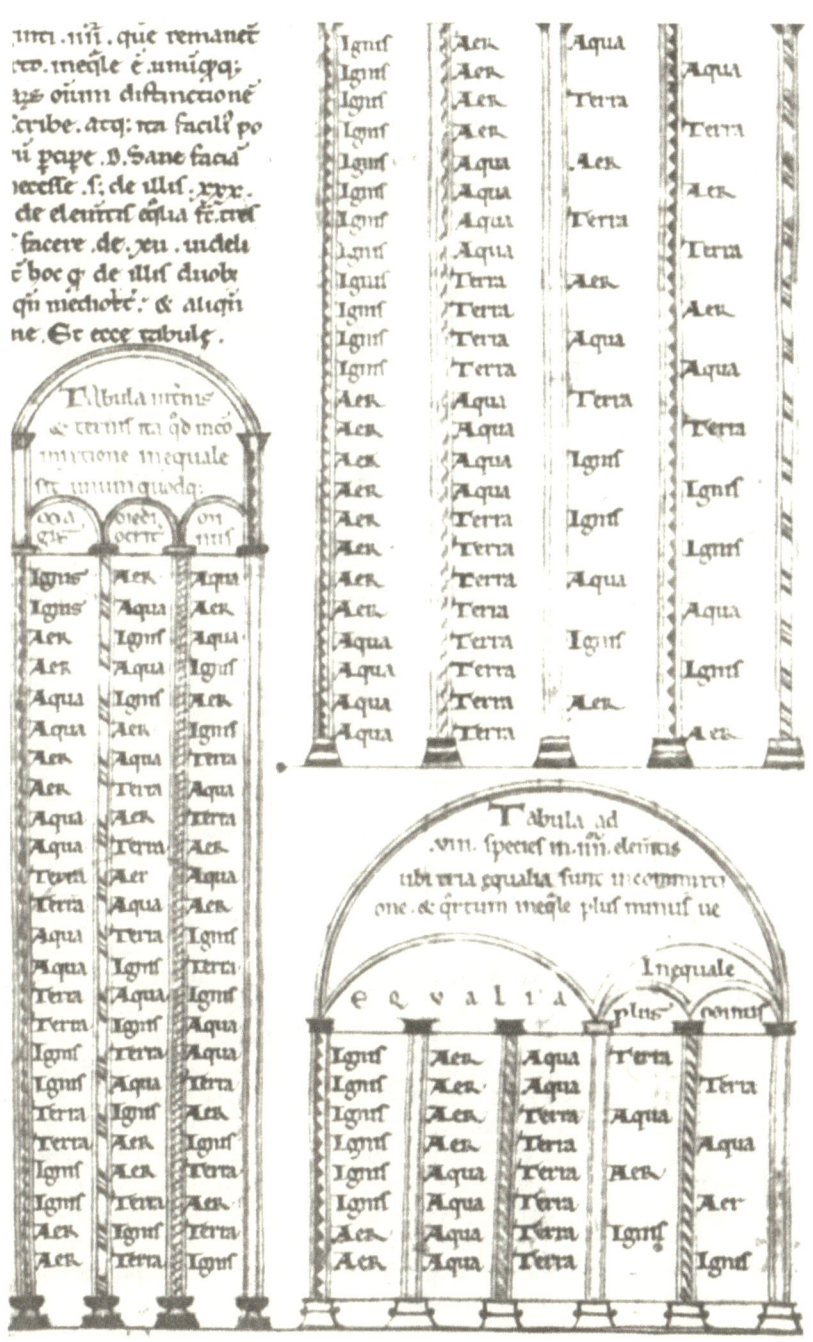

Fol. 195r (see pp. 12-13, 115, 117, 119)

Primū	Secdm	Tercium	Quartum
Ignis	Aer	Aqua	Terra
Ignis	Aer	Terra	Aqua
Ignis	Aqua	Aer	Terra
Ignis	Aqua	Terra	Aer
Ignis	Terra	Aer	Aqua
Ignis	Terra	Aqua	Aer
Aer	Aqua	Terra	Ignis
Aer	Aqua	Ignis	Terra
Aer	Terra	Aqua	Ignis
Aer	Terra	Ignis	Aqua
Aer	Ignis	Aqua	Terra
Aer	Ignis	Terra	Aqua
Aqua	Terra	Ignis	Aer
Aqua	Terra	Aer	Ignis
Aqua	Ignis	Terra	Aer
Aqua	Ignis	Aer	Terra
Aqua	Aer	Terra	Ignis
Aqua	Aer	Ignis	Terra
Terra	Ignis	Aer	Aqua
Terra	Ignis	Aqua	Aer
Terra	Aer	Ignis	Aqua
Terra	Aer	Aqua	Ignis
Terra	Aqua	Ignis	Aer
Terra	Aqua	Aer	Ignis

Aer	Aqua
Aer	Terra
Aqua	Terra

Quorum temperiem singulorum diligenter considerabis quemadmodum de composito illo ostensum est quod posset conficere terrę commixtio atque ignis. Deinde etiam elementa commisceas equaliter terna et terna, et quattuor tantum provenient inde composita, ita:

Ignis	Aer	Aqua		Ignis	Aqua	Terra
Ignis	Aer	Terra		Aer	Aqua	Terra

Sed et eorum temperiem diligenter quę sit considera, sed et postea tota IIII^{or} elementa commisce equaliter compositique temperiem considera diligenter et vide utrum similis sit temperiei illius compositi quod supra preceptum est observari memoriter.

D. Ego quidem et commiscebo et temperiem considerabo; atque consideratam tibi si placet monstrabo.

M. Iam ecce XII species compositorum invenimus nos fieri ex elementorum equali adiunctione, quarum una tantum invenitur in actu, reliquę vero undecim non nisi cogitatione. Ex inequali vero commixtione in binis quidem et binis, duodecim possumus reperire; in ternis vero et ternis XLVIII; viginti IIII^{or} quidem ita quod ipsorum trium inequale erit [195^A] unumquodque, et XXIIII^{or} quod duo erunt equalia et tercium inequale. In IIII^{or} autem totis septuaginta quattuor. In quarum VIII, III^a de elementis equalia sunt in commixtione et quartum inequale. Sunt autem sex alie, in quibus II° de elementis inter se sunt equalia, et altera duo inter se equalia, sed inequalitas est inter bina. Item sunt alię XXXVI, in quibus duo de elementis

which two of the elements are equal to each other, but the other two are unequal both to each other and to each of the other pair. And in the twenty-four which remain of the seventy-four, each element is unequal to each of the others in the mixture. If you wish, draw the distinction of all these kinds of mixtures in the form of a table, and you will be able to perceive each one of the mixtures more easily.

D. I shall gladly do this, for it is necessary; but in those thirty-six kinds in which two of the elements are equal, we ought to make three tables, namely for each one of the sets of twelve where one pair of elements remains constant while the other two elements vary as to more, equal, and less in the mixture. And here are the tables:

The table where two elements are mixed unequally

More	Less
Fire	Air
Air	Fire
Fire	Water
Water	Fire
Fire	Earth
Earth	Fire
Air	Water
Water	Air
Air	Earth
Earth	Air
Water	Earth
Earth	Water

Liber Secundus 113

equalia sunt inter se, duo vero inequalia et erga duo alia et inter se. Sed et in viginti IIII^{or} que remanent de LXXIIII^{or}, in commixto inequale est unumquodque ab alio. Quod si velis, harum omnium distinctionem specierum in tabulis subscribe, atque facilius poteris temperiem singularum percipere.

D. Sane faciam libenter, namque fieri est necesse; sed de illis XXXVI speciebus in quibus duo de elementis equalia sunt, tres tabulas oportet nos facere, de XII videlicet speciebus unaquaque propter hoc quod de illis duobus elementis aliquando plus, aliquando mediocriter, et aliquando minus est in compositione. Et ecce tabulę:

Tabula in binis et binis ex inequali commixtione

Magis	Minus
Ignis	Aer
Aer	Ignis
Ignis	Aqua
Aqua	Ignis
Ignis	Terra
Terra	Ignis
Aer	Aqua
Aqua	Aer
Aer	Terra
Terra	Aer
Aqua	Terra
Terra	Aqua

The table in which each of three elements is mixed in unequal parts

More	Moderate Amount	Less
Fire	Air	Water
Fire	Water	Air
Air	Fire	Water
Air	Water	Fire
Water	Fire	Air
Water	Air	Fire
Air	Water	Earth
Air	Earth	Water
Water	Air	Earth
Water	Earth	Air
Earth	Air	Water
Earth	Water	Air
Water	Earth	Fire
Water	Fire	Earth
Earth	Water	Fire
Earth	Fire	Water
Fire	Earth	Water
Fire	Water	Earth
Earth	Fire	Air
Earth	Air	Fire
Fire	Air	Earth
Fire	Earth	Air
Air	Fire	Earth
Air	Earth	Fire

Liber Secundus

Tabula in ternis et ternis ita quod in commixtione inequale sit unumquodque

Magis	Mediocriter	Minus
Ignis	Aer	Aqua
Ignis	Aqua	Aer
Aer	Ignis	Aqua
Aer	Aqua	Ignis
Aqua	Ignis	Aer
Aqua	Aer	Ignis
Aer	Aqua	Terra
Aer	Terra	Aqua
Aqua	Aer	Terra
Aqua	Terra	Aer
Terra	Aer	Aqua
Terra	Aqua	Aer
Aqua	Terra	Ignis
Aqua	Ignis	Terra
Terra	Aqua	Ignis
Terra	Ignis	Aqua
Ignis	Terra	Aqua
Ignis	Aqua	Terra
Terra	Ignis	Aer
Terra	Aer	Ignis
Ignis	Aer	Terra
Ignis	Terra	Aer
Aer	Ignis	Terra
Aer	Terra	Ignis

Table in which the elements are mixed three at a time, so that two are equal to each other, the third unequal, either more or less.

Equals		Unequal	
		More	Less
Fire	Air	Water	
Fire	Air		Water
Fire	Air	Earth	
Fire	Air		Earth
Fire	Water	Air	
Fire	Water		Air
Fire	Water	Earth	
Fire	Water		Earth
Fire	Earth	Air	
Fire	Earth		Air
Fire	Earth	Water	
Fire	Earth		Water
Air	Water	Earth	
Air	Water		Earth
Air	Water	Fire	
Air	Water		Fire
Air	Earth	Fire	
Air	Earth		Fire
Air	Earth	Water	
Air	Earth		Water
Water	Earth	Fire	
Water	Earth		Fire
Water	Earth	Air	
Water	Earth		Air

Item tabula in ternis et ternis ita quod in commixtione duo sint
equalia et tercium inequale, plus equalibus vel minus equalibus

Equalia		Inequale	
		Plus	Minus
Ignis	Aer	Aqua	
Ignis	Aer		Aqua
Ignis	Aer	Terra	
Ignis	Aer		Terra
Ignis	Aqua	Aer	
Ignis	Aqua		Aer
Ignis	Aqua	Terra	
Ignis	Aqua		Terra
Ignis	Terra	Aer	
Ignis	Terra		Aer
Ignis	Terra	Aqua	
Ignis	Terra		Aqua
Aer	Aqua	Terra	
Aer	Aqua		Terra
Aer	Aqua	Ignis	
Aer	Aqua		Ignis
Aer	Terra	Ignis	
Aer	Terra		Ignis
Aer	Terra	Aqua	
Aer	Terra		Aqua
Aqua	Terra	Ignis	
Aqua	Terra		Ignis
Aqua	Terra	Aer	
Aqua	Terra		Aer

Table of the eight kinds of mixtures of all four elements, where three are equal and the fourth is unequal, either more or less.

	Equals		Unequal	
			More	Less
Fire	Air	Water	Earth	
Fire	Air	Water		Earth
Fire	Air	Earth	Water	
Fire	Air	Earth		Water
Fire	Water	Earth	Air	
Fire	Water	Earth		Air
Air	Water	Earth	Fire	
Air	Water	Earth		Fire

Table for the six kinds of mixtures of all four elements where two elements are equal to each other and are more than half of the mixture, and the other two are equal to each other and are less than half, and the two sets are unequal.

Larger Pair of Equals		Smaller Pair of Equals	
Fire	Air	Water	Earth
Water	Earth	Fire	Air
Fire	Water	Air	Earth
Air	Earth	Fire	Water
Fire	Earth	Air	Water
Air	Water	Fire	Earth

Tabula ad VIII species in IIII^{or} elementis ubi tria equalia sunt in commixtione et quartum inequale plus minusve

	Equalia		Inequale	
			Plus	Minus
Ignis	Aer	Aqua	Terra	
Ignis	Aer	Aqua		Terra
Ignis	Aer	Terra	Aqua	
Ignis	Aer	Terra		Aqua
Ignis	Aqua	Terra	Aer	
Ignis	Aqua	Terra		Aer
Aer	Aqua	Terra	Ignis	
Aer	Aqua	Terra		Ignis

Tabula ad VI alias species in IIII^{or} elementis, ubi sunt equalia inter se duo in maiori, et duo in alia inter se equalia in minori, sed inequalitas est inter bina.

Equalia In Maiori		Equalia In Minori	
Ignis	Aer	Aqua	Terra
Aqua	Terra	Ignis	Aer
Ignis	Aqua	Aer	Terra
Aer	Terra	Ignis	Aqua
Ignis	Terra	Aer	Aqua
Aer	Aqua	Ignis	Terra

Table for the twelve kinds of mixture of all four elements, where two of them are equal to each other, and the other two are unequal both to each other and to the other pair; but the pair of equals constitutes more than half of the mixture; one of the unequals is less than either one of the equals, and the other is still less.

Equal to each other, but more in the mixture than of the unequals		Unequals	
		Less than of the equals	Least of all
Fire	Air	Water	Earth
Fire	Air	Earth	Water
Fire	Water	Air	Earth
Fire	Water	Earth	Air
Fire	Earth	Air	Water
Fire	Earth	Water	Air
Air	Water	Fire	Earth
Air	Water	Earth	Fire
Air	Earth	Fire	Water
Air	Earth	Water	Fire
Water	Earth	Fire	Air
Water	Earth	Air	Fire

Liber Secundus

Tabula ad XII^cem species in IIII^or elementis, ubi duo de ipsis inter se sunt equalia, et alia duo inequalia et inter se et erga alia que sunt equalia, sed de equalibus plus est in compositione quam de inequalibus; de inequalibus vero, de altero minus equalibus et de altero minori minus.

Equalia inter se sed plus est in commixtione quam de inequalibus		Inequalia	
		Minus quam de equalibus	Minus quam de omnibus
Ignis	Aer	Aqua	Terra
Ignis	Aer	Terra	Aqua
Ignis	Aqua	Aer	Terra
Ignis	Aqua	Terra	Aer
Ignis	Terra	Aer	Aqua
Ignis	Terra	Aqua	Aer
Aer	Aqua	Ignis	Terra
Aer	Aqua	Terra	Ignis
Aer	Terra	Ignis	Aqua
Aer	Terra	Aqua	Ignis
Aqua	Terra	Ignis	Aer
Aqua	Terra	Aer	Ignis

Table for the second twelve kinds of mixture of all four elements, where two are equal to each other, and the other two are unequal both to each other and to the equals, but there is a small amount of the equals in the compound; but one of the unequals is greater than the pair of equals, the other less.

More than of the Equals	Equal to each other		Less than of the Equals
Water	Fire	Air	Earth
Earth	Fire	Air	Water
Air	Fire	Water	Earth
Earth	Fire	Water	Air
Air	Fire	Earth	Water
Water	Fire	Earth	Air
Fire	Air	Water	Earth
Earth	Air	Water	Fire
Fire	Air	Earth	Water
Water	Air	Earth	Fire
Fire	Water	Earth	Air
Air	Water	Earth	Fire

Liber Secundus

Tabula ad alias XII species in IIII^or elementis, ubi duo de ipsis inter se sunt equalia, et alia duo inequalia et inter se et erga alia, que sunt equalia, sed est de equalibus mediocriter in compositione; de inequalibus vero, de altero magis quam de equalibus, de altero autem minus quam de equalibus.

	Inequalia		
Magis quam de equalibus	Equalia inter se		Minus quam de equalibus
Aqua	Ignis	Aer	Terra
Terra	Ignis	Aer	Aqua
Aer	Ignis	Aqua	Terra
Terra	Ignis	Aqua	Aer
Aer	Ignis	Terra	Aqua
Aqua	Ignis	Terra	Aer
Ignis	Aer	Aqua	Terra
Terra	Aer	Aqua	Ignis
Ignis	Aer	Terra	Aqua
Aqua	Aer	Terra	Ignis
Ignis	Aqua	Terra	Aer
Aer	Aqua	Terra	Ignis

Table for the third of the twelve kinds of mixtures of all four elements, where two of them are equal to each other, the other two unequal to each other and to each of the other pair; the pair of equals constitutes less than half of the mixture, and each of the two unequals is greater than either of the two equals.

Unequals		Equal to each other but less than both	
More of it than in the equals	The greater of the two unequals		
Water	Earth	Fire	Air
Earth	Water	Fire	Air
Air	Earth	Fire	Water
Earth	Air	Fire	Water
Air	Water	Fire	Earth
Water	Air	Fire	Earth
Fire	Earth	Air	Water
Earth	Fire	Air	Water
Fire	Water	Air	Earth
Water	Fire	Air	Earth
Fire	Air	Water	Earth
Air	Fire	Water	Earth

Liber Secundus

Tabula ad tercias XII species in IIII^{or} elementis, ubi duo de ipsis inter se sunt equalia, et alia duo inequalia et inter se et erga alia que sunt equalia, sed est de equalibus in compositione, de altero magis quam de suo inequali et de altero magisquam de equalibus; de (e)qualibus vero minus quam de omnibus.

Inequalia		Equalia	
Magis quam de suo in equalibus	Magis quam de inequalibus	inter se et est minus quam de inequalibus	
Aqua	Terra	Ignis	Aer
Terra	Aqua	Ignis	Aer
Aer	Terra	Ignis	Aqua
Terra	Aer	Ignis	Aqua
Aer	Aqua	Ignis	Terra
Aqua	Aer	Ignis	Terra
Ignis	Terra	Aer	Aqua
Terra	Ignis	Aer	Aqua
Ignis	Aqua	Aer	Terra
Aqua	Ignis	Aer	Terra
Ignis	Aer	Aqua	Terra
Aer	Ignis	Aqua	Terra

Table for the twenty-four kinds of mixtures of all four elements where each one is unequal to the other; there is less of the second than of the first, less of the third than of the second, and least of all of the fourth.

First	Second	Third	Fourth
Fire	Air	Water	Earth
Fire	Air	Earth	Water
Fire	Water	Air	Earth
Fire	Water	Earth	Air
Fire	Earth	Air	Water
Fire	Earth	Water	Air
Air	Water	Earth	Fire
Air	Water	Fire	Earth
Air	Earth	Water	Fire
Air	Earth	Fire	Water
Air	Fire	Water	Earth
Air	Fire	Earth	Water
Water	Earth	Fire	Air
Water	Earth	Air	Fire
Water	Fire	Earth	Air
Water	Fire	Air	Earth
Water	Air	Earth	Fire
Water	Air	Fire	Earth
Earth	Fire	Air	Water
Earth	Fire	Water	Air
Earth	Air	Fire	Water
Earth	Air	Water	Fire
Earth	Water	Fire	Air
Earth	Water	Air	Fire

[196^A] Tabula ad XXIIII species, ubi in composito de IIII^or elementis, est inęquale unumquodque ab alio; de secundo videlicet minus quam de primo, de tercio minus quam de secundo, de quarto minus quam de omnibus

Primum	Secundum	Tercium	Quartum
Ignis	Aer	Aqua	Terra
Ignis	Aer	Terra	Aqua
Ignis	Aqua	Aer	Terra
Ignis	Aqua	Terra	Aer
Ignis	Terra	Aer	Aqua
Ignis	Terra	Aqua	Aer
Aer	Aqua	Terra	Ignis
Aer	Aqua	Ignis	Terra
Aer	Terra	Aqua	Ignis
Aer	Terra	Ignis	Aqua
Aer	Ignis	Aqua	Terra
Aer	Ignis	Terra	Aqua
Aqua	Terra	Ignis	Aer
Aqua	Terra	Aer	Ignis
Aqua	Ignis	Terra	Aer
Aqua	Ignis	Aer	Terra
Aqua	Aer	Terra	Ignis
Aqua	Aer	Ignis	Terra
Terra	Ignis	Aer	Aqua
Terra	Ignis	Aqua	Aer
Terra	Aer	Ignis	Aqua
Terra	Aer	Aqua	Ignis
Terra	Aqua	Ignis	Aer
Terra	Aqua	Aer	Ignis

M. You have done well; you have drawn the tables well. Therefore, you can know from this that eighteen kinds of composite result when you mix all four elements in groups of two, one pair equal and the other unequal. But, when you join the mixture of three at a time equal and unequal, it makes fifty-two. When you add all four equally and unequally mixed, seventy-five. If you add them all up together, you will find 145, of which you will perceive some by a bodily sense, but others you will only understand in your mind.

D. Now I understand in part from those mixtures of the elements, and especially from the seventy-five, what things, consistent with and similar to them, composed of the four elements, can be found among the created things of the world. And I see this to be an argument that animals, plants, and minerals are composed of the four elements. But I still wish that you might demonstrate this matter more clearly.

M. Very well. If someone should give you some milk and ask you to which of the 145 kinds of mixture it was similar, what would you answer him?

D. It is known immediately that milk is liquid, thick, and greasy—exceedingly liquid, somewhat less thick than liquid, but more so than it is greasy. And water is liquid, earth is thick, air is greasy. We cannot find fire in it visibly, but we can prove by experience that it is present, for a man is warmed up as a result of drinking milk. Therefore, it can truly be said that there is less of fire than of anything else in milk. And so I might answer that milk is similar to that kind of mixture in which there is much water, less earth, still less air, and least of all of fire.[48]

M. You would answer correctly. But so that you may understand the same thing better, I would like you now to divide that composite of milk and separate each element from the others, for thus you would have a clearer and stronger argument.

D. I wish you would show me how to do this.

---

[48] *Cf.* Isaac, *De dietis particularibus** (*Opera omnia*, Lyons, 1515, fol. CXL) and *De dietis universalibus** (*ed. cit.*, fol. LXXXIv-LXXXIIr)

Liber Secundus

M. Bene fecisti; bene tabulas descripsisti. Iam igitur ex hoc nunc scire potes quia de quattuor elementis binis et binis equaliter et inequaliter commixtis, X^{cem} VIII° proveniunt compositorum species. Sed ternis vero et ternis equaliter et inequaliter adiunctis, LIIe. De IIII^{or} autem totis equaliter et inequaliter simul iunctis, LXX^{ta} V^{que}. Quas si omnes simul connumeres, CXLV invenies, quorum quasdam corporeo sensu percipies, alias vero nequaquam nisi ratione intelliges.

D. Iam quidem partim cognosco ex elementorum commixtionibus his, et maxime ex LXXV, que de IIII^{or} elementis quidem convenientia atque similia in mundi valeant inveniri creaturis. Et hoc utique video ego esse argumentum quod animalia, virentia et congelata de IIII^{or} sint composita elementis, sed idem vellem adhuc si possis lucidius approbares de ipsis.

M. Si ergo aliquis lac tibi afferret et cui harum CXLV specierum simile esset inquireret, quid inde ei responderes?

D. Notum profecto est lac esse liquidum, spissum, et pingue, liquidum quidem valde, spissum vero minusquam liquidum, sed plusquam pingue. Et liquidum est aqua, spissum terra, pingue aer. Ignem vero in eo nequaquam possumus visibiliter invenire, sed possumus experimento approbare ipsum in eo esse, calefit enim [196^{B}] homo ex lactis comestione. Vere igitur dici potest de igne minusquam de omnibus esse in lacte. Responderem itaque lac esse simile speciei illi ubi magis est de aqua, minus de terra, minus etiam de aere, minimum vero omnium de igne.

M. Recte quidem responderes, sed ut idem melius intelliges, vellem modo compositum lactis illud divideres et elementa unumquodque ab alio separares, ita enim lucidius atque potentius argumentum haberes.

D. Volo illud quomodo faciam insinues.

---

10. que] + sunt *del.*   25. minimum] mininum *cod.*

M. I shall gladly show you. But first answer a question. If someone now wished to tear down a certain house which had been built of wood, iron, and stones, could the house revert to anything but wood, iron, and stones?[49]

D. Indeed, it would return to that which it was before it became a house.

M. And if someone agitated milk, would not a greasy substance—that is, butter—appear on the top?

D. Yes it would.

M. Then if he removes the greasy substance and puts what remains into a jar, and does to it what one does in making rosewater, you should know that fresh and potable water comes forth from it. But if he also burns the waste matter which remains in the bottom of the jar, it will turn into ashes, and thus earth.

D. I see clearly that earth and water come from the milk; but concerning the greasy substance which you said was air, I do not understand that it is air.

M. Except for air, it would not nourish fire at all, for it is visibly apparent to all by what fire is nourished.[50]

D. You have explained clearly about earth, water, and air. But how will you show fire to be in milk?

M. Indeed, there is only a very small amount of fire in it, and for that reason, it can be perceived only by reason. But it can also be said that that little bit joined itself to the other fire when the denser part of the mixture was burned. So behold! You have a clear and evident argument that animals and other things we mentioned before are all composed of a joining of the four elements. And indeed it is asserted of two of the things made up of the four elements, namely animals and plants, that none of them lives long if any of the four elements is completely absent from it.[51] But concerning the third, that is, minerals, dif-

---

[49]*Cf.* Macrobius, *In somnium Scipionis** 2 12 13 (*ed. cit.*, p. 132), Constantine, *Pantegni*,* *Theorice*, I 5, Arist., *Meteor.* IV 7 (383b) and *De long. et brev. vitae* V (466a)

[50]*Cf.* Isaac, *De dietis universalibus** (*ed. cit.*, fol XXXIXrb)

[51]*Cf.* Isaac "Chapter on the Elements,"* pp. 45-46, *Isaac Israeli*, pp. 122-123, and perhaps Eriugena, *De divisione naturae* I 54 (*ed. cit.*, 498A)

M. Libenter utique ostendam, sed prius michi responde quod queram. Siquis modo diruere vellet domum quandam que ex lignis et ferro lapidibusque esset composita, nunquid redigi posset nisi in ferrum, lapides atque ligna?

D. Profecto in id rediret quod erat antequam domus fieret.

M. Si itaque aliquis lac moveret, nunquid non statim pinguedo, hoc est butirum, superemineret?

D. Utique faceret.

M. Quod si emissa pinguedine quod remanet in vas commiserit, ac sicut de aqua rosata fit de eo fecerit, scias quia dulcis inde atque potabilis aqua exibit. Si vero etiam fecem que in vasis fundo remanserit comburet, cinis quidem atque ita terra fiet.

D. De terra et aqua patenter video quod ex lacte redit; de piguedine vero quam aerem esse dixisti, non intelligo quod aer sit.

M. Quippe nisi aer, nequaquam ignem dietaret, sed ignem inde dietari cunctis visibiliter apparet.

D. Bene ostensum est de terra, aqua et aere; sed quomodo ostendes in lacte ignem esse?

M. Parum nempe est in eo de igne, quare et percipi non valet nisi ratione; sed et dici potest quoniam illud parum alii igni se adiunxit in spissitudinis combustione. Ecce igitur lucidum atque evidens habes argumentum quod ea que prediximus animalia et cetera composita sunt cuncta ex adiunctione IIII^{or} elementorum. Et quidem hec duo, animalia scilicet atque virentia, ex IIII^{or} elementis sint facta, assertio est quod nullum eorum diu vivit ubi de ipsis IIII^{or} elementis aliquod omnino defecerit. De tercio vero, videlicet de congelatis, diverse date sunt sententię ab antiquis. Quidam enim ex duobus, alii ex tri-

---

11. potabilis *corr. ex* potabiles

ferent opinions are given by the ancients. Some say that they are composed of two, others of three, and still others of four elements. But I, following what I believe to be the truer authority, say that there are four elements in them.

D. And how is it that there are in the world almost innumerable kinds of composite bodies; and yet you, in your analysis, have divided them into only 145 kinds?

M. If you multiply these 145 kinds either by increasing or decreasing the parts, you will undoubtedly find them innumerable. There are only seven in which you cannot either diminish or increase the elements: one, the mixture of all four elements in which they are all equal in the composite; the six others, the mixtures of two elements at a time in which the two similarly are equal in the composite.

D. I wish you would clear up one other thing for me. For I have heard a saying by the ancients that there are only nine complexions of things. I want you to explain to me how this is.

M. Do you concede that in the mixture where the four elements are equal—do you concede, I say, that there are two temperaments in it?

D. Yes, I concede it; one between cold and hot, and the other between wet and dry.

M. You speak well. But if you leave the temperament which is between dry and wet as it is, but you wish to destroy the temperament between cold and hot, you should know that you can only do this in two ways. Either there will be more of heat, and then the composite will be hot but temperate between dry and wet; or there will be more of cold, and so the composite will be called cold but temperate with respect to wet and dry. But if you leave that temperament which is between cold and hot as it is, and you wish to destroy that which is between dry and wet, there are similarly only two ways you can accomplish this destruction: there will either be more of humidity, and then the composite will be called moist but tempered between heat and cold; or there will be more of dryness, and thus the composite will be dry but tempered between cold and heat. There! You have now discovered four complexions, but not nine of them.

bus, et alii ex IIII^{or} dicunt ea esse composita elementis. Ego autem, veriorem reor auctoritatem secutus, IIII^{or} dico esse elementa in ipsis.

D. Et quid est quod in mundo sunt compositorum species fere innumerabiles, et tu ea in CXLV tantum ratione partitus es?

M. Si has CXLV species secundum partes sive crescendo sive decrescendo multiplices, innumerabiles eas proculdubio invenies. Septem tantum excipies in quibus neque diminuere elementa neque augmentare multiplicando vales, unam quidem in IIII elementis in qua equalia sunt in composito cuncta elementa, sex vero reliquas in binis et binis in quibus illa II° similiter sunt in compositione equalia.

D. Est aliud de quo me volo certifices. Audivi enim dictum ab antiquis novem tantummodo rerum esse complexiones. Quod quomodo sit, michi queso explanes.

M. [196^C] Concedis tu in ea compositione ubi sunt equalia IIII^{or} elementa, concedis, inquam, duas temperies esse in ea?

D. Concedo equidem, alteram scilicet inter frigus et calorem et alteram inter humiditatem atque siccitatem.

M. Bene dicis. Verum si eam temperiem quę est inter siccitatem et humiditatem ut est dimiseris, eam vero que inter frigus et calorem destruere velis, scias quia non poteris efficere, nisi duobus modis: quatinus vel de calore sit magis, et tunc erit compositum calidum sed inter siccitatem et humiditatem temperatum; vel sit magis de frigore, et ita compositum appellabitur frigidum sed temperatum humiditate atque siccitate. Si vero illam temperiem dimiseris que est inter frigus et calorem illamque delere volueris quę inter siccitatem et humiditatem, duobus similiter tantum modis facies illam distructionem, videlicet ut vel de humiditate sit amplius, et tunc dicetur compositum humidum sed temperatum inter calorem et frigiditatem; vel sit amplius de siccitate, et ita compositum erit siccum sed inter frigus et calorem temperatum. Ecce igitur iam IIII^{or} invenisti complexiones sed nequaquam de illis IX. Item IIII^{or} alias reperire

---

17. temperies] teperies *cod.*   34. sed nequaquam add. *i.m.*

Likewise, you will be able to find four other complexions, but only if you destroy both the temperaments we have mentioned, so that there will either be more of heat and humidity in the composite, and thus it will be hot and moist; or there will be more of heat and dryness, and then it will be hot and dry; or there will be more of cold and moisture, and thus it will be cold and moist; or more of cold and dryness, and it will be cold and dry. The ninth is that first complexion in which all four elements were equally tempered. Therefore, it was said by the ancients in accord with necessary reason that only nine complexions of things can be discovered, nor will you be able to discover more.[52]

D. You have explained well about the nine complexions. But now there arises one other problem which I should very much like to be explained to me. Why is it that those composites in which there is more of fire and air are not always found up above, since those in which there is more earth and water always remain below?[53]

M. You should know that if you take an earthy body and join to it a fiery body equal to it in length, breadth, and width, even if there should be more of the fiery body than there is of earth—I am speaking with regard to weight in the earthy body only—the earthy will always drag the fiery downward after it and, if possible, even all the way to the center. For example: If you take a very small wick in your hand and, after smearing it thoroughly with some oil, light it, even though the flame may leap up two or three times the size of the wick, nevertheless if you take your hand away and let go of the wick, you will see the wick will immediately fall and drag the flame down after it. The reason for this is that the motion of the earth, which moves toward the lowest places, has greater power here in its own place than the motion of fire, which moves toward the highest places; nor should this be wondered at, because all things have greater power in their own place than elsewhere.

---

[52] *Cf.* Constantine, *Pantegni*,* Theorice, I 6 and ps.-Galen, *De spermate* (Galeni *Opera*, Venice, 1597, fol. 41). See above, "Introduction," p. 28

[53] *Cf.* Arist., *De caelo* IV 5 (312b)

poteris complexiones, sed nequaquam nisi ambas quas diximus delebis temperies, quatinus vel de calore et humiditate sit magis in composito, et ita erit calidum et humidum; vel sit de calore magis atque siccitate, et tunc erit calidum et siccum; vel sit de frigore et humiditate magis, et sic erit frigidum et humidum; vel magis de frigore et siccitate, eritque frigidum atque siccum. Nova vero est illa complexio prima in qua equaliter temperata sunt IIII^{or} elementa. Dictum est igitur ab antiquis necessaria ratione novem tantummodo rerum complexiones inveniri posse, neque enim plures poteris invenenire.

D. Bene de novem complexionibus explanasti, sed nunc ecce subit unum quod michi multum vellem aperiri. Cur enim composita illa in quibus magis est de igne et aere non inveniuntur semper sursum, cum ea ubi magis est de terra et aqua semper consistant deorsum?

M. Scias quia si acceperis corpus unum terreum et coniectes illud cum alio equali sibi longitudine, latitudine et altitudine quod sit igneum, etiam si magis sit de igneo quam sit de terra—secundum pondus loquor in terreo tantum—terreum semper trahet igneum post se deorsum et, si permittatur, etiam usque ad centrum. Verbi gratia: si lichinum exiguissimum manu tua acceperis atque aliqua pinguedine perunctum accenderis, licet surgat flama maior duplo sive triplo quam sit lichinus, si tantum manum subduxeris lichinumque dimiseris, statim et lichinum decidere et post se flammam deorsum trahere [196^D] videbis. Hoc autem est argumentum quia motus terrę que movetur ad infima maiorem habet virtutem hic in loco suo quam motus ignis qui movetur ad suprema, nec hoc mirandum quia in loco suo maiorem vim quam alibi habent cuncta.

---

6. atque *corr. ex* et   21. lichinum *corr. ex* lichinium

D. Now I understand clearly from your explanation that those things which are found in earth, water, and air are all composed of the four elements. But I wish you would reveal to me by what means this is done.

M. I shall do this gladly, and I shall begin by talking about those things which are clearer and easier to demonstrate—that is, I shall first treat of minerals. Have you ever seen a goldsmith cast silver or gold in a pot?

D. Yes. I have seen this many times.

M. And do you know that the pot is made of earth ground up with water; and when gold or silver is cast in it time and again and many times over, have you seen that at some point it usually expands[54] and also becomes transparent like glass and can hardly be seen?

D. I have also seen this many times. Nor does this happen only to a goldsmith, but also to all those who are accustomed to dissolve copper or iron and the rest of the metals in a pot.

M. Therefore, it ought not to seem wonderful to you, or impossible, if the earth creates glass within itself in the same way.

D. Indeed, I think this too is possible. But how could so great a heat—such as fire produces—be found inside the earth, by which the earth might be cooked and glass made?

M. Don't you know that a small amount of heat maintained for a long time has just as much strength as a great heat maintained for a short time?

D. Indeed, this is evident to everyone. But I do not yet see, nor does my mind lead me to concede, that there is any heat in the earth, either large or small.

M. This we can also prove visibly. The argument for this is that in the winter the water in wells is warm with respect to the coldness they have in summer; but also the deeper the wells, the warmer the water is in them in winter.[55]

---

[54]*virescere* literally means "to turn green;" a derivative meaning is "flourish, grow." In view of what would actually happen to the pot, I have taken some liberty and translated it "expand."

[55]*Cf.* Salernitan question B 117 (fol. 128) and P 11 (fol. 3v); William of Conches, *Dragmaticon*, pp. 204-205; and the authorities cited by Lawn, *Salernitan Questions*, p. 198, *putei latices*

Liber Secundus

D. Iam nunc patenter intelligo ex tuo sermone ea quę inveniuntur in terra, aqua, et aere, ex IIII^{or} elementis composita cuncta esse. Sed modum quo fiat volo te michi aperire.

M. Libenter faciam, ac de his quę patentiora sunt et ad ostendendum leviora incipiam, de congelatis videlicet primum agam. Vidisti itaque unquam auri artificem argentum vel aurum in urceo fundere?

D. Vidi utique et sepe.

M. Et nosti tu quia de terra macerata cum aqua fit urceus ille; et cum in eo funditur aurum vel argentum semel et iterum ac multa vice, vidisti quia soleat quandoque virescere et fieri perlucidum, quasi vitrum, atque ultra visum recipere?

D. Et hoc quoque vidi multa vice, neque contingit hoc aurifici tantum, immo his omnibus qui cuprum vel ferrum et metalla reliqua in urceo solent dissolvere.

M. Non itaque mirum videri tibi debet, aut impossibile, si eodem modo vitrum tellus procreet intra se.

D. Et hoc quidem fieri reor possibile. Sed quomodo tantus calor intra terram poterit inveniri quo terra excoqui ac vitrum fieri valeat sicut igni?

M. Nunquid non nosti quod tantundem valeat longo tempore calor parvus quantum breviori tempore calor magnus?

D. Hoc nempe est perpatens omnibus; sed nondum video, nec fert michi animus ut concedam, quod in terra sit calor sive magnus sive parvus.

M. Et hoc quoque visibiliter possumus nos approbare. Inde enim argumentum est quod tempore hiemali calide in puteis inveniuntur aquę respectu frigiditatis quam habent in ęstate; sed et putei quanto profundiores sunt, tanto calidior est in eis aqua in hieme.

---

14. aurifici *corr. ex* artifici   18. fieri *add.*

D. Therefore, according to you it must be said that earth be called hot and not cold.

M. No indeed! For that heat is in the earth only in winter. If the earth were actually hot, then heat would be in it both in summer and in winter.

D. What is the cause of that heat?

M. When the surface of the earth is heated by the heat of the sun in the summer, the moisture and vapors which are mixed with bits of earth are heated up. But in the winter, the heat recedes to the interior of the earth as if fleeing from its contrary, namely the cold which encircles the surface of the earth at that time; and therefore the earth is cold on the surface, but its interior is hot at that time.

D. How do you mean that heat flees, since it is an accident and you cannot find it by itself separated from substance?

M. Indeed, I mean that the vapors which are mixed with earth flee downward, and thus they take the heat in them into the interior.

D. That is enough concerning this question. But I wish you would point out to me how each contrary flees its contrary, which you apparently meant above.

M. Truly, every contrary tries and works to demolish and destroy its contrary, as cold tries to destroy heat, and humidity dryness, and the opposite.

D. Isn't heat one of the qualities of bodies, and isn't it an accident?

M. It is.

D. And how can one quality so abhor another that it tries to demolish and destroy it, since a quality has no discretion nor does it know what it ought to do?

M. Do you know that sleeping and waking are contraries?

D. Yes, I know this.

M. And do you know that when sleep approaches, a man ceases to be awake, and the other way around, and that the one perishes when the other returns?

D. I know this too.

D. Ergo secundum te dici est necesse terram calidam nec frigidam esse.

M. Non utique. Est enim calor ille in terra tantum in hieme; quod si terra calida esset, et in estate et hieme equaliter in ea esset calor ille.

D. Quę est caloris illius causa?

M. In diebus quidem estatis calefacta superficie terrę calore solis, calefiunt humiditas et vapores qui commiscentur terrę glebis. Diebus vero hiemis, secedit calor ad interiora telluris utpote suum contrarium fugiens, frigus videlicet quo terrę superficies circumvenitur tunc temporis, et ideo tellus superficietenus quidem frigida, interius vero semper calida est diebus illis.

D. Et quomodo dicis quoniam fugiat calor ille, cum accidens sit, nec a substantia separatum per se valeas invenire?

M. Dico equidem vapores ad ima fugere qui terrę permixti sunt, sicque in se ad interiora calorem deferunt.

D. [197ᴬ] De hoc quidem satis est, sed quomodo unumquodque contrarium suum fugiat contrarium queso ostendere velis, quod ecce superius dicere voluisse videris.

M. Revera omne contrarium suum semper nititur et laborat perdere contrarium ac delere, quemadmodum calorem frigus atque humiditas siccitatem, id est, econverso et a regione.

D. Nunquid non est calor de corporis qualitatibus et est accidens?

M. Est.

D. Et quomodo potest qualitas una ita aliam abhorrere quod eam perdere nitatur ac delere cum nec discrecionem habeat aliqua qualitatum, nec scit quid debeat facere?

M. Nosti quia contraria sunt dormire et vigilare?

D. Novi utique.

M. Et nosti quia surreppente somno desinit homo vigilare, et econverso, atque perit ita alterum altero redeunte?

D. Et hoc quoque.

---

14. ille] + cum *del. man. rec.*   24. calor *add.*

M. Thus it should be understood about heat and cold, moisture and dryness.

D. You have well laid bare a great secret, insofar as I understand what you have said. For a quality brings about nothing; the effective agent is the body in which the quality inheres. For if a body is hot, it causes heat; if cold, it causes cold; if moist it makes a thing wet; and if it is dry it causes dryness. But if a hot body is also dry, if both heats and dries. If, however, it is hot and moist, it causes heat and moisture. But if it is cold and dry, it makes coldness and dryness. And if it is cold and moist, it causes coldness and wetness. If, however, it has been tempered with respect to heat, cold, humidity and dryness, it works no change. It is clear from this, therefore, that bodies have nine complexions, as we have said above, and that eight of these are the effects which bodies exercise with other bodies. The ninth complexion is the temperament of the others, and, as has been said, it does nothing. But now I ask that you return to your interrupted discourse and set forth how minerals are made in the earth.

M. The heat existing in the interior of the earth heats the mud within until, after many, many years, it is turned into glass, just as the enormous heat of the furnace turns the pot of the goldsmith into glass.

D. I understand clearly.

M. Do you also know that the jar of a potter is a kind of glass? But because it was not cooked long, it is therefore not glass. But if it were cooked for a long time by the fire, it would be turned into clear and glittering glass, like the pot of the goldsmith. Now, therefore, you can observe how stones are created in the body of the earth because of insufficient fire; if the fire were greater, the process would be completed and these stones would be turned into glass. Of this sort are the stones we use for the construction of houses, and marble of various colors, and the little white stones which are found on the banks of rivers. There are many kinds of these because of the varieties of earth of which there are many kinds—I do not mean earth properly speaking—and because of the variation in the amount of heat

M. Sic sane intelligendum est de calore et frigore, humore, ac siccitate.

D. Archanum magnum bene enucleasti, in quantum ego de sermone tuo intelligo. Qualitas enim nichil operatur, sed opera sunt corporis quod qualitati subicitur. Corpus enim si calidum est, et calidum facit; si vero frigidum, frigidum facit; si autem humidum, humidum facit; si vero siccum, aridum facit. Verum si corpus calidum et siccum est, et calefacit et siccat. Si autem calidum et humidum, calidum et humidum facit. Si vero frigidum et siccum, gelidum et aridum facit. Si vero frigidum et humidum, gelidum et madidum facit. Si autem calore, frigore, humore, ac siccitate contemperatum fuerit, nichil operatur. Inde igitur patet corpora novem habere complexiones, ut superius dictum est, et octo esse opera que corpora cum aliis corporibus exercent. Nona enim complexio aliarum temperamentum est et, ut dicitur, nichil operatur. Sed nunc ad sermonem intermissum nostrum redeas, et qualiter congelata in terra fiant nunc queso propales.

M. Calor in interioribus terre existens lutum intus usque adeo decoquit, donec in vitrum post annos innumeros redigatur, quemadmodum urceum aurifabri vis ignis inmensa decoquens in vitrum redigit.

D. Perspicue equidem intellexi.

M. Nostin etiam amphoram figuli quandam vitri speciem esse? Sed quia ab igne non diu decocta fuit, ideo nec vitrum est. Si enim ab igne diu coqueretur, in vitrum clarum et nitidum ut aurifabri urceus redigeretur. Nunc igitur animadvertere potes qualiter lapides in terrę corpore ignis procreantur inopia in quibus, si ignis admodum operaretur, in vitrum verterentur. Huiusmodi sunt lapides quos in domuum constitutione ponimus, et colorum diversorum marmora quique in fluviorum ripis reperiuntur lapilli, quibus inest diversitas ob terre diversitates cuius multę sunt species—non dico terrę proprię—et ob diversitatem quantitatis coquendi. Terra enim solida et levis, cuius multum [197ᴮ] in ventre terre durat decoctio, lapides solidos et

---

8. corpus calidum *tr.*

they receive. For light and solid earth which is heated for a long time in the interior of the earth makes solid and heavy stones similar to glass. Of this type are flintstones, from which we are accustomed to strike fire. But from light and rough earth, which is not heated long in the earth's interior, light and brittle stones come forth. Indeed, this same thing is a kind of glass existing in the earth's interior. For that glass which is made from solid, light and clear earth and which is heated in the earth's interior for many years is turned into jacinth when it is heated up by that very great heat which is in the eastern regions. Indeed, jacinth is a kind of glass, but because of such great heat it does not melt. Undoubtedly, this happens because the force of the fire works on it so long that all its moisture is dried out and all its parts are compressed tightly[56] so that the fire cannot enter its parts. And this is why it is not damaged by fire as other stones are. But if that glassy substance is heated and dried out more than jacinth, it is transformed into a stone which is called diamond. But that glass which is made from pure, light, and clear earth, and which is not heated so much as jacinth, is made into crystal or beryl. But if a greater heat pervades these stones, they are changed into alebandina or carnelium. But if the earth is coarse and impure and not heated for a long time, it will be turned into ordinary glass. But if greenness of copper is added to any of the previously mentioned kinds of glass, the stone will be of a green or bluish color. For example: If light, pure, and clear earth were mixed with water and cooked by a heat sufficient to produce jacinth, and if it were mixed with the greenness of copper, it would be made into an emerald. However, if that earth were cooked with a small amount of heat for a short time, it would be turned into a prase. But if the copper were well-cooked, it would be made into a turquoise. But if the earth is coarser than in the previously mentioned cases, it will be made into an azurite.

D. I understand the making of stones, for the most part.

---

[56]*arte* is given by the scribe as an alternate spelling for *arce*, "tightly."

ponderosos efficit, vitro similes. Cuiusmodi sunt silices, ex quibus ignem excudere solemus. Ex terra autem levi et aspera quę non diu in ventre telluris coquitur, lapides leves et fragiles proveniunt. Idem nempe vitri modus est in telluris ventre existentis. Illud enim vitrum quod de terra solida et levi claraque fit quodque in terrę visceribus non paucis annis coquitur, illo calore maximo qui in plaga orientale est, in iacinctum vertitur. Iacinctus quippe quedam species est vitri, sed propter ignem tantum non defluit. Hoc absque dubio inde contingit quod vis ignis in ea tam diu operatur donec universum eius exsiccet humorem, et partes universas eius arce (vel arte) comprimat, quare ignis illas partes subintrare nequit. Et hęc est occasio quare ab igne sicut et alii lapides non ledatur. Verum si vitreum illud plus iacincto decoquitur et exsiccatur, in lapidem qui adamas nuncupatur transformatur. Illud vero vitrum quod de terra munda et levi ac clara fit et quod non quantum iacinctus excoquitur cristallus vel berillus efficitur. Si autem maior adveniens calor hos lapides infecerit, in alebandinam vel sardium rediguntur. Quod si terra grossa et inmunda fuerit nec diu decocta, in rectum vitrum vertetur. Si vero alicui predictarum specierum vitri cupri adhibeatur viriditas, lapis coloris erit viridis vel azurei. Verbi gratia: Si terra levis et munda ac clara et cum aqua mixta fuerit caloreque illo bene decocta qui ad iacinctum efficiendam sufficere posset, et si cum cupri viriditate conmixta fuerit, in smaragdum formabitur. Si autem terra illa calore parvo parumque coquetur, in prassium vertetur. Quod si cuprum bene combustum fuerit, in turchesiam redigetur. Si vero terra preter hec supradicta grossa fuerit, in azurum formabitur.

    D. Lapidum maxime partis facturam intelligo. Hoc autem

---

6. annis] amnis *cod.*   11. vel arte *add.*   22. terra *add.*   24. viriditate] viritate *cod.*

But I wish you would explain this, whether each of the four elements, or three of them, or two, are in glass.

M. It has been made clear above that every composite body in this lower world consists of four elements. Therefore, we may assume from this that glass consists of the four elements. Nevertheless, I shall explain this clearly so that you may understand better.[57] But the eyes of your mind are necessary for the understanding of this. Since unless you understand this, you will never be able to comprehend properly any composite body on earth.

D. I shall do my best.

M. Do you not understand that air is changed into fire, and thus each of the elements into another?

D. How could I fail to understand this, when it has been explained so clearly in the beginning of this book?

M. If someone should say to you that air, before it is changed into fire, is potentially fire, he would speak nothing false. I say potentially, because air has a certain natural potential to be turned into fire.

D. What you say is true.

M. Now it appears most evidently that that thing which is changed into another, before it is changed into it, is potentially the thing it is changed into.[58] But as soon as it is changed into that thing, it is it actually. For example: a boy must become an old man, unless he is first seized by death. Therefore, he who is a boy can be called an old man potentially. But when he has grown old, he will be called an old man actually. It is thus also with air. For while it is still air, it is fire potentially. But when it has become fire, it can be called fire actually.

D. You have spoken clearly. From this, I judge that physicists have called species of plants hot and cold, dry and moist, as is apparent of a pepper. For when we touch it, it feels cold,

---

[57] *Cf.* Arist., *De gen. et corr.* I 10 (327b-328a) and II 7 (334a). See also H. H. Joachim, "Aristotle's Conception of Chemical Combination," *The Journal of Philology*, XXIX (1904), 72-86, Otto Apelt, "Die Schrift des Alexander von Aphrodisias über die Mischung," *Philologus*, XLV (1886), 82-99, and Robert Multhauf, *The Origins of Chemistry*, pp. 122-123, 149-153

[58] *Cf.* Arist. *Phys.* IV 5 (213a) and *De caelo* III 2 (302a).

Liber Secundus

edisseras volo, an elementorum IIII^{or} unumquodque, an ex illis tria, an duo, vitro insint.

M. Superius enucleatum est omne compositum in hoc mundo inferiori ex IIII^{or} constare elementis. Inde igitur animadverti potest ex IIII^{or} vitrum constare elementis. Manifeste tamen illud ut potius intelligas propalabo. Verumtamen ad hoc intelligendum tui cordis oculi sunt necessarii. Quoniam nisi hoc intellexeris, aliquid in terra compositum nequaquam considerare poteris.

D. Ego pro posse meo operam dabo.

M. Nunquid non intelligis aerem in ignem mutari et sic elementorum unumquodque in aliud?

D. Quare ego id optime non intelligerem, cum in huius libri primordio evidentissime declaratum sit?

M. Si aliquis aerem, priusquam in ignem mutetur, ignem potentia dicat esse, nichil falsi dicet. [197^C] Potentia quippe ideo dico, quia aer potentiam quandam naturalem in ignem mutari habet.

D. Nichil revera falsi loqui.

M. Modo evidentissime apparet rem illam quę in aliam mutatur priusquam in eam mutetur esse eam potentia in quam mutabitur. Sed simulac in ipsam mutabitur, ea in actu erit. Verbi gratia: Nequit esse quin puer senex fiat, nisi morte preoccupetur. Ergo qui puer est, senex potentia vocari potest. Quando autem senex fuerit, senex actu dicetur. Sic quoque de aere est. Dum enim aer adhuc est, ignis potentia; cum vero ignis fuerit, actu ignis dici potest.

D. Manifeste dixisti. Hincque autumo phisicos herbarum species calidas et frigidas, siccas et humidas vocasse, sicut de pipere apparet. Cum enim illud tangimus, frigidum non cali-

---

1. elementorum *corr. ex* elementum   11. M *add.*   12. elementorum *add.*

not hot. But when we eat it, our body becomes hot. But if too much of it is consumed, it will burn the inside of the body of the person eating it. Therefore, when a pepper is touched by the hand, it is not actually hot, since it does not heat up the hand; but it is hot potentially.[59] For it is changed into a hot thing if it is eaten or drunk. And thus I understand you mean it is with the other elements.

M. Thus I wish to understand, my dear pupil, that when the four elements make up any body, none of them is found actually in the composite body except insofar as it is there potentially. For example: In a fruit composed of the four elements, none of them is found there actually, but only potentially.[60] For if fire were actually in the fruit, that fruit would undoubtedly be found to be hot. But if air were actually in the apple itself, the fire existing in it actually would destroy that air, and the fruit would not be durable. But we know that a fruit lasts for many months. If, however, water were actually in the fruit, it would either certainly flow out, or it would be turned into vapor by the force of the fire existing in it actually. But if earth were in the fruit actually, its own heaviness would clearly be the cause of its destruction. Another argument: If the four elements were actually in the fruit, one of them would not be able to exist even for an hour together with another. For it has been established that fire flees from water, and conversely, as has been set forth above in this book. Therefore, it is clear that a fruit can only exist if each one of the elements in it is changed into something other than it was before it became a fruit. But when fire encounters water in the composition of an apple, fire operates on water, and water undergoes its operation; also in the same way water operates on fire, and fire undergoes the operation of water. And each one of them tries to alter the other from its own nature, since when fire operates on water, it heats it up and dries it out; and conversely when water operates on

---

[59] *Cf.* Constantine, *Pantegni,* * Theorice, I 6 and Isaac, *Liber de elementis** (ed. Lyons, 1515, fol. VIv)

[60] *Cf.* Isaac, *De dietis universalibus** (*ed. cit.*, fol. LVIIva) and William of Conches, *Dragmaticon** (*ed. cit.*, pp. 232-233)

dum sentimus. Verum cum illud comedimus, corpus nostrum calescit. Quod si ipsius piperis immodica pars sumetur, vescentis corpus interius cremabit. Piper ergo, cum manu tangitur, non actu quoniam manum non calefacit, sed potentia calidum est. In calidum enim mutatur si mansum aut bibitum fuerit. Et sic de aliis esse elementis velle te dicere intelligo.

M. Sic, discipule mi dilecte, intelligas volo quod cum elementa IIII^{or} corpus aliquod componunt, nullum illorum in corpore composito actu invenitur nisi potentia dum taxat. Verbi gratia: In pomo ex IIII^{or} elementis composito, nullum illorum actu sed potentia reperitur. Si enim ignis in pomo actu esset, absque dubio calidum reperiretur. Si vero aer ipsi malo actu inesset, ignis in eo actu existens ipsum aerem pessundaret, pomumque durabile non esset. Sed multis mensibus pomum durare cernimus. Si autem aqua pomo actu inesset, vel certe diflueret vel ob vim ignis in eo actu existentis in vaporem redigeretur. Quod si terra pomo actu inesset, sua sine ambiguitate gravitas esset sibi causa ruinę. Aliud argumentum: Si illa IIII elementa in pomo in actu essent, unum illorum vel una hora cum alio consistere nequiret. Ratum est enim ignem aquam fugare, et econverso, sicut in hoc libro superius explanatum est. Manifestum igitur est pomum consistere nequire nisi unumquodque quod in eo est elementorum in aliud mutetur quam esset priusquam pomum fieret. Cum vero ignis in mali compositione aquę obviet, ignis in aqua operatur, et aqua eius opera suscipit; aqua quoque eodem modo in igne operatur, et ignis aquę opera suscipit. Unumquodque autem eorum aliud a natura sua removere nititur; quoniam cum ignis in aqua operatur, calefacit eam et siccat; et cum econverso aqua in igne operetur, ipsum frigidum humidumque reddit. Cumque eodem modo in pomi constitutione terrę aer obviet, utrumque eorum alterum a natura sua propellere luctatur, et alterutrum in altero operatur [197^D] et

---

3. corpus *corr. ex* cropus   5. si *add.*   13. actu *corr. ex* actum   20. fugare *corr. ex* fuget

fire, it imparts cold and moisture. And when in the same way air encounters earth in the composition of the fruit, both of them struggle to drive the other from their own nature, and each of them operates on the other and undergoes the operation of the other. When earth operates on air, it bestows solidity and dryness on it; but when air operates on earth, it makes it hot and moist. For this reason, therefore, there is made from the four elements another mixture, another temperament, and another complexion than existed before, since each one of them, from that state of actuality in which it existed earlier, is changed into something else. Nor will any of them be found in the fruit in that previous state of actuality, since each one is changed.

D. I understand very clearly what you have said. For earlier I heard you affirming that when two contrary elements oppose each other, each of them seeks to alter the other from its own nature until it itself is altered from its own nature which previously existed actually. For example: When fire is joined potentially with an equal amount of water, so that there is not enough fire to destroy the water nor so much water that it puts out the fire, each of them operates on the other and undergoes the operation of the other. For if fire operates on water, it lessens its coldness and moistness. But if water operates on fire, it diminishes the heat which was previously in it and the dryness. And thus one fights against the other until they come together, and from them a third thing is made, of which it can truly be said that fire is not in it actually, but potentially; and thus also water is not in it actually, but rather potentially. Since if any of them were in it actually, they would not come together, nor would a third body be composed of them which is similar to none of them. But if that body is destroyed by force, each one of the elements will again exist actually as before. And in this aforesaid manner I understand a fruit and whatever consists of the four elements to exist. Therefore, it can well be said that the fire which is in the fruit was actually fire before the apple was made out of it. But when the fruit was made of it, the fire was turned into a different thing than it was before, and so some-

alterius suscipit opera. Cum enim terra in aere operetur ipsum gelidum aridumque reddit. Cum autem aer prius in terra operetur, illam calidam humidamque efficit. Hac itaque de causa ex illis IIII^or elementis alia commixtio, alia contemperatio, aliaque complexio quam prius esset efficitur, quoniam unumquodque eorum ex eo genere quod prius in actu erat in aliud mutatur. Nec aliquod eorum in pomo eius generis cuius prius fuerat reperietur, cum unumquodque mutetur.

    D. Quod dixisti optime intelligo. Audivi enim superius te affirmantem quod cum duo elementa contraria sibi obviaverint, utrumque eorum aliud a natura sua removere laborat quousque a natura sua quę prius in actu fuit removeatur. Verbi gratia: Quando ignis aquę pari addicione in potentia sic adiungitur quod ignis non pars tanta adsit quę ad aquę perdicionem sufficiat, neque aquę tantum quod ignem queat extinguere, utrumque eorum in altero operatur et alterius opera suscipit. Nam si ignis in aqua operatur, et eius geliditatem ac humiditatem minuit. Si vero in igne aqua operatur, caliditatem quę prius infuerat siccitatemque aminuit. Sicque unum alii repugnat donec illa conveniant, et ex eis res tercia efficiatur quę sane dici potest quod ignis in eo non actu immo potentia est sicque ętiam aqua non actu verum potentia inest. Quoniam si quodlibet eorum in eo actu esset, non convenirent, nec corpus tercium ex eis componeretur, quod nulli illorum simile est. Quod si corpus illud vi defecerit, unumquodque elementorum ipsorum in actu sicut prius erit. Et hoc modo predicto intelligo pomum esse et quodcumque de IIII^or constat elementis. Bene itaque dici potest quod qui ignis pomo inest, prius in actu ignis fuit quam ex eo compositum malum esset. Cum vero compositum fuit ex eo pomum, ignis in rem alterius se generis transtulit quam prius esset, sicque ex eo aliud effectum est. Et eodem ipso modo, se alia habent elementa ex quibus constat. Dum vero durabit

---

6. mutatur *corr. ex* mutetur   16. utrumque *corr. ex* utrum

thing different was made from it. And the other elements of which it consists behave in the very same way. For while the fruit endures, each one of the elements of which it consists will be in it potentially. But when it rots or is burned, each one of the elements will be removed and will exist actually, as they did before.[61] But if it is eaten, it will change into a thing of the same kind as the thing by which it is eaten. Also, each one of those elements can be extracted *per se*, as we have previously established in the case of milk. Therefore, it is now clear to everyone that all minerals consist of the four elements. All the elements are present in these minerals potentially before they are freed from them. But when they are set free, each one of them will be the removed element actually. It is thus also in truth with both animals and plants.

M. May the Lord bless you for understanding my words correctly. So now let us return to your question, for the sake of which what we just said was inserted. Your question is whether or not the four elements are present in glass. For you did not believe them to be present before I explained these things to you. Do you now believe them to be present or not?

D. I believe very well and I know that the four elements are present in glass potentially, even though its greatest part is earthy. Therefore I wish that you would now make clear how they are mixed in it.

M. In its beginning, water was necessary for glass to soften the earth until there was enough of this muddy substance to be turned into glass. Next, fire was necessary, by whose heat the mud was made liquid. Also, it is clear that air, of necessity, is in the glass, since there is no place in the world in which anything is made without air; for no place is empty. Also, we shall show that air is actually present in glass, since we have already proved that it is present potentially. For when fire is applied to glass, it forces it to break; and this is the reason: When the air which is actually in the glass receives heat from the force of the fire, it expands and requires a greater place. When it cannot find room

---

[61]*Cf.* William of Conches, *Dragmaticon** (*ed. cit.*, p. 233)

Liber Secundus 151

(pomum), unumquodque (elementorum) ex quibus (constat) in eo potentia erit. Si autem putridum ac combustum fuerit, unumquodque elementorum removebitur ac in actu ut prius fuit existet. Si vero mansum fuerit, in rem eiusdem generis abibit, cuius res a qua comedetur fuerit. Elementorum quoque illorum unumquodque per se extrahi potest, sicut de lacte superius declaratum est. Liquet ergo nunc omnibus quod congelata omnia ex IIII^{or} constant elementis. In quibus congelatis priusquam deficiant, omnia insunt potentia elementa. Cum autem defecerint, unumquodque eorum remotum elementum in actu fuerit. Sic quoque in rei veritate et de animalibus et de virentibus est.

M. Benedicaris a domino qui sermones meos recte intelligis. Redeamus itaque ad questionem tuam cuius causa hec predicta sunt inserta. Est utique questio tua utrum vitro IIII^{or} insint elementa necne. Non enim ipsa inesse credebas antequam hec tibi [198^A] explicarem. Credisne vel adhuc ea inesse an non?

D. Optime credo ac scio vitro IIII^{or} inesse elementa potentia, verumtamen maxima pars eius terrea est. Volo igitur nunc ut qualiter ipsa in eo commixta sint aperias.

M. In suo primordio, vitro aqua erat necessaria, unde terra maceraretur quoad multum tale unde vitrum fieri posset redigeretur. Ignis deinde necessarius erat, cuius ex coctione lutum fieret liquidum. Aerem etiam necessario vitro inesse constat, cum nullus mundi locus in quo aliquid fit absque aere sit. Nullus enim locus vacuus est. Aerem item actu etiam vitro inesse monstrabimus, quandoquidem eum inesse potentia probavimus. Nam ignis vitro adhibitus ipsum cogit dissilire; et hec est causa: Cum aer qui vitro actu inest calorem a vi ignis suscipit, dilatatur maioremque locum exigit. Quo non reperto, fisso vitro prodit. Sed si vitrum igni paulatim propius adhibeatur, non dissiliet.

---

1. Dum...constat *add. i.m.* (pomum), (elementorum), (constat) *supplevi; exciduntur*   3. actu *corr. ex* tactu   4. generis *corr. ex* generes   17. ea *corr. ex* eam   21. aperias *corr. ex* aperies   32. dissiliet *corr. ex* dissilet

to expand, it bursts forth by cracking the glass. But if the glass is gradually put closer to the fire, it will not crack.[62] And this happens because when the glass is heated up gradually, the air escapes a little at a time. It can also be proved by another argument that air is actually present in glass; since a kind of glass can be set on fire when it is mixed with salt or sulphur, and this would not happen if no air were present.

D. I have understood perfectly what you have perfectly explained. And I can also prove what is evident and established by another argument. The argument for this is that glass is very different from earth in being not nearly so heavy, dry, or cold, and this is because there is air in it. For if it were not present, glass would be heavy, dry and cold, as earth is.

M. That is a good argument, and thus you ought to understand about all the things which are composed of the four elements. Likewise, it ought to be conceded that all minerals are composed of the four elements. But most of the minerals have a greater abundance of earth than of the other elements. However, there are some of their number in which there is more fire and air, such as sulphur, orpiment, petroleum, and sal ammoniac. There is not so much of fire and air in sal ammoniac as is perceived to be in the others. And this is clear because each one of them is burned quickly, but nevertheless one more quickly than the other. There is an abundance of water in quicksilver, and for that reason it is very similar to cold water and ice and is readily congealed. But there is a small amount of fire and air in it; and this is clear because it does not burn easily. For if there were an abundance of air in it, it would burn easily, like sulphur. And if there were much fire in it, it would burn the tongue of one tasting it, as sal ammoniac does. And so, the water—of which we have proved it to have a large amount—forces it to scatter if it is thrown into a fire. It should be noted that all six kinds of metals are composed in the earth of quicksilver and sulphur,[63] namely gold, silver, copper, iron, lead, and tin. This

---

[62] *Cf.* Nicolaus of Damascus, *De plantis* II 2 (ed. E.H.F. Meyer, p. 28)
[63] *Cf. Liber Apollonii de secretis naturae* (*MS cit.*, fol. 11r-12r)

Hocque inde evenit quod paulatim calescente vitro, paulatim exit aer. Alio item argumento probari potest aerem vitro actu inesse: Quoniam vitri species cum sale vel sulphure mixta accendi potest; quod non fieret si aer abesset.

D. Perfecte intellexi quod perfecte explicasti. Quod evidens esse atque ratum ego quoque alio preterea potero probare argumento. Est enim argumentum ad hoc, quod vitrum longe diversum est a terra cum ipsum tanta gravitate, siccitate vel frigiditate nequaquam participet, hocque ideo est quia aer in eo est. Si enim abesset, admodum terrę grave, siccum ac frigidum esset.

M. Bonum est argumentum, sicque intelligere debes de universis quę ex IIII^{or} sunt elementis composita. Item concedendum est quod omnia congelata ex his IIII^{or} sunt composita elementis. In maxima vero parte congelatorum maior est habundantia terrę quam cuiuslibet reliquorum elementorum. Sunt autem quedam de eorum numero in quibus ignis et aer plus habundant, ut sulphur, auripigmentum, petroleum, sal amoniacum. Sali amoniaco non tanta inest ignis et aeris habundantia quanta reliquis inesse comprehenditur. Hocque inde manifestum est quod unumquodque eorum cito comburitur, attamen aliud alio citius. In vivo quidem argento est aque habundantia, et iccirco simillimum est aquę frigidę et glaciei, et constringi prompte. Ignis vero et aeris parva pars ei inest; hocque inde manifestum est quod non facile ardet. Si enim aeris ei inesset habundantia, facile ut sulphur arderet. Quod si ignis multum inesset, linguam gustantis quemadmodum sal amoniacum cremaret. Itaque aqua—qua ipsum habundare probavimus—si in ignem proiciatur, cogit ipsum diffugere. Notandum quidem est omnia sex metallorum genera ex vivo argento et sulphure in terra componi, aurum videlicet, argentum, cuprum, ferrum, plumbum, et stannum. Hoc quoque inde verum esse probatur,

---

2. actu] potentia *cod.*   17. de eorum *corr. ex* deorum   29. diffugere *corr. ex* diffigere

fact can also be proved true from this, that when these are liquefied in a fire, they are similar to quicksilver. Therefore, gold is made from pure quicksilver mixed with pure sulphur heated deep in the earth for a long time. And both because of the long time taken in the cooking of gold and because its material was pure, its parts were pressed closely together until it became solid and heavy. Therefore, it neither rots inside the earth nor can it easily be burned by fire. Silver, however, is made from pure quicksilver mixed with a small amount of reddish sulphur for a short time. And because a small amount of reddish sulphur was present, therefore, it did not have the same reddish-yellow color as gold. Copper was made from impure quicksilver mixed with very dirty and somewhat dense red sulphur, and it was cooked for a long time—even longer than gold—at an extremely high heat. And because it underwent a great force of combustion, it therefore has much redness in it. Also, its body was so loosened up that the vapor of vinegar is able to enter its body and give it a greenish color, which is called 'flower of brass.' Iron was made from dense quicksilver mixed with sulphur of a color half-way between red and white, and it was cooked for a long time, even longer than copper, by a moderate heat, and from this is derived its great solidity; nor does it become fluid from the force of fire as copper does, since it was cooked for a long time. And because a moderate heat was present, its body did not become loose like copper. And because the sulphur contained a small amount of redness, therefore if iron should lie undisturbed for a long time, it becomes rusty and takes on a reddish color. Tin was made from pure quicksilver mixed with pure white sulphur. But it was cooked for a short time. For if, in cooking it, the heat were small and the time were great, it would be turned into silver. Lead was made from coarse quicksilver mixed with coarse sulphur which was white with just a little red. And that it was made from white sulphur is clear, because when vinegar is applied to it, it takes on a white color. But that the sulphur was slightly reddish is clear when lead burns, for then it is of a reddish color.

D. What you promised about minerals, namely that they

quod quando hec in igne liquescunt, vivo argento consimilia sunt. Aurum igitur fit ex vivo argento claro mixto cum sulphure claro in cor-[198^B]-de terrę longo excoctis tempore. Et quia et magna mora in auro decoquendo et ipsius materia clara fuit, strinxerunt sese partes queque ad aliam quoad solidum graveque fieret. Ideoque nec sub terra putrescere nec ab igne facile comburi valet. Argentum vero factum est ex vivo argento claro cum parva parte sulphuris parumper rubei mixto. Et quia parum sulphuris aliquantulum rubei adfuit, iccirco non admodum auri fulvum fuit. Cuprum autem factum est ex vivo argento non bene claro mixto cum sulphure rubeo multum turpitudo et aliquantulum spisso, fuitque tempore longo, auro etiam diucius, excoctum calore maximo. Et quia multam vim combustionis passum est, ideo multo rubore est infectum. Laxavit quoque ita corpus suum ut vapor aceti corpus suum intrare queat. Unde etiam fit color viridis, qui flos eris dicitur. Ferrum quidem factum est ex vivo argento spisso mixto cum sulphure medii coloris inter rubeum et album, fuitque tempore longo, cupro etiam diutius, excoctum calore modico, quare magnam sortitum est soliditatem, nec ad virtutem ignis ut cuprum defluit, quoniam longo excoctum fuit tempore. Et quia modicus affuit calor, non laxavit ut cuprum corpus suum. Et quia sulphur rubedine aliquantulum fuit infectum, iccirco si ferrum sine exercitio diu iaceat, ferrugine infectum rubeum contrahit colorem. Stannum vero factum est ex vivo argento claro mixto cum sulphure claro et albo. Sed mora parva in coquendo fuit. Si enim in coquendo calor parvus et mora magna esset, in argentum verteretur. Plumbum quidem factum est ex vivo argento grosso mixto cum sulphure grosso, albo et aliquantulum rubeo. Et quod ex sulphure albo factum sit, inde patet quia cum acęto adhibetur albedinem contrahit. Quod vero sulphur aliquantulum rubeum fuerit patet in plumbo cum ardet, tunc enim rubei coloris est.

 D. Quod de congelatis pollicitus es, ea videlicet ex IIII^{or}

---

5. ad *rep.* diucius *tr.*   6. fieret *corr. ex* fierent   9. aliquantulum *corr. ex* aliquantum   13. etiam
20. ut] ubi *cod.*

are made up of the four elements, I think has now been sufficiently treated. Now, if you please, speak about plants.

M. Do you understand perfectly what things are called plants?

D. I know that plants are growing bodies. For I see a certain tree, at first small, which after a long lapse of time I see to be huge. And in the same way, a branch which we first see to be small, after the passage of much time is observed to be huge.

M. Do you know any more about them?

D. What more should I know about them?

M. You ought to know that they move.

D. How do they move?

M. Have you seen that when the tree is small, there is a certain space between its top and the sky? But when the mature tree has become large, its top is nearer the sky, and the space is less. It is clear to all that whatever thing is a given distance from some other thing, and is later close to that same thing, must have moved.

D. I see well that plants do not exist without motion. I also notice from the lucid explanation of your discourse what the difference is between the motion of a growing thing and the motion of an animal. When an animal moves, it moves from place to place with its whole body. A growing thing, however, does not move with its whole body, but rather with a part of it, and never changes its place when it moves.

M. I should say that you have understood excellently if you have understood the principle of motion involved in such growth.

D. Indeed, I do not understand, but I wish you would make it clear to me.

M. Have you ever seen grain and other seeds being sown?

D. Many times.

M. Then, in your opinion, when the seed falls from the hand of the sower, does some principle of growth fall with it, which gives life to the seed until it grows into a tree, and is held in innumerable roots? Or do you think rather that the motion

Liber Secundus 157

constare elementis, sufficienter iam dictum esse arbitror. Nunc autem de virentibus si placet eloquere.

M. Intelligisne perfecte que vocentur virentia?

D. Scio quia virentia corpora sunt crescentia. Video namque quandam arborem primitus parvam quam post longo elapso tempore inmensam conspicio. Eodemque modo ramus quem primitus parvum videmus, post multi decursum temporis inmensus cernitur.

M. Nunquid amplius de illis intelligis?

D. Quidnam amplius de eis intelligerem?

M. Intelligere debes quia moventur.

D. Quomodo moventur?

M. Videsne quod quamdiu parva est arbor inter sumitatem illius et celum quoddam spacium est? Cum vero arbor adulta inmensa effecta est, cacumen illius celo afinius est spaciumque illud minus. Patet quidem omnibus quia quęcumque [198^C] res primo remota ab aliqua alia, postea appropinquata eidem fuerit, nequit esse absque motu.

D. Bene video non sine motu virentia existere. Animadverto etiam ex lucida verborum tuorum ratione que sit differentia inter rei virentis motum et animalis. Animal enim quando movetur, cum toto corpore de loco ad locum movetur. Sed res virens non cum toto corpore, immo cum parte, numquam locum mutans movetur.

M. Optime te intellexisse dicerem si principium motus prout est intellexisses.

D. Non equidem intelligo, sed tu queso illud michi velis aperire.

M. Vidisti unquam frumentum ac cętera semina seminari?

D. Multociens.

M. Estimasne igitur semine de manu serentis labente quia quispiam vegetator cum illo cadat qui ipsum vegetet quoad in arborem crescat, et in innumeris teneatur radicibus? An potius

---

1. esse *add*.   9. M *add*.   10. eis] eius *cod*.   16. quia *add*.   21. virentis] virentibus *cod*.   31. Estimasne *corr. ex* Estimansne

by which the tree is given life is extended into all parts from the center of the grain?⁶⁴

D. I think that the motion proceeds from the center of the grain. But I do not know how it comes forth.

M. Do you know that grain becomes moist and swells up when it is planted in the earth?

D. It seems so to me.

M. How then do you think that moisture enters the grain—by force? Or rather does the grain attract it?

D. I think that the grain attracts it. For I have often seen a jar full of water placed on grain in the evening, and in the morning the grain was found to be moister and heavier.

M. You have spoken well, but you will still hear more. If you place a sack full of grain somewhere near water in the evening, in the morning you will find that grain moister and heavier. It is clear that the water did not enter the grain, since it stayed where it was and did not come any closer. Therefore, such power is in the grain that it can attract moisture to itself. For if it had lacked this power, it would not thus attract the water. You ought therefore to know that there is an appetitive power in all plants. This can also be proved by another argument: If, in the morning, someone should sprinkle the vines with water when they have clusters of grapes on them, in the evening he will see the grapes swollen with moisture. Obviously it is contrary to the nature of water to rise upward. Therefore, if the vine lacked the appetitive power, it would never have drawn the water upward contrary to its nature.⁶⁵

D. You have explained clearly that there is an appetitive power in all plants.

M. Let me explain more fully. A grain grows, swells up, and bursts when it forces the seed from itself; and the seed,

---

⁶⁴"Marius' principal source is probably ps.-Arist. *De elementis* (*i.e.* "Ibn Ḥasdāy's Neoplatonist").* *Cf.* Isaac, "Chapter on the Elements" (Altmann and Stern, *Isaac Israeli*, pp. 124, 125), *Book of Substances* (*ed. cit.*, pp. 90, 91, 94), *Book on Spirit and Soul* (*ed. cit.*, p. 109) and *Liber de elementis* (*ed. cit.*, fol. Xra); Constantine, *Pantegni*, Theorice, IV 1-2 (Bodl. MS Auct. F. 3. 10, which is translated in Lawn, *Salernitan Questions*, p. 23, n. 2); William of Conches, *Dragmaticon* (*ed. cit.*, p. 251); and Nicolaus of Damascus, *De plantis* I 7 (*ed. cit.*, p. 12)

⁶⁵*Cf.* Isaac, *De dietis universalibus** (*ed. cit.*, fol. LVIrb)

credis motum quo vegetatur arbor a centro grani in omnes partes se distendere?

D. Autumo motum a grani prodire centro. Sed quomodo prodeat ignoro.

M. Scisne granum sub terram proiectum humectari atque tumescere?

D. Sic michi videtur.

M. Qualiter igitur opinaris humiditatem illam granum subintrare, vi videlicet, an potius grano ipsam attrahente?

D. Puto quia granum ipsam attrahit. Vidi enim sepius vas aqua plenum sero in frumento poni, et mane triticum humidius ponderosiusque reperi.

M. Bene dixisti, sed plus iam audies. Si saccum frumento refertum in vespere alicubi prope aquam posueris, mane ipsum frumentum humidius graviusque invenies. Liquet quidem aquam granum non intrasse, cum etiam nec appropinquasse constat. Talis igitur grano virtus inest quod sibi humiditatem attrahere potest. Si enim hac caruisset virtute, non sic eam alliceret. Scire itaque debes universis virentibus virtutem appetitivam inesse. Quod etiam alio potest approbari argumento. Siquis in racemorum tempore vineas aqua asperserit mane, sero racemos tumidos videbit. Constat sane alienum esse a natura aquę sursum conscendere. Itaque si vitis virtute careret appetitiva, nequaquam aquam contrario sue naturę modo sursum traheret.

D. Perspicue explicuisti omnibus virentibus virtutem inesse appetitivam.

M. Amplius: Granum crescit, tumet ac rumpitur dum ex se germen trudit, quod terram aperiens in aerem se erigit. Radices

---

14. alicubi] alicui *cod.*   20. appetitivam *corr. ex* appetivam   24. appetitiva *corr. ex* appetiva   24. sue] sine *cod.*   27. appetitivam *corr. ex* appetivam

pushing its way up through the ground, raises itself into the air. Also, the grain sends out its roots like veins under the earth this way and that seeking for nourishment.

D. This is manifest and known to everyone.

M. Therefore, when the grain forces all this out from itself, is not that which is produced by it often more than twice the quantity of the grain itself?

D. That is true. And with the passage of time, it produces ears loaded with many grains.

M. How then do you think that all this can come forth from the grain except as a result of the attracted moisture which took on the nature of the grain itself? Or do you think it is otherwise?

D. I do not think it is otherwise than you have explained it. For I see trees of different kinds, one bitter and one sweet, which have been planted in the same field of earth, grow and produce fruit; and the sweet tree produces sweet fruit, while the bitter one produces bitter fruit. From this it is clear that the moisture attracted by the tree is changed into the nature of the tree.

M. Do you believe, I ask, that the moisture changes into the nature of the tree of its own accord, or rather that there is some power in the tree which forces it to be changed into its own nature?

D. I do not believe that the moisture is changed by itself into the nature of a tree. For if this were so, it would be changed in the same way in all trees.

M. Therefore, the power which is in the tree forces the moisture to change into the nature of the tree. And so we have found another power, that is, the digestive, to be in the grain, which changes the nourishment which the tree attracts to itself into its own nature.

D. That is true.

M. I don't think you are unaware that there is yet a third power in the grain, namely the retentive, which retains the moisture until the digestive power has done its work.

D. I do not doubt this. For unless there was something

quoque sub terra venis consimiles ad dietam perquirendam huc illucque expandit.

D. Manifestum est hoc et notum omnibus.

M. Cum igitur granum hoc totum ex se trudat, nonne sepius id quod ab eo producitur duplo maius est ipsius grani quantitate?

D. Verum est, tempore quoque labente spicas producit multis granis oneratas.

M. Quomodo ergo totum hoc ex grano prodire posse arbitraris nisi per attractam humiditatem quę in ipsius grani secedit naturam? Anne aliter esse putas?

D. Non puto aliter esse nisi sicut explicuisti. Video enim in eadem terrę platea insertas diversi generis arbores, unam videlicet amaram et [198^D] aliam dulcem, crescere fructusque facere; et arbor dulcis dulces fructus, amara vero amaros producit. Hinc itaque patet humiditatem ab arbore attractam in ipsius transmutari naturam.

M. Credisne quęso humiditatem ipsam in naturam arboris sponte secedere, an potius arbori talem inesse virtutem quę ipsam in naturam suam transferri cogat?

D. Non credo humiditatem illam per semet ipsam in arboris naturam transmutari. Si enim hoc esset, eodem modo in omnes se transferret arbores.

M. Igitur virtus quę arbori inest humiditatem illam in sui naturam secedere cogit. Invenimus itaque aliam virtutem, id est, digestivam, grano inesse, quę dietam quam allicit sibi arbor in naturam ipsius transmutat.

D. Verum est.

M. Non equidem te latere reor terciam adhuc grano virtutem inesse, retentivam scilicet, quę humiditatem illam retinet quoad virtus digestiva opus suum faciat.

D. Non inde dubito. Nisi enim esset aliquid quod attrac-

which detained the attracted moisture, it would immediately go back to where it came from.

M. Do you think that each one of these three powers always completes its work in the same way, or that some one of them sometimes cannot complete its work?

D. I believe that it can well be that one of them might sometimes fail to complete its work.

M. Therefore, if the digestive power should fail to complete its work, and there is in the tree no expulsive power which would expel that which was left undigested, do you think the tree can endure?

D. I do not think it would last very long. For since the nourishment that is in it is not fully digested but is corrupted, it will be foreign to the tree's nature to grow taller, and this will be a cause of the corruption of the tree.

M. You should know that, when a plant once begins to grow, there is an expulsive power in it which casts out that which is contrary to its nature. The exudations of gum from a tree also indicate that this power is present in the tree. Therefore it is clear that these powers which we have often spoken of are present in the aforementioned grain.

D. It is true these are found in grain and in all plants.

M. Indeed, these powers always cause the aforementioned grain to grow until it reaches the limit set for it, and then the seed makes innumerable plants completely similar to itself, just as each species of animal makes seed not dissimilar to itself.

D. I have understood well what you have said, and it is evident. But it seems to me that I can consider, from what you have said, that you wish to assert that there is a soul in plants, from which these four powers proceed.

M. You have considered well; it was to make this point that I have given the preceding discourse. And this is usually called the 'viridal soul' by philosophers. This soul has no powers beyond those four we have just mentioned. For it does not, in the manner of the animal soul, have in itself the power of sensing or understanding, or even of moving about from place to place. And yet we ascribe to it the power of a certain

tam detineret humiditatem, profecto illuc unde discessit reverteretur.

M. Putasne unumquamque harum trium virtutum semper eodem modo opus suum complere, an earum aliquam quandoque complere non posse?

D. Credo quia bene esse potest quod aliqua earum quandoque in opere suo complendo deficiat.

M. Si igitur virtus digestiva in opere suo complendo deficiat, nec sit in arbore virtus expulsiva quę quod ab alia compleri nequivit foras expellat, putasne posse arborem durare?

D. Non eam diuturnam esse arbitror. Cum enim quę ei inest, dieta non plene digesta sed corrupta est, erit arbori a natura sua alienum altius crescere, hecque erit causa corruptionis arboris.

M. Cum igitur res virens modo inchoata crescat, noscas in ea virtutem esse expulsivam, quę quod nature eius contrarium est, eicit. Gummi etiam ex arbore prodeuntia ipsi arbori eam inesse designant. Patet igitur has sepedictas virtutes grano memorato inesse.

D. Verum est has in grano universisque virentibus inveniri.

M. Semper quidem granum prefatum usque ad diffinitum seminatum terminum crescit, et tunc semen facit gramina innumera sibi omnino consimilia, quemadmodum quęque species animalis semen sibi ipsi non dissimile facit.

D. Quod dixisti, bene intellexi, et patens est. Sed ex verbis tuis, ceu michi videtur, perpendere possum animam virentibus inesse te velle asserere, ex qua hec IIII[or] procedunt virtutes.

M. Bene perpendisti, ideo enim hec superiora adduxi, et hec a philosophis anima viridalis dici solet. Hęc quidem nullam preter IIII[or] predictas habet virtutem. Non enim ad modum bestialis animę habet in se virtutem sentiendi vel intelligendi, sed nec de loco ad locum movendi. Attamen cuiusdammodi sen-

---

4. aliquam] aliquem *cod.*   17. prodeuntia *corr. ex* providentia *man. rec.*

kind of sentience. For the appetitive power attracts what it senses to be good for itself, and thus the expulsive power retains what it senses to be good but expels what is bad.

D. I perceive well from your words how plants are composed of the four elements; yet something about plants still troubles me, which I should like you to make clear to me. There are some plants which grow from seeds, such as wheat and barley; some from grafted twigs, such as most trees; some, neither sown nor planted, grow by themselves, such as happens to a chance shrub in a place where the air, water, and heat of the sun are favorable.

M. Previously in this book, I mentioned that in the beginning, the Lord created all things from the four elements. Therefore, when these elements come together under the earth near its surface in the sort a mixture from which something is to be made, then that what is made from it grows and presses against the earth and raises itself into the air. And if it came forth from a seed, it will not even stop growing so long as it is furnished the principle of growth by the seed. That seed will grow similarly if it is saved by man until the proper time and placed in the ground, after the example of the first parents doing this concerning the first created things. For God commanded and bestowed the power upon the viridal soul to be able to preserve its own kind always in its own form and seed. The only reason man plants trees (instead of depending on wild ones) is so he may enjoy the convenience of the fruit more quickly. For they grow in the same way from seed, only this takes a little more time. If you had wandered through as many regions as I have traversed, you could have seen apple trees, oranges,[66] pear trees, and wild grapevines, growing in groves without having been planted by man.

D. You have now answered my question satisfactorily. But now I wish you would explain why such lovely flowers of plants are of such a variety of colors.

---

[66]*cinos (cinus,-i)* is not listed in any dictionary I know. Because of the context and the fact that oranges were (and in some places still are) known as "China apples," I have guessed at "oranges" for the translation.

sibilitatis virtutem ei ascribimus. Nam virtus appetitiva quod bonum sibi esse sentit, attrahit, sicque expulsiva, quod bonum sentit, detinet; quod vero malum, expellit.

D. Bene ex verbis tuis percipio qualiter virentia ex IIII^{or} sint composita elementis, adhuc tamen [199^A] quiddam de virentibus me movet, quod te michi vellem aperire. Sunt quędam virentium quę de seminibus crescunt, ut triticum et ordeum; quędam de ramis insitis, ut pleręque arbores; quędam nec sata nec plantata, sed per se crescunt, ut herbę locum sortitę, qui aeris, aquę, solisque caloris accensum habeat.

M. In superiori huius pagina voluminis, dominum in principio omnia ex IIII^{or} creasse elementis memoraveram. Cum igitur ipsa elementa sub terra prope eius superficiem in tali complexione conveniant unde aliquid componi oportet, id quod tunc inde componitur crescit ac terram pulsat, seque in aerem erigit; ac si de semine prodiret et non desinit crescere quoad fecundetur semine. Crescet similiter semen illud si ab hominibus reservatum apto tempore in terram iactetur primorum exemplo parentum ita de primis creaturis facientium. Nam deus precepit atque virtutem animę viridali contulit speciem suam semper in forma et semine suo posse reservare. Arborum autem plantatio non fit ob aliam causam, nisi ut homines fructuum commoda celerius capiant. Eodem enim modo de semine, etsi cum temporis dilatione, crescerent. Quod si tot regiones quot ego perlustravi pererrasses, malos, cinos, piros, vitesque silvestres, absque hominis plantatione in nemoribus crescentes vidisse potuisses.

D. Iam peticioni meę satis fecisti. Nunc autem volo ut aperias cur tam decentes virentium flores tot diversis coloribus sint colorati.

---

7. de *add.*   21. posse *add.*   26. vidisse *corr. ex* vide

M. I shall gladly tell you what has been said about them by the philosophers.⁶⁷ They assert that in the springtime, the viridal soul has its greatest power, since this is a temperate time, by whose complexion things are vivified. The soul, as it spreads outwards, shows its beauty and splendor in the various colors of the flowers. But there are some philosophers (although they are not the best) who affirm that growing things have, in the springtime, a certain kind of sense, similar to the senses of hearing and sight, and therefore they then produce flowers in which they delight. And when these fall, they lose the power of this sense.

D. Tell me now why it happens that some growing things wither immediately, such as grasses; some more slowly, such as almonds and peaches; and others after a very long time, such as palms and carobs.

M. Plants which are delicate and slender and are fastened by small roots, such as the grasses, wither in a single year. But slender and soft trees whose roots are slender and short can endure so long as the heat of the sun is not able to corrupt their natures. But as the power of the heat corrupts their natures after a long time, they then wither. But other trees, huge and solid, and having long and thick roots firmly connected to the soil, although the sun sometimes dries out their moisture, nevertheless recover it because of their immense roots and do not wither right away. And for this reason they cannot be injured by the winter cold. For their solidity and density neither permit the internal heat to escape nor the winter cold to enter. The long and thick roots take heat from the earth for themselves, by which they defend themselves against the cold of winter.⁶⁸

D. It can be well understood from your words what the reason is that some of its leaves fall from a tree when winter approaches, and some do not. For those which are slender and are weakly affixed to the tree fall at the approach of winter. But those which are thick and firmly attached do not fall.⁶⁹

---
⁶⁷*Cf.* Isaac, *Book of Substances** (*ed. cit.*, p. 94)
⁶⁸*Cf.* Isaac, *De dietis universalibus** (*ed. cit.*, fol. LVIIvb)
⁶⁹*Cf.* Lawn, *I Quesiti Salernitani*, p. 234, n.C

M. Quod inde a philosophis dictum est, libenter tibi memorabo. Asserunt namque in vere maxima virtute animam viridalem pollere, quoniam tunc est tempus temperatum, cuius complexione res vivificantur. Anima quidem, se foras diffundens, decorem splendoremque suum in variis florum ostentat coloribus. Sunt autem quidam philosophorum, sed non de summorum numero, qui affirmant virentia in vernali tempore cuiusdammodi sensum sensui auditus et visus affinem habere, et iccirco flores in quibus delectantur tunc producunt. Quibus cadentibus predicti sensus destituuntur virtute.

D. Iam nunc michi unde contingat eloquere quod virentium quędam ilico arescunt, ut herbę; quędam tardius, ut amigdali et persici; quędam post multi temporis diuturnitatem, ut palmę et carrublę.

M. Illud ex virentibus quod tenerum est et exile, parvisque innixum radicibus, ut herbę, unoquoque arescit anno. Arbores vero exiles et laxę, quarum radices exiles sunt ac curtę, quamdiu solis calor earum nequit corrumpere naturas, durare possunt. Sed ut virtus caloris post longum tempus ipsarum corripit naturas, ilico arescunt. Verum alię arbores, inmensę et solidę ac cum radicibus longis grossisque firmiter humi connexę, licet sol quandoque sumpta sibi virtute ipsarum exsiccet humiditates, recuperatis tamen illis ab inmensis radicibus non cito arescunt. [199^B] Hacque de causa ab hiberno frigore minime possunt corrumpi. Soliditas namque ac spissitas illarum nec calorem internum exire, nec frigus hibernum intrare permittunt. Longę etiam ac inmensę radices a terra sibi calorem alliciunt, per quem se ab hiemis frigore defendunt.

D. Bene ex verbis tuis percipi potest qua de causa quędam arbore eorum foliorum imminente hieme cadant, quedam non. Nam illa quę exilia sunt et arbori debiliter herentia, imminente hieme, occidunt. Quę vero grossa firmiterque sunt herentia, minime cadunt.

---

5. diffundens *corr. ex* difundens
10. cadentibus *corr. ex* candentibus
8. habere] haberet *cod.*
30. arbore] arbor *cod.*
9. tunc *lec. inc.*
32. sunt *add.*

M. You have foreseen well what I was going to say.

D. Now I hope that you may be willing to discuss the tastes of plants, of which some are sweet, some bitter, some sour, some sharp, some dull, some astringent, some salty, some pungent, some tasteless.

M. I once read a book by some philosopher,[70] in which I found the substances and complexions of the flavors, in the way this table will make clear. This is how that philosophical book says the substances and complexions of the tastes are, but since I do not know how the elements came together to create these tastes, I do not have any lesson to show you this. In order that it not be difficult to show you this, I shall try, in a table, to show as accurately as I can the mixture of the elements.

Tastes	Substances	Complexions	Tastes	Earth	Water	Air	Fire
Sweet	Coarse	Temperate	Sweet	Medium	Medium	Much	Much
Bitter	Coarse	Hot	Bitter	Medium	Little	Little	Much
Sour	Fine	Cold	Sour	Little	Much	Medium	Little
Sharp	Fine	Hot	Sharp	Little	Little	Medium	Much
Dull	Fine	Temperate	Dull	Little	Medium	Much	Medium
Astringent	Temperate	Cold	Astringent	Medium	Little	Little	Much
Salty	Temperate	Hot	Salty	Medium	Little	Little	Much
Pungent	Coarse	Cold	Pungent	Much	Little	Little	Much
Tasteless	Temperate	Temperate	Tasteless	Much	Much	Much	Little

These quantities—much, medium, and little—are not equal in all the tastes. For example, although there is much fire in salty and bitter, nevertheless it is not equal in each of them, but more in one, less in the other. And thus it is with the other quantities.

D. Can someone make these flavors artificially?

M. Yes, he can. If you wish to make a salty flavor, cook honey and it will become salty. If you wish to make a bitter taste, cook honey for a long time, and it will become bitter.[71]

---

[70] Cf. *Liber Apollonii de secretis naturae* (MS cit., fol. 27r)

[71] Cf. Isaac, *De dietis universalibus** (ed. cit., fol. XXXVIva)

M. Bene quod dicere proposueram previdisti.

D. Nunc quidem precor ut de virentium saporibus agere velis, quorum quędam sunt dulcia, quędam amara, quędam acida, quędam acuta, [quedam pingua], quędam constipativa, quędam salsa, quędam pontica, quędam insipida.

M. Legi siquidem cuiusdam philosophi librum in quo saporum substantias et complexiones quales hec tabula declarabit inveni. Hoc modo esse saporum substantias et complexiones liber ille philosophicus refert, sed, cum ego quomodo ipsa elementa ad hos procreandos sapores convenerunt ignorem, tuo documento ad hoc videndum indigeo. Ne tibi hoc ad intelligendum difficile fiat, in tabula quadam ipsorum commixtionem elementorum quam verissime potero ostendere conabor.

Sapores	Substantie	Complexiones	Sapores	Terra	Aqua	Aer	Ignis
Dulcis	Grossa	Temperata	Dulcis	Mediocriter	Mediocriter	Multum	Multum
Amarus	Grossa	Calida	Amarus	Mediocriter	Parum	Parum	Multum
Acidus	Subtilis	Frigida	Acidus	Parum	Multum	Mediocriter	Parum
Acutus	Subtilis	Calida	Acutus	Parum	Parum	Mediocriter	Multum
Pinguis	Subtilis	Temperata	Pinguis	Parum	Mediocriter	Multum	Mediocriter
Constipativus	Temperata	Frigida	Constipativus	Mediocriter	Parum	Parum	Multum
Salsus	Temperata	Calida	Salsus	Mediocriter	Parum	Parum	Multum
Ponticus	Grossa	Frigida	Ponticus	Multum	Parum	Parum	Multum
Insipidus	Temperata	Temperata	Insipidus	Multum	Multum	Multum	Parum

Istę quidem quantitates, multum videlicet, mediocre et parum, non in omnibus saporibus ęquales sunt. Verbi gratia: Cum in salso et amaro ignis habundet, non in utroque tamen equaliter, sed in alio plus, in alio minus. Sicque est de cęteris quantitatibus.

---
2. saporibus *add. i.m.*   4. quedam pingua *supplevi; om. cod.*   12. quadam] quedam *cod.*
13. ipsorum commixtionem *tr.*

But if you wish to prepare an acid flavor, mix wine with water and put it in the sun, and it will become sour. If, however, you wish to make a sharp taste, allow an excellent wine to lie quietly for a long time, and it will become sharp. By these and by many other arts, the platonic book affirms that flavors are to be altered.

D. Why are growing things green more than any other color, and their leaves much more so?[72]

M. You should know that green consists of two colors, namely black and yellow.[73] Earth mixed with water is made black, as we can plainly see. The color yellow is made from fire and air. For we see many times that when air is joined to fire, the tip of the rising flame is of a yellow color. Therefore, when these two composites come together, the color of green is made from them. Nevertheless, colors sometimes deceive the sight, as Aristotle explains in his book.[74]

D. Tell me please why some leaves are round and perfect, but others are split, some more, some less.

M. There is very little dryness in round and perfect leaves. But those which have some dryness are somewhat split, and those which have more, more.[75]

D. I think you have now treated of growing things sufficiently, though briefly, in accordance with my capacity. For this reason, you may now be willing to treat fully the subject of animals, so that you might keep your promise to me to treat created things, namely minerals, plants, and animals.

M. I agree. But tell me first, please, whether or not you perfectly understand what transitive motion is.

D. I think that transitive motion is the movement of a thing from one place to another.

M. Do you know how the kinds of transitive motion, namely simple and composite, differ from each other? I call

---

[72] *Cf.* Salernitan question B 237 (fol. 144) and N 39 (Bibl. nat. MS lat. 18081, fol. 219v); and Lawn, *I Quesiti Salernitani*, p. 224, n. 15, *viror in flore*

[73] *Cf.* ps.-Arist. *De coloribus* V (794b) and *Liber Apollonii de secretis naturae* (MS cit., fol. 13r)

[74] Perhaps Marius' source is ps.-Arist., *De elementis*. *Cf.* Isaac, *De dietis universalibus* (ed. cit., fol. Lra), Arist., *Meteor.* I 5 (342b) and *De anima* II 6 (418a) and II 7 419a)

[75] *Cf.* Isaac, *De dietis universalibus* (ed. cit., fol. LVIvb) and Salernitan question B 60 (fol. 123)

Liber Secundus

D. Potestne aliquis hos sapores arte machinari?

M. Potest. Nam si salsum saporem vis facere, coque mel, et fiet salsum. Si vero amarum vis machinari, coque mel multum, et fiet amarum. Quod si acidum vis parare saporem misce vinum cum aqua et pone ad solem, sicque fiet acidum. Si autem acutum saporem vis fieri, sine vinum optimum quiete longo iacere tempore, et fiet acutum. His et aliis multis artibus platonicus liber sapores innovandos esse affirmat.

D. Cur sunt virentia viridi colore plusquam alio colorata et eorum [199^C] folia multo magis?

M. Scias colorem viridem ex duobus coloribus, nigro scilicet et croceo constare. Terra quidem ab aqua suffusa, ut intuitui nostro patet, nigra efficitur. Croceus autem color ab igne et aere fit. Videmus enim sepissime quod quando aer igni coniungitur, flamę surgentis apex crocei coloris est. Cum igitur duo hec composita conveniant, ex eis color viridis efficitur. Colores tamen visus quandoque fallunt, sicut Aristotiles in libro explicat.

D. Dic queso cur foliorum quedam rotunda sint et integra, quędam autem fissa, alia magis, alia minus.

M. Foliis rotundis et integris parum inest siccitatis; illa vero quę aliquantulum habent siccitatis aliquantulum finduntur, et que plus, plus.

D. Sufficienter iam nunc licet breviter de virentibus pro ingenii mei capacitate tractum esse opinor. Quamobrem de animali nunc velis compendiose agere, ut promissio tua adimpleatur qua pollicitus es te de tribus tractaturum esse creaturis, de concretis videlicet virentibus et animali.

M. Annuo. Sed dic prius queso si quid sit motus transitivus perfecte intelligis necne.

D. Motum transitivum esse reor corporis transitionem de uno loco ad alium.

M. Scisne qualiter inter se differunt motus transitivi species, scilicet simplex motus et compositus? Simplicem voco solis

---

4. acidum *corr. ex* accidum   5. autem *add.*   6. quiete *add.*   7. iacere tempore *tr.*
12. suffusa] + est *del.*

simple the motion of the sun, lacking rest; and I call composite the motion of animals, consisting of rest and quiet. For while one animal is moving, another is resting.

D. I have thought about both kinds of motion sufficiently. And from this, I understand the motion of a stone from a high place to a low place, and the motion of fire rising upward, to be cases of simple motion.

M. You understand well. You should know furthermore that animals differ from plants through transitive motion. (Nevertheless, many animals lack transitive motion, such as oysters and things similar to them.) There can also be noted in an animal yet another motion which plants lack. For if a plant is pricked by a sharp object, it does not move. But if an animal is pricked, it immediately becomes frightened and moves in such a way that the motion of all its parts is evident to our sight. And this movement is sensibility; that is, a thing which moves in this way is said to be sensible by itself. And this motion is common to all animals.

D. You have already explained how animals and plants differ; now explain their similarities.

M. You have posed a philosophical question. You should know that they are alike in that they increase and decrease in size. It has been said above that growth is one of the six motions. For by it, plants which were small are made large, and those which were short are made long. And we said that this motion has a beginning, middle, and end. Indeed, the ancient philosophers assert that plants have a cycle similar to the phases of the moon, which has a beginning—that is, when it is waxing, a middle—that is, a stationary period when it is full and does not grow any larger, and an end—that is, a decline, when its light decreases until it cannot be seen. It is the same with plants. For at first they are so small they can hardly be seen. Afterward, they do not stop growing until they attain their proper degree of length, breadth and height. Next they remain stationary, so that they neither increase nor decrease in size. And finally, slowly losing their life force, they begin to decrease and thus to die. And in the same way, without any doubt, an animal has a begin-

motum requie carentem; compositum vero animalis ex requie et quiete constantem. Dum enim animal unum movet, alter interim quiescit.

D. Utrosque motus satis perpendo. Inde etiam percipio motum lapidis de superiori ad inferius labentis et ignis sursum conscendentis simplicem esse.

M. Bene intelligis. Sciendum preterea est animal virentibus per motum transitivum distare. Pleraque tamen animalia motu carent transitivo, ut ostrea et his similia. Potest quoque in animali adhuc alius motus quo carent virentia notari. Nam si virentia cum re acuta pungantur, nequaquam movebuntur. Sed si animal pungitur, ilico expavescit, moveturque ita quod universarum ipsius partium motus visibus nostris patent. Et hic motus sensibilitas, id vero quod movetur, per ipsum sensibile dicitur. Hic quidem motus cuilibet animali convenit.

D. Iam in quo animal et virentia differant explicuisti, nunc in quo conveniant aperi.

M. Questionem philosophicam fecisti. Scias itaque quia in crescere et decrescere conveniunt. Dictum est quidem superius incrementum de VI motibus unum esse. Nam eo virentium quę parva fuerunt, magna; quę vero curta, longa fuerunt effecta. Et hunc ipsum motum exordium, medium, ac finem habere memoravimus. Asserunt quippe antiqui philosophi virentia cum luna convenire quę habet principium, id est, augmentum, et medium, id est, stationem, cum ipsa plena iam amplius non crescit, et finem, id est, defectum quando videlicet claritas sua decrescit quoad videri nequeat. Sic quoque est de virentibus; primitus enim adeo sunt parva quod [199^D] vix visibus nostris subiacent; postea crescere non desinunt donec ad unam quantitatem longitudinis, latitudinis et altitudinis quodque eorum perveniat. Tunc vero in statione manent ita videlicet quod neque crescunt neque decrescunt. Denique incipiunt virtutem paulatim amittentia decrescere et sic ad defectum pervenire. Et eodem modo absque ulla ambiguitate animal inicium habet; postea crescit

---

13. partium *corr. ex* partivum   24. habet *corr. ex* habent

ning. Later it grows until it has reached its proper size, and then it remains stable for a time. Finally it slowly declines until it perishes utterly. You can consider therefore that an animal shares growth and decay with the plants, but that they differ with regard to sensibility and transitive motion. It is clear therefore that if any one defining an animal should say that it is a thing which grows and declines, is mobile and sensible, he would not deviate from the truth of the matter.

D. Now I know very well what the differences and similarities are between animals and plants. Now I ask whether or not there is anything in addition to sensibility and transitive motion which might to any extent be added to a plant, by which something different from the plant or animal might be brought about. I do not question that oysters, which grow like plants and do not move from place to place, nevertheless have feeling like animals.[76] And there are other things intermediate between minerals and plants, such as coral, which is heavy, solid, cold, dry, and flat. We know that this, while it is in its native place under the ocean waves, grows without having branches or roots. But I am asking about a thing which is not an animal, not a plant, and not intermediate between these.

M. Do you know that plants have motion, but not transitive motion?

D. Yes.

M. Indeed, nothing can be added to a plant except motion and rest. If you should add rest, when the motion ceases it will be like a mineral. But if you add motion, it will either be of doing something, of decaying, of growing larger or smaller, or even of changing into something else. If the motion of doing something is added, decay necessarily follows. For that from which anything was made now ceases to be what it was. If, however, the motion of decay has been added, it is clear to everyone that it will decay. If the motion of growing larger or smaller has been added, the plant will remain as before, only more or less. But if the motion of changing into something else were added, there is no doubt that it ought to be changed into an animal or

---

[76]*Cf.* Nicolaus of Damascus, *De plantis* I 3 (*ed. cit.*, p. 7)

donec ad unam quantitatem veniat, et tunc aliquandiu in statione manet. Demum paulatim deficit quoad omnino pessundetur. Perpendere igitur potes animal cum virentibus in augmento ac detrimento convenire, differre vero per sensibilitatem et motum transitivum. Patet itaque siquis animal diffiniens ipsum dicat esse rem crescibilem ac decrescibilem, mobilem ac sensibilem, non a rei veritate deviat.

D. Optime iam nosco quę sit differentia, quę convenientia, inter animal et virentia. Modo quero si preter sensibilitatem et motum transitivum aliquid unde efficeretur quidpiam a re virenti et animali diversum adici rei virenti quoquammodo posset vel non. Ostrea nequaquam quero quę, sicut virentia crescunt et non moventur de loco ad locum, sentiunt quidem ut animalia. Sunt et alia inter concreta et virentia media, ut corallus, quę est gravis, solida, frigida, sicca et plana. Hanc sane dum in loco natali sub unda equorea est, non ramorum non radicum expertem crescere novimus. Sed de re quero quę non est animal, non res virens, non intermedia hec.

M. Scisne virentia motum, sed non transitivum habere?
D. Scio.
M. Nichil sane virenti adici potest nisi motus aut quies. Si quietem addideris, motu deficiente fiet quasi congelatum. Si vero motum, aut ille erit faciendi aut corrumpendi aut crescendi aut decresendi, aut etiam transmutandi. Si motus faciendi adicietur, necessaria subsequitur corruptio. Illud enim de quo fit aliquid iam desinit esse quod fuit. Si autem corrumpendi motus adiectus fuerit, patet omnibus quia corrumpetur. Si vero motus crescendi vel decrescendi fuerit additus, manebit res virens ut prius, sed maior vel minus. Quod si motus transmutandi addetur, non est ambiguum quin in animal vel congelatum transmutari oporteat. Hoc autem esse nequit. Nam huius motus virtus non unam speciem in aliam sed unam qualitatem in aliam

---

8. nosco *corr. ex* cognosco   24. aut decresendi *add.*

mineral. But this cannot be, for the power of this motion cannot change one species into another, but only one quality into another. Green can become more red or yellow, as we see in apples and pears, and bitter can become sweet, as is evident in grapes. But never can the plants be changed as a result of changes of their qualities. Therefore, nothing by which something can be brought about different from an animal or plant, can be added to plants except sensibility and transitive motion. And nothing can exist in the world except animals, vegetables, and minerals. You should know, therefore, that this is the foundation of this whole art.

D. I have understood well what you have said. Indeed, there is no doubt that there are innumerable kinds of animals, just as there are of plants. Therefore, I earnestly request that you reveal the usefulness of each kind and of its members.

M. What you ask me to explain does not pertain to the subject of this book. Indeed, it's a book in itself. But if you want to know the answer to your question, read through the writings of the ancient philosophers who treated this subject, and you will find it.

D. If God is willing, I shall examine their writings carefully, and in this way I shall discover what I now seek. But now I pray that you will not refuse to say a few things briefly about the five senses.

M. I would do as you ask most gladly, but these things are not pertinent to the subject of this book. But as soon as I come to the end of this book, I shall set out to compose a whole book on this subject, with God's help, and therefore I shall put off treating the matter here.

D. May God grant you his help to complete this work. But there are still some things about animals which trouble my mind,[77] about which I should like to hear what you think.

M. What are the things about which you have doubts?

D. Why, of all the animals, is only man wise, rational, and able to speak?

M. Because he has a rational soul.

---

[77] *quandam* is very clear and uncorrected in the MS. but it doesn't seem to fit. I have ignored it in the translation.

Liber Secundus 177

transmutare valet. Viride quippe plerumque fit rubeum vel croceum, ut in malis et piris videmus; et acre dulce, sicut in racemis patet; numquam tamen per qualitatum mutationes virentia possunt transmutari. Constat igitur virenti preter sensibilitatem et motum transitivum nichil posse addi, unde aliquid ab animali et virenti diversum efficiatur. Constat etiam nichil in mundo preter animalia et virentia et congelata posse existere. Noscas ergo hoc tocius artis huius esse fundamentum.

D. Bene quod dixisti intellexi. Animalis quidem prout [200^A] virentium innumeras esse species minime est ambiguum. Quare ut uniuscuiusque specierum eius et menbrorum eius utilitates aperias efflagito.

M. Quod me aperire postulas nequaquam ad hunc librum pertinet. Siquidem de hoc per se liber est. Sed si hoc scire desideras, antiquorum philosophorum de hoc tractantium scripta percurre et invenies.

D. Si deo libitum fuerit, scripta illorum scrutabor scrutansque quod nunc quero inveniam. Sed precor nunc ut super quinque sensibus corporeis pauca compendiose dicere non fastidias.

M. Precibus tuis libentissime, etsi de eis ad hunc librum agere minime pertinent. Sed simulac et huius voluminis metam perventum fuerit, librum integrum de eis deo opitulante componere aggrediar, ideoque hic de ipsis agere pretermittam.

D. Opem suam deus ad complendum quod satagis tibi indulgeat. Sed de animali adhuc quedam quandam mentem meam vexant, de quibus vellem audire quid sentias.

M. Quę sunt ea de quibus dubitas?

D. Cur de universis animalibus solus homo sapiens, fabilis et rationalis est?

M. Quia se ei anima rationalis indidit.

---

19. compendiose *corr. ex* comprehendiose   23. de eis deo opitulante *tr. ex* deo opitulante de eis

D. And why was this given to him rather than to some other creature?

M. Because he has a more temperate complexion than any of the other animals, and is the most handsomely formed creature of all of them.[78]

D. What argument do you have to prove this?

M. I have three arguments at hand to prove this assertion. One of them is that human skin is of a temperate complexion, because if it were not of a temperate complexion, it would not be able to sense contraries like cold and hot and what is tempered from both of them, and other sensible things.[79] Another argument is that man is also able, without harm, to eat contrary substances. But if his body were not temperate, he would not be able to eat both a thing and its contrary. The third argument is that he has temperate motions of the soul and body. However, that he has the most attractive form of all the animals does not need a proof, for it is sufficiently clear by itself.

D. What is this rational soul which you claim man has?

M. A substance which does not perish.

D. What argument have you to prove this?

M. To treat this question is not pertinent to the topic of this book. But it has been treated clearly enough by the philosophers, in whose writings you will find evident and necessary arguments concerning this. Also, in another book I have written called *On Human Welfare*, I have clearly treated this matter sufficiently. But nevertheless I shall now give you a clear and succinct argument. You do not doubt that wisdom and foolishness are contraries, and between them is a difference, as between two contraries.

D. I do not doubt it.

M. You also know that the rational soul is their subject, just as substance underlies qualities.

D. That is true.

M. Since, therefore, the soul can take on contrary qualities

---

[78] *Cf.* Constantine, *Pantegni*,* Theorice, I 9, William of Conches, *Dragmaticon** (*ed. cit.*, p. 261) and Isaac, *De dietis universalibus** (*ed. cit.*, fol. XXXIIva)

[79] *Cf.* Constantine, *Pantegni*,* Theorice, I 9, William of Conches, *loc. cit.*, and Isaac, *loc. cit.*

D. Et cur magis ei quam cęterorum alicui?

M. Quia temperatioris complexionis est quam cęterorum animalium quodlibet, et eorum omnium decentissima creatura.

D. Quod argumentum ad hoc ostendendum habes?

M. Tria certe argumenta ad hoc declarandum in promptu habeo. Est autem unum eorum quod cutis humana temperate complexionis est, quod si temperate complexionis non esset, nequaquam contraria sentire posset, ut frigidum et calidum et ex utroque temperatum, et cętera sensibilia. Aliud autem argumentum est quod homo ętiam absque danno contraria dietare potest. Quod si corpus eius temperatum non esset, nequaquam aliquo et suo contrario vesci posset. Tercium vero argumentum est quod animi et corporis motus habet temperatos. Quod autem decentissime omnium animalium formę sit, probatione non indiget, satis enim per se evidens est.

D. Quid est illa anima rationalis quam ei esse inditam perhibes?

M. Substantia quę non perit.

D. Quod argumentum ad hoc ostendendum habes?

M. De hoc agere ad hunc librum minime pertinet. Satis enim aperte inde tractaverunt philosophi, in quorum scriptis argumenta evidentia et necessaria de hoc invenire poteris. In libro quoque alio quem *de humano proficuo* feci satis evidenter de hoc ego. Sed tamen iam argumentum lucidum et compendiosum tibi faciam. Sapientiam et stulticiam esse contraria et inter eas differentiam, sicut inter duo contraria esse non ambigis.

D. Non dubito.

M. Noscis quoque animam rationalem earum esse subiectum, prout est qualitatum substantia.

D. Verum est.

M. Cum igitur anima absque sui corruptione contrariorum

---

1. magis *add.*   4. ostendendum *corr. ex* ostendum   11. temperatum *corr. ex* temperamentum   12. aliquo *add.*

without being corrupted itself—when one is present, the other must necessarily be absent, and conversely—it is necessarily a substance.[10] For thus the philosophers have defined substance. However, this is not the same kind of substance we were talking about before. This one is incorporeal, that one corporeal.

D. You have presented a short but good argument. But now I wish that you would finish what you promised at the beginning of this book, namely, show how all ten categories can be found in the four elements.

M. The four simple and most important categories—that is, substance, quantity, quality, and relation—no one denies are found in man.

D. How could any one deny what we know to exist? For we know that man is a substance, and that he does not lack quantity—that is, length, breadth, and depth, nor quality—that is whiteness, blackness, and other qualities. Relation is also in man, for it relates son to father, and servant to master, and conversely.

M. But this also ought not to be contradicted, that a man does, or writes, or teaches something, or something of this sort. And if he writes or teaches, there must be something which is written or taught. Now two categories have been discovered, namely doing and undergoing.

D. That is true.

M. But four things are necessary for an agent: a place where we may do something, and time when he may do it, and position, i.e., sitting or standing, or something of this sort; state is also necessary, for he ought to be in a state appropriate to the action. Therefore, as I promised, I have completed the ten categories.

D. You have made such a sufficient division of the ten categories that it is not necessary to add or subtract anything. Also, I have just realized that if the four simple categories are in man, he will necessarily either move or be at rest. If he is at rest,

---

[10] *Cf.* Gundissalinus, *De anima* (ed. J. T. Muckle, p. 37). See above, p. 93 and "Introduction," pp. 23, 26

sit susceptibilis, quorum unum cum adest, alterum abesse necesse est, et econverso, necessario [200ᴮ] substantia est. Sic enim philosophi substantiam diffinierunt. Non est autem hec substantia de aliarum genere; est enim incorporea, ille vero corporeę.

D. Breve sed bonum argumentum fecisti. Vellem autem modo ut quod in huius libri exordio pollicitus es compleres, scilicet quomodo in IIII^{or} elementis X predicamenta complere inveniri queant.

M. Quattuor simpla et maxima predicamentorum, id est, substantiam, quantitatem, qualitatem, relationem, in homine reperiri nemo negat.

D. Quomodo negaret quispiam quod stare scimus? Scimus enim hominem substantiam esse, et ipsum quantitate non carere, id est, longitudine, latitudine, altitudine, nec qualitate, id est, albedine, nigredine, et ceteris qualitatibus. Relatio etiam in homine est, refertur enim filius ad patrem et servus ad dominum et econverso.

M. Sed nec hoc quoque contradici debet quin homo aliquid agat, vel scribat, vel doceat, vel aliquid huiusmodi; et si scribit vel docet, oportet aliquid esse quod scribatur vel doceatur. Ecce duo predicamenta iam propalata sunt, scilicet facere et pati.

D. Verum est.

M. Agenti vero IIII^{or} sunt necessaria: locus ubi aliquid faciat, et tempus quando faciat, et positio, scilicet sessio vel stacio, aut aliquid huiusmodi; habitus etiam necessarius est, habere enim ipsum unde quid faciat oportet. Igitur, ut promisi, X^{cem} predicamenta complevi.

D. Divisionem adeo sufficientem de ipsis X^{cem} predicamentis fecisti quod nichil addi vel minui necesse sit. Innotescit etiam michi quod si IIII^{or} predicamenta simpla in homine sunt, necessario aut movet aut quiescit. Si quiescit, est quasi mortuus.

---

6. Breve *corr. ex* Beve

he is as if dead. But if he moves, that motion is one of the ten categories, namely, doing something. And so five things are necessary for an agent: undergoing something, place, time, posture, condition.

M. My words have taken root in you well. You should know furthermore that five things ought to be investigated in man. One is that he is composed of the four elements; another that he is similar to the minerals; third that he is similar to plants; fourth that he is an animal; fifth that he is similar to the angels.

D. I know well enough that nothing is an animal which is not also composed of the four elements. Therefore, man is composed of the four elements. I also know that he is, in a certain way, similar to minerals. For if he is lifted up, he will fall to the earth like a mineral. And after death he can be counted among the minerals. He is also similar to plants, for he grows like a plant. That he is an animal, no one denies. He is also similar to the angels, for he is rational like an angel.[61]

M. You have understood well. You are also able to know now that what I said is true, namely that man was composed of the four elements, and that he is similar to minerals, plants, and even angels, and that he is an animal. Therefore he is called a small world by philosophers. May He Who raised him above all the composite things of this world be blessed through all the ages. Amen.

---

[61] *Cf.* Gregory the Great, *Hom. in Evang.* 29 (*PL*, LXXVI, 1214), William of St. Thierry, *De natura corporis et animae* (*PL*, CLXXX, 710), Salernitan question B 23 (fol. 120v), and John Blund *De anima* 310 (edd. D.A. Callus and R.W. Hunt). See also M.-Th. d'Alverny, "Le Cosmos symbolique du XIIe siècle," *Archives d'histoire doctrinale et littéraire du Moyen Âge*, XX (1953), 46-47

Si autem movet, motus ille est unum ex X^{cem} predicamentis, scilicet actio. Agenti vero sunt quinque necessaria—passio, ubi, quando, situm, esse—habere.

M. Bene sermo meus in te radicat. Preterea scias in homine quinque esse investiganda. Unum est quod ex IIII est compositus elementis, aliud quod congelatis similis est, tercium quod virentibus similis est, quartum quod est animal, quintum quod angelis similis est.

D. Satis scio nullum esse animal quin etiam IIII^{or} componatur elementis. Homo igitur ex IIII^{or} compositus est elementis. Scio quoque illum quodammodo esse congelatis similem. Si enim sullevatur, ut congelatum in terra labitur. Post mortem vero inter congelata computari potest. Virentibus etiam similis est, crescit namque ut virentia. Animal eum esse nullus abnegat. Angelis etiam similis est, rationalis namque est ut angelus.

M. Bene intellexisti. Scire quoque modo potes hoc verum esse quod dixi, scilicet hominem ex IIII^{or} compositum esse elementis, et eum esse similem congelatis, virentibus, ac etiam angelis, et quod animal est. Ideoque a philosophis minor mundus nuncupatus est. Qui ipsum super huius seculi universa composita sullimavit, sit benedictus in secula seculorum. Amen.

Bibliography

Manuscript Sources

Anonymous, *Compendiosus tractatus de philosophia et eius secretis*. Vatican MS Barb. lat. 283, folios 45-106 (*saec.* XIV°)

Anonymous, Untitled book on astronomy. Paris, Bibliothèque nationale MS lat. 15015, folios 200-223v (*saec.* XII°)

Apollonius, *De secretis naturae*. Paris, Bibliothèque nationale MS 13951, folios 1-31 (*saec.* XII°). Title in upper margin: "Hermetis Trimegesti liber de secretis naturae et occultis rerum causis ab Apollonio translatus." Incipit: "Liber Apollonii de principalibus rerum causis, et primo de celestibus corporibus et stellis et plantis, et etiam de mineriis et animantibus, tandem de homine."

Avicenna (pseudo-Aristotle), *De mineralibus*, translated by Alfred Sareshel. University of Paris MS 507, folios 220-230 (*saec.* XIII°)

Marius, *De elementis*. London, British Museum MS Cotton Galba E. IV, folios 190-200 (saec. XII[ex.])

Printed Sources

Adelard of Bath, *Quaestiones naturales. Die Quaestiones Naturales des Adelardus von Bath*, ed. Martin Müller (Münster i.W., 1934). *Beiträge zur Geschichte der Philosophie und Theologie des Mittelalters*, XXXI.2

Al-Kindi, *De essentiis. Die philosophischen Abhandlungen des Ja'qūb ben Ishāq Al-Kindi*, ed. A Nagy (Münster i.W., 1897). *Beiträge zur Geschichte der Philosophie des Mittelalters*, II.5

Algazel, *Metaphysica. Algazel's Metaphysics: A Medieval Translation*, ed. J. T. Muckle, C. S. B. (Toronto, 1933)

Anonymous, *De elementis*. "Anonymi *De elementis*: From a Twelfth-Century Collection of Scientific Works in British Museum MS Cotton Galba E. IV," ed. Richard C. Dales, *Isis*, LVI (1965), 174-189

Pseudo-Aristotle, *De causis proprietatum elementorum. Aristotelis opera cum Averrois commentariis*, VII (Venice: Junta, 1574; repr. Frankfort, 1962), 204v-220v

Avicenna (ps.-Aristotle), *De mineralibus. Avicennae De congelatione et conglutinatione lapidum*, edd. E. J. Holmyard and D. C. Mandeville (Paris, 1927)

Calcidius, *Timaeus, Translation and Commentary. Timaeus a Calcidio translatus commentarioque instructus*, ed. J. H. Waszink (London and Leyden, 1962). *Plato Latinus*, IV

Constantine the African, *Pantegni.* Isaac Israeli *Opera* (Lyons, 1515), folios 1-144. Constantinus Africanus, *Opera*, 2 vols. (Basel, 1536, 1539). Costantino l'Africano, *L'Arte della Medicina (Pantegni)*, Parte I - Libro I, edd. Marco T. Malato and Umberto de Martini (Rome, 1969)

Dominicus Gundissalinus, *De anima.* "The Treatise *De anima* of Dominicus Gundissalinus," ed. J. T. Muckle, C. S. B., *Mediaeval Studies*, II (1940), 23-103

Pseudo-Galen, *De spermate.* Galeni *Opera ex septima Iuntinarum editione* (Venice: Junta, 1579)

Isaac Israeli (Judaeus), *Opera* (Lyons, 1515). "Isaac Israeli's 'Chapter on the Elements' (Ms Mantua)," ed. Alexander Altmann, *Journal of Jewish Studies*, VII (1956), 31-57. A. Altmann and S. M. Stern, *Isaac Israeli* (Oxford, 1958). *Scripta Judaica*, I. Contains the texts, in English, of *The Book of Definitions, The Book of Substances, The Book on Spirit and Soul, The Mantua Text* (i.e., "Chapter on the Elements"), and an excerpt from the *Book on the Elements.*

John Scotus Eriugena, *De divisione naturae.* Joannis Scoti ΠΕΡΙ ΦΥΣΕΩΣ ΜΕΡΙΣΜΟΥ id est *De divisione naturae. Patrologia Latina*, CXXII, 439-1022

Macrobius, *Commentarii in somnium Scipionis. Macrobius*, ed. J. Willis, II (Leipzig, 1970). *Saturnalia. Macrobius*, ed. J. Willis, I (Leipzig, 1970)

Nemesius of Emesa, *De natura hominis. Nemesii Episcopi* Premnon Physicon sive ΠΕΡΙ ΦΥΣΕΩΣ ΑΝΘΡΩΠΟΥ *Liber a N. Alfano, Archiepiscopo Salerni in Latinum Translatus*, ed. C. Burkhard (Leipzig, 1917). *Gregorii Nysseni (Nemesii Emeseni)* περί φύσεως ἀνθρώπου *liber a Burgundione in Latinum Translatus*, ed. C. Burkhard, *Jahresberichte des k. k. Staatsgymnasium* (Vienna, 1891-1902). "An Unnoticed Translation of Nemesius' *De natura hominis*," ed. Richard C. Dales, *Medievalia et Humanistica*, XVII (1966), 13-19

Nicolaus of Damascus (pseudo-Aristotle), *De plantis. Nicolai Damasceni de Plantis Libri Duo Aristoteli Vulgo Adscripti*, ed. E. H. F. Meyer (Leipzig, 1841)

Philo of Byzantium, *De ingeniis spiritualibus. Anecdota Graeca et Graecolatina*, ed. V. Rose, 2 vols. (Berlin, 1864-1870)

Priscianus Lydus, *Solutiones*, ed. I. Bywater (Berlin, 1886). *Supplementum Aristotelicum*, I.2

Urso of Calabria (of Salerno), *Aphorismi* and *Glossae.* "Die medizinisch-naturphilosophischen Aphorismen und Kommentare des Magister Urso Salernitanus," ed. R. Creutz, *Quellen und Studien zur Geschichte der Naturwissenschaften und der Medizin*, I (Berlin, 1936), 1-192. *Der Salernitaner Artz Urso... und sein beiden Schriften* De effectibus qualitatum *und* De effectibus medicinarum, ed. C. Matthaes (Borna-Leipzig, 1918)

William of Conches, *Dragmaticon. Dialogus de substantiis physicis ante annos ducentos confectus a Vuilhelmo Aneponymo Philosopho*, ed. G. Gratarolus (Strassburg, 1567; repr. 1967). *Glossae in Timaeum*. Guillaume de Conches, *Glosae super Platonem*, ed. Edouard Jeauneau (Paris, 1965)

Secondary Works

Apelt, Otto, "Die Schrift des Alexander von Aphrodisias über die Mischung," *Philologus*, XLV (1886), 82-99

Baumgartner, M., *Die Philosophie des Alanus de Insulis* (Münster i. W., 1896). *Beiträge zur Geschichte der Philosophie des Mittelalters*, II.4

Birkenmajer, Alexandre, "Le Rôle joué par les medecins et les naturalistes dans la réception d'Aristot au XIIe siècle," *La Pologne au VIe congrès international des sciences historiques, Oslo, 1928* (Warsaw, 1930), 1-15

Cadden, Joan, *De Elementis: Earth, Water, Air and Fire in the Twelfth and Thirteenth Centuries*, unpublished M.A. thesis, Columbia University, 1968

Dales, Richard C., "Marius 'On the Elements' and the Twelfth-Century Science of Matter," *Viator*, III (1972), 191-218

d'Alverny, Marie-Thérèse, "Notes sur les traductions médiévales d'Avicenne," *Archives d'histoire doctrinale et littéraire du Moyen Âge*, XIX (1952) 337-359

d'Irsay, Stephen, *Histoire des universités françaises et étrangères des origines à nos jours*, 2 vols. (Paris, 1933-1935)

Dronke, Peter, "New Approaches to the School of Chartres," *Anuario de estudios medievales*, VI (1969), 117-140

Duhem, Pierre, *Le Système du monde: Histoire des doctrines cosmologiques de Platon a Copernic*, II (Paris, 1913; repr. 1958). "Du temps où la scholastique latine a connu la Physique d'Aristot," *Revue de Philosophie*, XV (1909), 63-178

Garufi, C. A., *Necrologio del Liber Confratrum di S. Matteo di Salerno* (Rome, 1922)

Grabmann, Martin, *Forschungen über die lateinischen Aristoteles Übersetzungen des XIII Jahrhunderts* (Münster i. W., 1916). *Beiträge zur Geschichte der Philosophie des Mittelalters*, XVII.5-6. *Handschriftliche Forschungen und Mitteilungen zum Schrifttum des Wilhelm von Conches* (Munich, 1935). *Sitzungsberichte der Bayerischen Akademie der Wissenschaften* (Philos., philol. und hist. Klasse), X

Haskins, C. H., *Studies in the History of Mediaeval Science* (Cambridge, Mass, 1924; repr. 1960)

Hauréau, B., *Notices et extraits de quelques manuscrits latins de la Bibliothèque nationale*, I (Paris, 1890)

James, M. R., *Lists of Manuscripts Formerly Owned by Dr. John Dee* (Oxford, 1921). *Transactions of the Bibliographical Society.* Supplement 1

Joachim, H. H., "Aristotle's Conception of Chemical Combination," *The Journal of Philology*, XXIX (1904), 72-86

Klibansky, Raymond, *The Continuity of the Platonic Tradition during the Middle Ages* (London, 1939; repr. 1950)

Kristeller, Paul O., "The School of Salerno," *Bulletin of the History of Medicine*, XVII (1945), 138-194; repr. in Kristeller, *Studies in Renaissance Thought and Letters* (Rome, 1956), 495-551

Lawn, Brian, *I Quesiti Salernitani*, tr. Alessandro Spagnuolo (Salerno, 1969), an Italian translation, with much additional material, of the following item. *The Salernitan Questions* (Oxford, 1963)

Lemay, Richard J., *Abu Ma'shar and Latin Aristotelianism in the Twelfth Century* (Beirut, 1962)

Otte, James K., "The Life and Writings of Alfredus Anglicus," *Viator*, III (1972), 275-291

Rose, V., ed., *Anecdota Graeca et Graecolatina*, 2 vols. (Berlin, 1864-1870)

Rouse, Mary A. and Richard H., "The Texts Called *Lumen Anime*," *Archivum Fratrum Praedicatorum*, XLI (1971), 5-113

Rouse, Richard H., "Bostonus Buriensis and the Author of the *Catalogus Scriptorum Ecclesiae*," *Speculum*, LXI (1966), 471-499

Schipperges, Heinrich, *Die Assimilation der arabischen Medizin durch das lateinischen Mittelalter* (Wiesbaden, 1964). *Sudhoffs Archiv für Geschichte der Medizin und der Naturwissenschaften*, Beiheft 3

Schneider, Arthur, *Die abendländische Spekulation des zwölften Jahrhunderts in ihrem Verhältniss zu Aristotelischen und judisch-arabischen Philosophie* (Münster i.w., 1915). *Beiträge zur Geschichte der Philosophie des Mittelalters*, XVII.4

Silverstein, Theodore, "Elementatum: Its Appearance among the Twelfth-Century Cosmogonists," *Mediaeval Studies*, XVI (1954), 156-162. *Medieval Latin Scientific Writings in the Barbarini Collection* (Chicago, 1957)

Steinschneider, *Die europäischen Übersetzungen aus dem Arabischen bis Mitte des 17. Jahrhunderts* (Vienna, 1905-1906; repr. 1956). *Sitzungsberichte der kaiserlichen Akademie der Wissenschaften* (philos.-hist. Klasse), CXLIX.4, CLI.1

Talbot, C. H., *Medicine in Medieval England* (London, 1967)

Tanner, Thomas, *Bibliotheca Britannico-Hibernica*, ed. D. Wilkins (London, 1748)

Thomson, Rodney, "*Liber Marii De elementis*: The Work of a Hitherto Unknown Salernitan Master?" *Viator*, III (1972), 179-189

Thorndike, Lynn and Pearl Kibre, *A Catalogue of Incipits of Medieval Scientific Writings in Latin* (Revised and augmented edition; Cambridge, Mass., 1963)

Thorndike, Lynn, "Questiones Alani," *Isis*, LI (1960), 181-185

Vieillard, C., *Gilles de Corbeil* (Paris, 1909)

Yahia, Boubaker ben, "Constantin l'Africain et l'école de Salerne," *Cahiers de Tunisie*, IX (1955), 49-59

Index to Introduction and Notes

Single numbers refer to pages in the introduction; numbers separated by a colon refer to page and line number in the Latin text of *De elementis* cited in the notes to the translation.

Abu Ma'shar
 Introductorium in astronomiam 19
Adamarius 9
Adelard of Bath 5, 41
 Quaestiones naturales 9, 15, 33; 65:15, 85:23
Alain de Lille 43-45
 Anticlaudianus 44
 Questiones Alani 44
Alexander of Aphrodisias, *see* Apelt, Otto
Alfanus of Salerno 3, 8-9, 18. See also Nemesius of Emesa
Algazel
 Metaphysics 5, 6, 12, 26-27, 34; 49:22, 51:31f., 53:16, 59:17, 61:7
  65:29, 67:27, 69:26, 73:6, 73:23, 99:26, 103:6, 103:29
'Ali Ibn 'Abbās 27, 34. See also Constantine the African
Al-Kindi
 De quinque essentiis 6, 23, 24, 25; 93:21
Altmann, Alexander, and S. M. Stern
 Isaac Israeli 83:23, 93:15, 129:28, 159:2
 See also "Ibn Ḥasdāy's Neoplatonist" *and* Israeli, Isaac
Alverny, M.-Th. d'
 "Le Cosmos symbolique du XIIe siècle" 183:15
Ambrose, St. 20
Animism 15
Apelt, Otto
 "Die Schrift des Alexander von Aphrodisias über die Mischung" 145:6
Apuleius
 De dogmate Platonis 71:10
Aristotle 7, 13-14, 18, 19-22, 24, 25, 29, 34, 41
 Categories 23; 93:10
 De anima 21; 171:18

De caelo 21, 22; 69:25, 73:6, 135:15, 145:22
De generatione et corruptione 22; 65:29, 103:29, 145:6
De longitudine et brevitate vitae 21; 131:4
Meteorology 21, 22, 31, 32; 55:11, 57:14, 95:6, 131:4, 171:18
Physica 8, 21; 53:16, 73:23, 99:26, 103:29, 145:22
Problems 101:7, 103:29
See also Joachim, H. H.
Ps.-Aristotle 9, 30
De coloribus 27; 59:17, 171:12
De elementis 5, 6, 24, 25, 34; 159:2, 171:18
De plantis, see Nicolaus of Damascus
See also *Liber de phisiognomia*
Augustine, St. 20
Aulus Gellius 20
Averroes 44
Avicenna 7, 18-19, 24, 44
De mineralibus 7, 18-19, 24

Bacon, Roger 36
Basil, St.
Hexameron 20
Blund, John
De anima 183:15
Boethius 20
Boston of Bury (Henry Kirkstede)
Catalogus scriptorum ecclesiae 2-3
Burgundio of Pisa 18
Bury St. Edmunds 2, 7, 35

Calcidius 23, 29, 34
Commentarius in Timaeum 12, 23, 29; 59:17, 65:29, 71:8, 71:19, 75:28, 77:14, 91:8, 93:22
See also Winden, J. C. M. van
Cassiodorus 20
Categories (of Aristotle) 29
Chartres 5, 35, 41, 42
Compendiosus tractatus de philosophia et eius secretis 4-5, 36
Constantine the African 25, 34, 42
Liber de herbis 9
Liber graduum 3, 9

Pantegni 4, 26, 27, 28, 42; 51:4, 57:28, 65:15, 95:27, 131:4, 135:10, 147:5, 159:2, 179:3, 179:9
Costa ben Luca 23
 De animae et spiritus discrimine 23, 24, 30

De urina mulieris 9
Dee, John 7, 9
Dionysius Exiguus 20
Dioscorides
 De virtutibus herbarum 9
Duhem, Pierre
 Le Système du monde 89:25

Elementatum theory 4-5
Elements, nature and properties of 12
Eriugena, John Scotus 5, 34
 De divisione naturae 5, 12, 27, 29; 71:8, 71:10, 73:23, 75:26, 77:27, 89:25, 91:13, 129:28
Eupho 9
Eustathius 20
Experimental method 10-11

Form, doctrine of 5, 20
Forma corporeitatis 11

Galen 44
Ps.-Galen 28, 34
 De spermate 9, 28; 135:10
Gerard of Cremona 6, 23, 25
Gilles of Corbeil 43
Grabmann, Martin 19
Gregory the Great
 Homiliae in Evangelia 183:15
Gregory of Nyssa 5, 29
 De opificio hominis 20; 89:25
Gundissalinus 26, 34
 De anima 5, 6, 23-24; 181:2

Henry of Eastry 7
Hippocrates 44

Ps.-Hippocrates
  Expositio quinte incisionis epidemiarum 9
  Liber de aere et aquis 8
Hugh of Santalla 24, 34

"Ibn Hasdāy's Neoplatonist" 12, 25, 26, 34
Isidore of Seville
  Etymologies 9
Israeli, Isaac 28, 34, 43, 44
  Book of Spirit and Soul 28, 43; 159:2
  Book of Substances 26, 28, 43; 159:2, 167:2
  "Chapter on the Elements" 5, 6, 24, 26, 28, 34, 43; 83:23, 93:15, 129:28, 159:2
  De dietis particularibus 26; 129:26
  De dietis universalibus 25, 26, 27, 28, 32, 42; 59:17, 129:26, 131:18, 147:11, 159:25, 167:28, 171:4 (168n), 171:18, 171:23, 179:3, 179:9
  Liber de elementis 26, 28; 147:5, 159:2
  See also Altmann, Alexander and S. M. Stern

Joachim, H. H.
  "Aristotle's Conception of Chemical Combination" 145:6
Joannitius
  Isagoge 28
John of Salisbury
  Metalogicon 42
John of Seville 4n

Kirkstede, Henry, *see* Boston of Bury

Lawn, Brian 9, 32
  I Quesiti Salernitani 167:33, 171:10
  Salernitan Questions 32; 137:30, 159:2
  "Some Observations on the Milieu of Marius' *De elementis*" 41-45
  See also Salernitan Questions
Lemay, Richard J. 19
Liber Apollonii 6, 24, 30, 34; 77:14, 93:21, 107:2, 153:30, 169:6, 171:12
Liber de phisiognomia 9
Liber Hermetis, see *Liber Apollonii*
Loxus 9

Macrobius
   Commentarii in somnium Scipionis   29; 65:15, 75:26, 131:4
   Saturnalia   29, 32; 95:6
Manuscript (British Museum Cotton Galba E. IV)   7-10
Marius
   De elementis   7-8, 10-17, 32, 35-37
   De humano proficuo   2, 17
Martianus Capella   20
Maurus   4, 35
Melancholicus, Johannes
   Liber de substantia urine   9
Mercury   15
Metals   15, 16
Milk   10
Mixtures   13
Montecassino   27
Montpellier   5, 6, 42-45
Multhauf, Robert
   The Origins of Chemistry   145:6

Neckam, Alexander   41, 42
Nemesius of Emesa   18
   De natura hominis   3, 4, 8, 18
Nicolaus of Damascus
   De plantis   30-31, 32, 33-34; 151:32 (152n), 159:7, 175:14

Odo of Meung
   Versus de virtutibus herbarum   9
Oresme, Nicole
   Quaestiones in De caelo et mundo   85:23
Oribasius
   De virtutibus herbarum   9
Orpiment   15
Ovid
   Metamorphoses   65:15

Palemon   9
Palladius
   De agricultura   9
Petroleum   15
Philo
   De ingeniis spiritualibus   49:2, 51:4

Picot   3, 9
Plants   16, 25
Platearius
   Liber de simplici medicina   9
Plato   41
   Timaeus   57:13, 65:15, 91:8
Pliny   20
Plotinus
   Enneads   89:25
Prima materia   11
Priscianus Lydus   20
   Solutiones   32; 55:11
Properties   12
Ptolemy   44

Raoul de Longchamp
   Cornicula   44
Rhazes   44

Sal ammoniac   10, 15
Salernitan Questions   31, 32, 33; 55:11, 65:7, 95:2, 95:6, 137:30, 171:10, 171:23, 183:15
   See also Lawn, Brian
Salerno   2-6, 28, 34, 35, 41, 45
Sareshel, Alfred   7, 19, 24, 30, 31, 34
Schneider, Arthur   19
Seneca   20
   Quaestiones naturales   31
Ps.-Soranus
   Isagoge   9, 28
Sources of Marius *On the Elements*   17-35
Substance, doctrine of   11-12
Sulphur   15

Talbot, C. H.   3, 9
Thierry of Chartres   35
Thomson, Rodney   2-4, 8
Transmutation   16

Urso of Calabria   4, 12, 31, 35, 41, 44

Aphorisms   44; 103:6
De commixtionibus elementorum   31; 55:11
Glossae   44; 51:4, 65:29

William of Conches   4, 5, 12, 33, 34, 35, 42, 44
  De philosophia mundi   44
  Dragmaticon   26, 27f, 28f, 31, 32, 33; 55:11, 69:22, 85:23, 137:30, 147:11, 151:4, 159:2, 179:3, 179:9
  Glossae in Timaeum   32, 33; 65:29, 73:23, 77:14, 77:27
William of St. Thierry
  De natura corporis et animae   183:15
Winden, J. C. M. van
  Calcidius on Matter   71:10
Wiscard   3, 9

Index to Text and Translation

Accident (Aristotelian sense) 71:13, 93:1
   Whether an accident, such as heat, may be said to flee 138:24
Act (Aristotelian category) 145:22
Agent 181:24, 183:2
Air 49:2, 53:4, 57:8, 59:2, 61:3, 63:6, 87:31, 95:17, 145:15 and *passim*
   Its nature 47:22
   Its property 53:17
   Upper limit of 57:15
Alebandina 143:18
Almond tree 167:12
Animal 107:1, 129:12, 171:25
   How it differs from plants 175:3
Appetitive power 159:19
Apple 165:25
Aristotle 57:14
   On the Elements 83:11, 93:8
Atom, *see* Particles
Azurite 143:28

Bellows 47:29, 49:19
Beryl 143:17
Body 69:3, 97:5, 103:11
   Composite 107:21, 133:1, 135:3, 145:3
   How it was created in the beginning 77:2
   Human 97:26, 179:13
   Is a substance lacking all quality, quantity, or relation 69:24, 71:11
   Natural 67:17, 69:11
Brazier (*focus*) 51:5
Bread 49:7
Butter 131:7

Candle 51:1, 65:8
Carob tree 167:14

Categories (the Aristotelian categories, or *praedicamenta*) 75:2, 83:28, 89:3, 181:8
Center, definition of 87:17. *See also* Motion
Cinus, translated "orange" 165:25
Clavis philosophiae ("key to philosophy," alchemical term) 79:21
Clouds 63:26
Cold 47:19, 57:27, 79:10, 81:21, 89:23, 95:1, 99:12
   Whether it is a quality 83:29
Color 89:13
   Of flowers 165:28
   Of plants 171:9
   Of stones 143:21
   Whether the pure elements have colors 59:16
Complexions, the nine 133:14, 141:9
   Of human skin 179:2
   Of tastes 169:6, 171:8
Contraries 95:25, 139:10, 179:26
Copper 137:14, 143:21, 153:31
   Its composition 155:10
Coral 175:14
Cordis armarium (treasure chest of the memory) 85:14
Cornelium (*sardium*) 143:18
Creation 77:1
Creator 83:13
Creature 107:26, 129:11, 179:3
Crystal 143:17

De humano proficuo (another book by Marius) 179:23
Desire (*appetitus*) 97:13, 99:7
Dew 63:32
Digestive power 161:26
Dimensions, three 69:20, 71:3
Dryness 53:29, 81:6, 89:24, 97:11, 99:1

Earth 57:28, 65:20, 67:5, 83:8, 87:2, 95:17, 139:1 and *passim*
   Its property 47:12
Element
   Ancient books on the elements 57:25
   Tables of the mixtures of the elements 107-129
   That each element can be turned into the others 63:20
   That elements arise from the motion of the firmament 83:10

That the pure elements are not perceived by sight or touch, but only by the mind 89:12
That the pure elements do not have colors, tastes, or smells 59:16
Emerald 143:25
Emptiness 101:19, 103:18
Experience (*experimentum*) 129:21
Expulsive power 163:16

Fat (*saginum*) 83:3
Fire 49:31, 55:6, 57:16, 59:1, 65:2, 87:29, 91:7, 95:3, 141:21 and *passim*
  Its nature 53:29
  Its property 53:33
  Three kinds of 55:32
Firmament 57:16
  Motion of 83:10
Flame 51:5, 55:2, 57:1
Flint (*silex*) 143:1
Flower 165:28
Flower of brass 155:16
Foolishness 179:25
Form 77:14, 89:29
Frankincense 83:3
Fruit (*pomum*) 147:10

Glass 141:20, 143:5, 151:15, 153:1
Gold 83:2, 137:6, 153:31
  Its composition 155:2
Goldsmith 137:6
Grain (*frumentum*) 159:11
Grain (*granum*) 159:1–161:11
Grapevines, wild 165:25
Gum 83:3, 163:17

Hardness 89:24, 97:25
Hearing, sense of 89:15
Heat 47:23, 53:29, 79:28, 81:5, 89:23, 95:1, 97:1, 99:1, 139:3
Heaviness 47:12, 57:28

Ice 65:24, 99:17

Iron   137:14, 153:31
  Its composition   155:16

Jacinth   143:7

Kettle (*lebes*)   49:11, 53:11, 63:24

Lead   153:32
  Its composition   155:28
Leaf   167:30, 171:19
Lightness   57:28, 87:30, 97:27

Man
  Contains all ten categories   181:11
  His temperate complexion   179:2
  Is a small world   183:19
  Is composed of the four elements   183:9
Mercury (quicksilver)   107:2, 153:22 – 155:29
Metals   83:2, 97:25, 107:3
  How the six metals are made   155:2
  That all metals are composed of sulphur and mercury   153:30
Microcosm (*minor mundus*)   183:19
Milk   129:15 – 133:3
Minerals (*congelata*)   107:2, 129:13, 131:29, 137:5, 153:15
Mist (*nebula*)   63:26. *See also* Vapor
Moon   61:15, 173:23
  Circle of   57:16
Motion   77:5, 93:19
  Circular   73:1
  Composite   171:34
  From the center   55:5, 73:2
  From the center of a grain   159:1
  Is sensibility   173:14
  Of decay   175:26
  Of doing something   175:24
  Of plants   157:19
  Simple   171:34
  Straight   73:1
  Toward the center   47:17, 73:2, 85:30
  Transitive   171:33, 175:19
Myrrh   83:3

Nature
    Of air 47:22
    Of fire 53:27
    Of water 47:2
Necessaria quinque (Al-Kindi's five essences) 93:17
Nitron 67:7
Nourishment (*dieta*)
    That air is the nourishment of fire 49:31, 95:9, 161:1, 179:10

Oil 51:6, 67:25, 83:2
Orange (fruit) 165:25
Orpiment 153:18
Oyster 173:9

Palm tree 167:14
Particles, very small (i.e., atoms) 99:24
Passion (Aristotelian category) 183:2
Patient (Aristotelian sense) 181:2
Peach 167:13
Pear 165:25
Pepper 145:30, 147:2
Petroleum 153:18
Philosophers 95:23, 97:9, 167:6, 173:23, 177:15, 181:3
Philosophy 83:1
Physician (*medicus*) 103:5
Physicists 47:18, 55:4, 97:17, 145:28
Pitch (*pix*) 61:21, 83:3
Place (*locus*) 93:20, 181:24. See also Position
    Proper or natural place 57:9, 67:20 – 69:16, 95:4, 135:27
Plants 107:7, 129:13, 157:4–165:3, 171:9, 173:7
    How they differ from animals 175:8
    Their motion 175:19–177:8
    Their powers 165:11–167:33
Plato 57:13
Position (*positio*) 181:25. See also Place
Position (*situs*) 183:3. See also Place
Potency (Aristotelian sense) 145:16–151:12
Prase 143:26
Property
    Of air 53:10

Of earth 47:12
Of fire 53:33
Of water 47:12

Quality 65:16, 69:22, 71:4, 75:28, 83:28, 97:18, 175:32
   That a quality brings about nothing 141:4
Quantity 69:25, 71:4, 73:24, 75:3, 89:13

Rain 63:25
Rest
   Solidification results from rest 81:3
   Things grow cold through rest 79:28
Retentive power 161:30
Rose water 131:10

Sal ammoniac 67:7, 153:18
Salt 65:28–67:12
Saracens 107:2
Seed (*semen*) 157:29, 165:16
Sense 89:10, 93:4, 177:19
Sight, sense of 89:12, 97:20
Silver 83:2, 137:6, 153:31
   Its composition 155:7
Skin
   Human skin is completely temperate 179:6
Sleep 139:32
Slipperiness 97:27
Smell, sense of 89:17
Softness 89:24, 95:29, 97:25
Solidification 81:3
Solidity 57:3, 95:30
Soul
   Rational 177:31, 179:28
   Viridal 163:29, 167:2
Soul, powers of
   Appetitive 159:26
   Digestive 161:26
   Expulsive 163:9
   Of sensing 163:31
   Of understanding 163:31

Retentive 161:30
State (*habitus*, Aristotelian category) 181:26
Stone 87:2
    That stones are made inside the earth by fire 141:19
Substance 69:24–79:12, 89:9, 93:10, 101:28
    Elemental 93:14, 103:18
    Formal 93:15
    How it is defined by philosophers 181:3
    Of the rational soul 179:16
    That it is not perceived by a bodily sense 89:30
Sulphur 61:22, 107:3, 153:18–155:32
Sun 57:13, 61:14

Taste (*sapor*)
    How flavors can be made artificially 171:1
    Table of the tastes 169
Taste, sense of 89:19
Temperament 133:17
Time 93:20, 181:25
Tin 153:32
    Its composition 155:25
Touch, sense of 89:21
Tree 161:18
Tube (*phistula*) 103:5
Turquoise 143:27

Vapor 49:6, 51:6, 55:3, 63:20. *See also* Mist
Vinegar 155:30

Water 47:1, 49:2, 53:2, 57:28, 59:1, 63:5, 65:17, 87:30, 95:1 and *passim*
    Its nature 47:2
    Its property 47:12
Wax 51:6, 61:22, 83:2
Wetness 47:8, 51:25, 81:5, 97:3, 99:3, 159:8
When (Aristotelian category) 183:3
Where (Aristotelian category) 183:2
Wick 55:7, 135:23
Wind 49:16
Wine 171:4
Wisdom 179:25
Wood 51:5

World
   Natural order of 95:25
   Small   183:19

www.ingramcontent.com/pod-product-compliance
Lightning Source LLC
Chambersburg PA
CBHW021706230426
43668CB00008B/748